Men of Influence is a profoundly w... ... p......... ....
men shaping men. Hendricks speaks into our culture's void of the critical role
all men play in developing the character and vision of the next generation.
If you need convincing that healthy mentoring relationships are critical
and the cure to many of our societal ills, read *Men of Influence*. This is the de-
finitive guide on mentoring for any organization, family, business, and church
that has a passion to see young men grow into who God intended them to be.
Our manufacturing company has a mentoring culture, with our class for
high school students, "Craftsman with Character." I've added *Men of Influence* to our required reading list for young and mature men to understand
not only our inherent value, but our *need* to both mentor and be mentored.

DAVID HATAJ
President, Edgerton Gear, Inc.

I have known the power of mentorship since I was a young man. Intentional
mentoring was not a popular thing in my childhood, but mentoring went on
anyway—in an unintentional way. The men I admired most, I would watch
and emulate. These men unintentionally altered my life's path. More so than
anything else short of my conversion to Christianity.
Today is different; the importance of mentorship, and even life coaching,
is widely recognized. In fact, I have run into several executive coaches in the
past few months. What millennials want is not our brain power; they value
our experience . . . lessons learned. I believe mentoring is the most powerful
way to change the world for the better, and it has to happen one person at a
time. There are no two people that I admire more around this topic than Bill
and Prof Hendricks! I would highly recommend this book for anyone with
a passion for mentoring and in effect changing this world for the better.

DAVE RIDLEY
Former Executive, Southwest Airlines

This work should be considered the "flagship" work illuminating the extremely important concept of the power in godly mentoring. In his prag-
matic description of what mentoring really is and his easy-to-follow steps
for those who want to be mentored, as well as those who are seeking to serve
as a mentor, Bill's work transcends personal position and station in life.
Bill provides the reader with inspiration as well as a practical methodology.
A must-read for anyone in a position of influence and those who are seeking
to be that person of influence.

EVAN SIMMONS
President, One in Christ Jesus International Ministries
Bailey Fellow, The Hendricks Center, Dallas Theological Seminary

When Howard and Bill Hendricks originally wrote *As Iron Sharpens Iron*, it was my first exposure to the concept of mentoring. As a young minister and man of faith, I devoured that first book and referred to it often through my years of working with men. Now, with this revision of that classic book, a whole new audience of men can pick up the mantle of investing in the next generation. Godly men are more needed than ever in our churches and in our world. The only way you can raise up godly men is by intentional mentoring. I cannot recommend this book strongly enough to men of all ages.

GEORGE M. HILLMAN, JR.
Vice President of Student Life and Professor, Dallas Theological Seminary

Men of Influence "hits the nail the nail on the head, not my thumb," as we strive to make a difference in the lives of people. That could be a Howie Hendricks quote! Bill Hendricks has crafted substance and practical guidance to lift the mystery-lid off this significant need. I am the product of my mentors. Some did not even know that they were mentoring me, but were simply two businessmen determined to reach kids for Christ. Both stayed in my life until they died. Later mentors were more intentional and aware. Howie Hendricks influenced me in many conversations. Others, like Lorne Sanny and J. Oswald Sanders, made a deep impact as I led the Navigators. We need mentors and are obligated to pass on what we have received. Whether in my Navigators leadership or my leadership in the military, I have deliberately done this—mentored and coached people for the future in both spiritual and secular contexts. I wish I could have had this superb book then.

JERRY E. WHITE
International President Emeritus, The Navigators
Major General, USAF (Retired)

Bill does a super job of presenting, in logical sequence, both *why* and then *how* successful, biblical mentoring relationships can exist, thrive, and produce complementary benefits to those engaged in this life-on-life, skill-sharpening interchange. Yet equally impressive is Bill's persuasive and passionate appeal to the reader, as he seeks to woo them (us) into taking and making this form of relational, cross-pollinating outreach a personal standard for life.

Bravo Bill, for another great work that is both lucid and life applicable! This book will no doubt be a key resource for us in our ministry to men.

JIM COTÉ
President, Master's Men

Men of Influence is a much-needed book in today's world, and I can think of no one better to write it than Bill Hendricks. Hendricks is a gifted mentor himself, and has added to his father Howard Hendricks's legendary legacy of helping men realize their God-given potential. The book's premise—that despite rapid cultural shifts, today's young men crave the mentoring of older men—is certainly confirmed in my work with men at the C.S. Lewis Institute. I intend to recommend and use this book within our own organization as a handbook full of mentoring wisdom. Hendricks' book is one that could be applied and used by leaders in the worlds of business, government, the military, the church, and so on as an approach to mentoring that is biblical, practical, and geared toward the particular needs of men in our culture today. If only a few men in every church were to pick up this book, read it, and put its principles into practice, it could have a transformative impact within the church and our world. If you desire to be mentored or feel that God may be calling you to mentor, this is a must-read book.

JOEL S. WOODRUFF
President, The C.S. Lewis Institute

All men are influenced by other men. God has gifted each man with unique abilities. Bill Hendricks has the deep understanding and clear perspective of the eternal significance of a man's giftedness and his need for relational mentoring.

Bill warmly communicates with engaging stories the profound effect of mentorship on a man's life. You will be captivated from the beginning and will find *Men of Influence* an applicable field manual for mentoring. I will be using this book for years as my guide for being mentored and as I mentor younger men.

RAYMOND H. HARRIS
Founder of a prolific architectural firm, author, and executive producer of films

Men, Hendricks nails it! This book is practical and motivating. It's not what you know, but who you are including regarding your failures, scars, and lessons learned the hard way.

Men, younger men need you! They need your perspective and wisdom gained from experience. They *want* you.

Men, if you want to make an impact in this world and the world to come, invest in mentoring men.

Men, if you want to be a man of influence, be a mentor and find mentors for the rest of your life.

STACY T. RINEHART
Founder, MentorLink International

Bill (and his dad) have given us THE book on every aspect of mentoring—from knowing *why* mentoring is so important in life transformation, to *when* and *how* to look for mentors, to *who* is ready to serve as a mentor, as well as *what* elements and expectations make for successful mentoring. *Men of Influence* is definitely in my own resource bag for consulting and coaching!

REGGIE MCNEAL
Author of *A Work of Heart: Understanding How God Shapes Spiritual Leaders* and *Kingdom Collaborators: 8 Signature Practices of Leaders Who Turn the World Upside Down*

Men today desperately need a mentoring revolution, and *Men of Influence* provides the resource to kindle the fire! Envision a society where every godly man invests in others, resulting in a new kind of manhood where men courageously follow Jesus, unselfishly commit themselves to others, and model integrity and emotional intelligence in a fraudulent world. The Hendricks duo dispels mentoring myths and provides up-to-date practical guidance on how to create mentoring a man's way. I'm cheering for this revolution, and so will every woman I know.

SUE G. EDWARDS
Professor of Educational Ministries and Leadership, Dallas Theological Seminary; coauthor, *Organic Mentoring*, *Leading Women Who Wound*, and author, *The Discover Together Bible Studies*

MEN
OF INFLUENCE

THE TRANSFORMATIONAL IMPACT
OF GODLY MENTORS

BILL HENDRICKS and **HOWARD HENDRICKS**

MOODY PUBLISHERS
CHICAGO

All Scripture quotations, unless otherwise indicated, are taken from the New American Standard Bible®, Copyright © 1960, 1962, 1963, 1968, 1971, 1972, 1973, 1975, 1977, 1995 by The Lockman Foundation. Used by permission. (www.Lockman.org)

Scripture quotations marked NIV are taken from the Holy Bible, New International Version®, NIV®. Copyright © 1973, 1978, 1984, 2011 by Biblica, Inc.™ Used by permission of Zondervan. All rights reserved worldwide. www.zondervan.com. The "NIV" and "New International Version" are trademarks registered in the United States Patent and Trademark Office by Biblica, Inc.™

Scripture quotations marked ESV are from The Holy Bible, English Standard Version® (ESV®), copyright © 2001 by Crossway, a publishing ministry of Good News Publishers. Used by permission. All rights reserved.

Scripture quotations marked MSG are from *THE MESSAGE*, copyright © 1993, 2002, 2018 by Eugene H. Peterson. Used by permission of Tyndale House Publishers, Inc.

Scripture quotations marked NKJV are taken from the New King James Version®. Copyright © 1982 by Thomas Nelson. Used by permission. All rights reserved.

Edited by Kevin P. Emmert
Interior and cover design: Puckett Smartt
Cover photo of two friends copyright © 2018 by Brimstone Creative / Lightstock (499019). All rights reserved.

All websites and phone numbers listed herein are accurate at the time of publication but may change in the future or cease to exist. The listing of website references and resources does not imply publisher endorsement of the site's entire contents. Groups and organizations are listed for informational purposes, and listing does not imply publisher endorsement of their activities.

ISBN: 978-0-8024-1932-3

We hope you enjoy this book from Moody Publishers. Our goal is to provide high-quality, thought-provoking books and products that connect truth to your real needs and challenges. For more information on other books and products written and produced from a biblical perspective, go to www.moodypublishers.com or write to:

Moody Publishers
820 N. LaSalle Boulevard
Chicago, IL 60610

1 3 5 7 9 10 8 6 4 2

Printed in the United States of America

CONTENTS

HOW AND WHY WE CAME TO WRITE THIS BOOK

In 1995, my father, Dr. Howard G. Hendricks, and I were privileged and pleased to work together in producing a book entitled *As Iron Sharpens Iron: Building Character In a Mentoring Relationship*. This is the second, updated and revised edition of that book.

Dad passed away in February 2013. Believe me, he was ready to go! During his life, he had such a spellbinding gift for teaching and communication that it made him a legend in his own time. For sixty years, he taught at Dallas Theological Seminary, where he was affectionately known as "Prof." But his influence extended far beyond the academy. By the 1990s, he had already spoken to millions of people worldwide who were eager to learn about God and the Bible and the transformational difference they make to everyday life.

That helped bring him to the attention of Promise Keepers (PK), an organization founded in 1990 by then-Coach Bill McCartney of the University of Colorado Boulder. PK was attempting to ignite a movement of men who would honor Christ as Lord in every area of their lives. Beginning with a rally of four thousand men at the Colorado Buffaloes' Folsom Field in 1991, PK attracted hundreds of thousands of men to football stadiums and other venues nationwide over the next six years.

It takes a rare gift to hold the attention of fifty thousand men in a sweltering stadium, but Dad possessed that gift. Not surprisingly, he became a favorite on the PK circuit. In 1993, he used a PK rally to talk about one of his most passionate interests—mentoring. If men need anything, he believed, they need mentoring. With his classic genius for driving home the point with a succinct, indelible image, he declared,

> Every man needs to have three individuals in your life. You need a Paul. You need a Barnabas. And you need a Timothy. You need a Paul—that is, you need an older man who is willing to build into your life. . . . You need a Barnabas—somebody who loves you but is not impressed by you. . . . And third, you need a Timothy. You need a younger man into whose life you are building yours.

That simple formulation of mentoring became a watchword for men in the PK movement and beyond. *As Iron Sharpens Iron* was written in that context. I'm pleased to say that after twenty-three years, the book remains useful to readers.

WHY THIS BOOK?

So, why do we need an updated and revised edition? And perhaps more to the point: If Prof Hendricks was such an iconic communicator, how in the world am I going to improve upon what was written before? The short answer is I'm not. I'm not even going to try and improve on it per se. But I do intend to build on it.

Times have changed since 1995. Many of the changes are obvious:

Then we accessed the internet through dial-up modems; today we use Wi-Fi and smart phones. Then we went to the library; today we Google. Then we shopped at malls; today we shop online. Then the oldest of the millennials were barely in their early teens; today some of them are running the world.

During the same era our world became more populated, more urban, more connected, and therefore much more global, multicultural, multiethnic, multinational, and pluralistic. 9/11 dragged the United States into the global scourge of terrorism. The economic crash of 2008 wiped out as much as $22 trillion of wealth in the US alone—along with many long-cherished assumptions about the American Dream. For young and old alike, the optimism of the 1990s began to give way—not merely to pessimism, but to outright cynicism. The meaning of "family" also shifted radically, to the point where "traditional families" (mom, dad, and kids) are no longer the majority. Perhaps that helped push the traditional American value on the individual toward the far more radical individualism and selfism (idolatry of self) that we see today.

So what does all of this mean for the mentoring of men? Doesn't a man still need a Paul, a Barnabas, and a Timothy? Yes, and more than ever! But consider that many men today who might hear Dad's clarion call to mentoring would have no clue as to who Paul, Barnabas, and Timothy were.

That's because in 1995, the form of Christianity most dominant in American culture tended to be white, middle- to upper-middle-class, and suburban.[1] To be sure, America was becoming increasingly secular. But our culture still retained remnants of a Judeo-Christian worldview and the values that stem from it—which meant that the winds of culture, so to speak, were at that church's back. You could talk about God, and no one objected. You could appeal to a moral code that generally valued ideals like honesty, integrity, courtesy, civility, equity, cooperation, and trust. Authorities were more or less obeyed, even if not always respected. And institutions were at least expected to fulfill their basic functions—or face severe consequences if they didn't.

Not anymore. We now live in a post-Christian society where it's much more complicated to identify as a "Christian." For one thing, that designation has become a marketing and political/demographic term—one of the unintended but unfortunate consequences, I'm afraid, of the rise of the Christian Right in the 1970s and '80s. (By the way, in the New Testament, "Christian" is only used as a noun, *never* as an adjective; we should pay attention to that!)

Post-Christians (especially people under forty) regard Christians much less favorably than non-Christians did in the 1990s. Some view us with open hostility. Others are more tolerant but remain suspicious. They tend to have a favorable view of Jesus; of Christians, not so much. Many assume Christians have a political agenda. They're too negative and judgmental. Their churches look male-dominated and oppressive to females and minority groups. They come off as arrogant in claiming that all other religions are wrong. They also take the Bible too literally and ignore science.[2]

So let's say you're a Christian who is a baby boomer, and you're in a position of management at your company. You've been assigned as a mentor to a younger leader-in-training. That person has never been to a church, except perhaps for a wedding or a funeral. You learn that his parents were divorced when he was ten, he lives with his girlfriend, he has $83,000 in student loan debt to repay (the 529 funds from his grandparents more or less evaporated in the 2008 downturn), and he thinks boomers have "pretty much screwed up the world." That's before he ever learns that you are a Christian. How much influence can you expect to have with that young man? More than you probably realize, I hope to show. But, obviously, it's pretty much impossible to mentor someone if he distrusts you.

Okay, what about mentoring someone who openly acknowledges that they are a Christian? Again, we can't assume anything anymore. What exactly does one mean when they say they're a "Christian"?

Barna research shows that 73 percent of Americans identify as Christian. But when you factor in whether they attend church even once a month[3] and whether they say their faith is "very important in their life," the percentage of "practicing Christians" drops to 31 percent.[4]

What happens if we then ask what those "practicing Christians" actually believe? According to Barna, 28 percent "strongly believe" that everyone prays to the same divinity, regardless of what they call it (that idea is not at all Christian, but comes from what is called New Spirituality). Thirty-two percent "strongly believe" that if you do good, you'll receive good, but if you do bad, you'll receive bad (the idea of karma, from Hindu and Buddhist thought). Ten percent "strongly believe" that science is the ultimate arbiter of what is true (which is naturalism or secularism). Twenty percent "strongly believe" that making as much money as you can will bring meaning and purpose in life (materialism). And 23 percent "strongly believe" that moral right and wrong depends on individual beliefs (postmodernism).[5]

The point is if you intend to influence someone—or be influenced—through a mentoring relationship, you have to understand the context that person is coming from. You can't assume they are more or less like you.

In 1995, Dad and I were writing for an audience that, to a large degree, was pretty much like us—white, educated, middle- to upper-middle class, married men who lived in suburbia, attended church (or at least hung out regularly with other Christian men), had some familiarity with the Bible, and were trying to get serious about following Jesus. We had a lot in common with those guys, and I'm pleased to say that a lot of them are still going strong.

But in talking about mentoring today, one of the first things to point out is that you have to pay a lot more attention to the background narrative of a person's life. They may well be coming from rather different circumstances from the ones you're familiar with.[6]

THINGS HAVE NEVER BEEN BETTER FOR MENTORING

That said, one of the main reasons I've been eager to update and revise this book is I'm more excited than ever about the opportunities and potential that mentoring relationships hold for men. For one, more than any generation before them, millennials—men and women alike—crave to be mentored. Not patronized, but equipped to succeed. Already the largest generation in the American workplace, millennials are estimated to comprise as many as 75 percent of workers by 2025.[7]

That's the future! And if you see the value in mentoring, it's a bright future, because the tide of history is on mentoring's side. No one has to convince young adults that they could benefit from a mentoring relationship. Quite the opposite! If anything, the question is: Where are we going to find enough mentors for the demand?

One of the biggest reasons we need to mentor millennials is they are quickly followed by what is being called Generation Z (who were just starting to be born around 1995). Having come of age in a time of unprecedented connectivity via smartphones, tablets, and computers, and already far more conscious of the implications of robotics and artificial intelligence than boomers will ever be, these tech-savvy "digitals" nevertheless understand the importance and value of the human touch. Indeed, one study shows that as they contemplate entering the workforce, they rank a supervisor who will mentor and coach them as their top priority (along with interesting and challenging work).[8] Guess who will be their supervisors? Millennials, for the most part. So, there's no time to waste in getting that older generation prepared for the task.

I suppose much of my optimism about mentoring (don't worry, I'm plenty familiar with the less-pleasant realities of the task, as well) has to do with the fact—or at least the hope—that I know more about mentoring than I did in 1995. At that time, Dad had spent nearly four decades in mentoring relationships. On top of that, he had read widely in the field and was rightly considered an expert on the subject. By contrast, I was forty-one years old and barely ten years into my career. I certainly knew about mentoring from having personally benefitted from dozens, if not scores, of mentoring figures in my life. And I also was starting to realize that a few people were regarding me as something of a mentor to them, which felt very humbling, as well as affirming. So as we wrote *As Iron Sharpens Iron*, I let Dad's voice and content dominate. Yes, I threw in a few of my own thoughts and experiences, but that book was a life message from my dad, of which I was honored to be the wordsmith.

Today, Dad is with the Lord, but he leaves behind a great legacy to build on—especially in regard to mentoring. So now it's time for me to build on that legacy. Much of what follows is identical to or adapted from *As Iron Sharpens Iron*. And why not? If it's still useful, then let's keep using it. But I also hope to take whatever knowledge and experience about mentoring I've accumulated in the past twenty-three years and use it to describe what it takes to mentor in today's world. The most important of those new insights have come from the numerous mentors I've had during that time, and even more from the lessons learned through interacting with literally hundreds of individuals in an effort to impact their lives toward maturity, wholeness, and Christlikeness.

WHY THE FOCUS ON MEN?

One criticism—or at least hesitation—I can hear some readers or reviewers levelling against this book regards its intentional focus on the mentoring of men. Don't women need to engage in mentoring, too?

Well, of course they do. But I'm not a woman, so I'm hardly the best person to speak to that. Even so, I could name a score or more of women whom I regard as my mentors. And there are numerous women who would say that I have functioned in the role of a mentor for them. So there is much that I could discuss on that. But that's a different book.

As for this book, it is, after all, an update of *As Iron Sharpens Iron*, which targeted men. In 1995, there weren't very many resources on mentoring for women, and there should have been. But that's hardly the case today. There are now many excellent titles written by and focused primarily on women.[9]

By contrast, there is little if anything being written today specifically for Christian men.[10] Without getting into why that might be, I'll just say that I'm writing this book about what I know best, which is the man-to-man mentoring relationship.

THE PLAN OF THIS BOOK

First, I will briefly set the table with a primer on what mentoring is and what difference it could make for you (chapters 1–3). In effect, I have to sell you on the notion of mentoring. And when I say "sell," I mean it as when someone describes a product. The more you hear about a product, at some point you likely say, "I want one of those," and it's no longer a matter of price but of value. You *have* to have that thing because you can't imagine living without it. It means that much to you.

If I can succeed in getting you to imagine not being able to live without mentoring, then you'll be ready to tackle one of the two (if not both) sections that follow, based on which side of the mentoring relationship you're interested in right now: an interest in finding a mentor (part 1), or an interest in serving as a mentor (part 2). Obviously, I'd love it if you read both parts and become a man who both is mentored and mentors. But my main concern is that you read the part that most applies to you and then immediately put into practice the suggestions given. I should note that whereas the first edition of this book was written primarily from my dad's perspective and "I" therein always referred to him, though of course I was very much a coauthor, this edition is written primarily from my perspective and "I" always refers to me, though, of course, my father's wisdom is retained in the content.

As Dad and I see it, the purpose of this book is to promote a movement of mentoring among men. The Greek mathematician Archimedes did not invent the lever, but he did explain the physics involved. He did that so well that he inspired another sage of his era to declare, "Give me a place to stand on, and I will move the Earth." I believe that mentoring provides that place to stand, spiritually speaking. It has enough power to move the world if enough men engage in it. I want you to join me in being one of those men.

THE NATURE OF
MENTORING

CHAPTER 1

AS IRON SHARPENS IRON

When you look at the moon, what do you see? Maybe just a bright rock hanging in the sky. But if you look at it through a high-powered telescope, you find that the moon's surface is pockmarked by countless circular dings, like round divots on a golf course. Scientists call those rings impact craters, formed by asteroids and comets colliding with the moon over countless millennia.

Let's look the other way, from outer space to the earth. From a satellite or the Space Station, you can see five huge bodies of water in the middle of North America called the Great Lakes. They are believed to have been formed thousands of years ago when a series of glaciers melted, forming five in-land, freshwater seas. Some of those glaciers were a mile thick. They carved deeply into the earth's crust—804 feet for Lake Ontario, 925 feet for Lake Michigan, and 1,335 feet for Lake Superior (by comparison, the Willis Tower in Chicago is 1,453 feet tall).

One more image: the iconic sculpture of *David*, by Michelangelo, that now stands in the Galleria dell'Accademia in Florence, Italy. The work universally inspires awe for many reasons, not least of which is its portrayal of the Renaissance ideal of human potential. Michelangelo spent at least two and a half years chiseling, carving, and crafting this masterpiece out of a single block of marble.[1]

So, what do the moon, the Great Lakes, and *David* have in common? They all display the product of impressions. In each case, they have been marked, shaped, formed—in the case of the *David*, fashioned—by things that made an impact on them, that came into contact and made a lasting difference.

HOW TO SHARPEN A TOOL

A similar phenomenon happens between people. Humans have a way of rubbing off on one another and leaving a mark or impression, of making a difference.

Solomon, who was king over Israel some 2,900 years ago, wrote a proverb to that effect:

> Iron sharpens iron,
> So one man sharpens another. (Prov. 27:17)

Anyone who lived in Solomon's day would have known exactly what he was talking about.[2] Everyone was familiar with knives, axes, saws, ploughs, chisels, hooks, and similar tools, as well as weapons such as knives, daggers, or swords. All relied on a sharp edge, and by then most all were fashioned from iron.

The iron of that period was much softer than the steel we commonly use today. Over time, the blade of an iron tool would dull and even bend—but usually not break, as had been the problem with bronze, a more brittle material that was the previous metal of choice.

How would you make an iron blade sharp again? To our modern way of thinking, you would grind the metal back down to a good edge. But that would have been the exact wrong thing to do, because before long, your tool would have been ground into uselessness and you'd have to get a new one.

Iron Age folks used the properties of iron to restore the edge of an iron tool: they used an iron mallet to bang on it and straighten it. In short, they used iron to sharpen iron.[3]

The proverb says that something analogous happens between two men: one of them "sharpens" the other. So what does that mean? As he does with most of the Proverbs, Solomon doesn't tell us exactly what he means. He just sets those two thoughts side by side—sharpening a tool, and one man interacting with another—and lets the reader ponder what he's driving at. That's a very common way of communicating in Hebrew culture.

So, then, what is he driving at? Quite simply that one man can have a positive impact on another man as they relate. And more deeply: *only* another man can do that. Like affects like. Just as the nature of iron makes it the best material with which to shape iron, so the nature of men makes a man the best means of influencing another man. In short, it takes a man to mark another man.[4]

Mentoring is one of the most effective means whereby a man can leave his mark on another man.

Please note: I say "mark" another man, not "make" that man. Only God *makes* persons. Therefore, when a man marks another man, *he is giving shape to something (or someone) that already exists*—namely the personhood of the other man. That's extremely important for mentoring relationships, as we will see. People do not come into the world as a blank slate.[5] They bring a unique personhood that is already ordained by God. As they interact with others—first parents, then siblings and other family members, then peers at school, teachers, coworkers, neighbors, and many others throughout their life—those people "rub off" on them. They leave an impression—sometimes miniscule, sometimes momentous. Those interactions turn out to be massively important. But the core of the person, their personhood, is already pre-established—similar to the marble from which Michelangelo chiseled the *David*. Similar to the iron of a tool that needs sharpening.

WHO HAS MARKED YOU?

So who are the people who have marked you in a positive way, thereby helping to make you who you are today? I'm referring to the people who have made a significant impact, a lasting impression, on your life. The individuals who, at a critical moment, redirected your path such that today you look back and say, "I never would have become who I am were it not for that person's influence."

Obviously, one or both of your parents may jump to mind. Legendary basketball coach John Wooden describes the invaluable blessing he had in a father who consistently guided him with words of wisdom and modeled the qualities of love, character, persistence, and compassion, as well as a lifelong love for learning.[6]

Or perhaps, as is the case for many who grew up in single-parent homes, your mother was the one who paved the way by responding to tough times with even tougher faith, rock-solid character, and a ferocious belief in you.

But I'm thinking primarily of individuals outside your family—a teacher or professor, a youth worker, a coach, a boss, an adult in your neighborhood, a man from your church—persons who had little if any vested interest in what would happen to you, but nonetheless invited you into their lives in a way that has indelibly marked your own.

If you can remember someone who fits that description, then you know by experience what a deep and lasting difference a relationship like that can make. If not, I hope that just hearing about it is kindling a desire in you to meet such a person, because you don't want to miss out on a very good thing.

MY SEVENTH-GRADE TEACHER

Frank Gibson was my seventh-grade teacher. And it was probably destined that he would make a fork-in-the-road impact on my life because by the time I got to seventh grade, the bar had been set pretty low. Things for me could only go up. You see, fifth grade had been something of a disaster.

To be fair, my teacher that year had her hands full with little Billy (as had all of my teachers before her). I was what, in those days, they called a "strong-willed child." With Billy in the room, a teacher faced a force to be reckoned with, and if they weren't careful, they might soon have most of their class spiraling out of control.

Now, I wasn't really a belligerent or rebellious kid, nor was I looking to stage any sort of mutiny with my classmates. In truth, my only "problem" was that I was a very energetic, active kid with a quick mind who tended to finish class exercises and quizzes before my peers—leaving me with Too Much Time. Most of my teachers thought they could solve that problem by simply saying, "Billy, sit quietly and wait for the others." Emphasis on the word *quietly*.

Well, good luck with that! Give my mind idle time, and I can get into all kinds of mischief. And boy did I ever! As a result, I spent the better part of fifth grade out in the hall, which was the punishment for misbehavior in those days. I suppose students today would think that getting to stand in the hall instead of sitting through a boring class would be great. But there was a degree of shame attached to standing in the hall.

Sixth grade was okay. Not bad, not great. I think I was somewhat worn out after the fifth-grade fiasco. Fortunately, my sixth-grade teacher had a lovely disposition. And, because I was just entering puberty and to my young eyes she was fairly attractive, I found myself for some strange, new reason motivated to please her. Plus, I was tired of standing in the hall!

MEET MR. GIBSON

Then came seventh grade. A new teacher had been hired—Mr. Gibson. The fact that he was a man is probably significant, given that I was a twelve-year-old boy. I had a great father at home. But at school I needed a great teacher. Mr. Gibson was born to that task! From day one he realized that what others had seen as misconduct and "lack of self-control" was actually a rocket on the launch pad, waiting for liftoff. All it needed was a destination and permission to launch, and the mission would be a go.

Mr. Gibson immediately solved the Too Much Time problem by giving me endless special projects to do—many of them aimed at developing leadership and responsibility. For example, part of his job was to teach us about government, so he had us create our own class government. Guess who was elected president? Bill (I think it may have been Mr. Gibson who from the beginning called me Bill, rather than the more boyish name of Billy). Nor was that position just a formality: Mr. Gibson drew up jobs and responsibilities for each governmental role and made a point of loading up my plate—and time.

He loved music and was a great piano player. So as an extracurricular activity he formed a combo (as music ensembles were called at the time) that featured the school's music teacher and another woman as the vocalists, my best friend on the trumpet and another friend on the flute, and me on the trombone. We practiced regularly and actually became pretty good—at least good enough for Mr. Gibson to book us for a few performances, both at school and around the city.

I could describe countless other strategies that Frank Gibson used to channel my energies into positive directions. However, I think his real contribution to me was to reverse some of the damage that my fifth-grade teacher (as well as others) had done by shaming me for what turned out to be my strengths. (We will see later that most men have probably been shamed at some level for what are actually their core strengths.) That's another way of saying he gave me permission to be me. What an invaluable gift that was! And I needed it so badly at that point in my life.

One other thing that Mr. Gibson did was to have a talk with my parents toward the end of the school year. He was quite knowledgeable about Texas state and county governments, and he had extremely good political instincts. As an educator, he was always analyzing the future of education in Texas, and he could see that the public schools in Dallas were struggling and would probably struggle much more in the near term. Knowing me as he did by then, he advised my folks in no uncertain terms to look into sending me to a private school that would be able to handle my energies.

That pivotal conversation with Mr. Gibson changed the course of my life. Because of their respect for him, my parents started looking for alternative schools, and in eighth grade I transferred to St. Mark's, an outstanding boys' school in Dallas. That turned out to be the best educational experience of my life, as well as the doorway to the Ivy League.

A FACT OF LIFE

Solomon said that just as iron sharpens iron, so one man sharpens another. Largely overlooked in his proverb is that he's describing something inevitable and unavoidable. Iron that strikes iron hard enough will change that iron in some way. It may improve it (by sharpening it). It may damage it (by denting it). But it *will* make a difference.

If that's true of iron, it's also true of men. A man who "strikes," or makes an impact, on another man *changes* that man in some way. He may change him for better or for worse. But neither man can escape the fact that men have a way of impacting each other. It's the nature of men. It's inevitable and unavoidable.

Again, mentoring is one of the most powerful ways in which men impact other men. So, looked at from the perspective of Proverbs 27:17, there's a sense in which mentoring takes place whether we want it to or not and whether we're aware of it or not. Was I aware that Mr. Gibson was mentoring me? By no means. As a twelve-year-old boy, I just liked the guy. Little did I realize what a profound and lasting impact he was having on me. And in truth, who knows how much he realized the impact he was having? For all I know, he may have just felt like he was simply doing his job as a teacher.

That's why I call mentoring a *phenomenon*. It's like gravity. It's just the way the world is. It's a fact of life. People have a way of rubbing off on one another. Men have a way of impacting and being impacted by each other.

That being the case, you can easily see that someone (many someones, actually) will end up shaping you, and you will end up shaping someone else (indeed, many someone elses). Again, in a given moment you may be totally unaware that that process is taking place. But I assure you it is, as does Solomon. It's just the way the world works.

TWO QUESTIONS

So let me ask: If some form of mentoring and being mentored (which we'll define in chapter 3) will inevitably happen for you, *why not be intentional about it?* Being passive brings no advantage. If you're already feeling a need for a mentor, why stand around and wait? Why not actively seek one and put yourself in opportunity's path? Likewise, if you can see that you're going to end up influencing other men, whether you realize or not, why not realize it? Why not be intentional about the influence you have, to the extent you can be?

Most men I know seem to love being in control. The truth is, you do have considerable control and choice about who will shape you and who will be shaped by you—*if* you are intentional about it.

A second question follows from the first: If some form of mentoring is inevitable, then it seems to me we can do it well or we can do it poorly. *So why not do it well?* Of course, doing it well is obviously tied to doing it intentionally.

This book is about men impacting and being impacted by other men, and how to make that happen more intentionally and effectively. In the next chapter, we'll discuss why that's not just a good thing if it happens, but something a majority of men *require* if they have any hope of thriving as a man.

CHAPTER 2

WHY MEN NEED MENTORING

As my dad stated, every man needs a Paul, a Barnabas, and a Timothy—an older man to build into us, a peer to walk beside us, and a younger man for us to build into.

That's an eloquent formulation. But if you're like me, you respond to it with a simple question: *Why do men need mentors, and why do they need to serve as mentors?* In this chapter, I want to build a case to answer that question. In fact, my objective is to show why mentoring is not just good but absolutely necessary, a *requirement*—something that men cannot live without if they hope to live their lives to the full. It all has to do with the nature of life and the nature of men:

- We all grow
- We all learn
- We all work
- We all need an identity and a purpose
- We all die

Mentoring is vital to each of those processes. Let me describe how that works.

WE ALL GROW

When I was growing up, our family had a growth chart on the back of a closet door. Dad would stand my sisters and brother and me, one by one, with our backs to the door, place a ruler on top of our head, mark a line on the door, measure the distance between the floor and that line, and then write our name, the date, and our height next to the line. Through that simple growth chart, each of us kids watched our growth from toddler to teen.

Physical growth is easy to see, and enormous research has gone into tracking what actually happens physiologically and chemically to the body as it matures from infancy to adulthood, and then into later adulthood, and finally into the last season of life.

But of course, people are more than a body. We are also a soul.[1] And while our body grows and then declines, our inner person can keep growing pretty much to the very end of our life—or at least as long as our body (and especially brain) allows us. For that reason, personal growth is a lifelong process (or can be and should be).

But note: *personal and spiritual growth always require other people.* No one learns language apart from others. No one learns values apart from others. No one learns to think critically apart from others. It is self-evident that no one learns to do relationships apart from others. And certainly no one grows in their walk with Christ apart from others.

Humans are designed to grow, and we are also designed to be relational creatures. So when we put those two realities together, we come to the profound truth that most growth requires getting into some kind of developmental relationship *with a person in a process over time.* That's just a fact.

"Thank You for Being a Role Model"

And as I said in the last chapter, we can engage in a relational process of growth unintentionally or intentionally, and it can be done poorly or done well. But that's just how personal growth works. It's the principle behind having a fitness trainer or signing up for Peloton. It's how the Boy Scouts have helped generations of boys grow into men and what drives the Officer Candidates School (Marines) at Quantico, Virginia. It's how farmers and artisans and sailors and cooks and seamstresses and woodworkers have learned their crafts for millennia, and how knowledge workers today learn to operate on brains and drill for oil and invest money and construct buildings and erect bridges and produce smartphones, films, and AI. Sadly, the same principle also operates rather effectively in training boys to become "good" gang members, drug dealers, and terrorists.

Yes, it's quite possible—and in some cases preferable—to develop a skill on your own. Plenty of people have taught themselves to blow bubblegum, play the guitar, read Hebrew, bake cookies, paint flowers, or do ollies and grabs on a skateboard. But matters of character and conscience, the attainment of wisdom, and the development of one's soul are never acquired by purely independent means.

For example, Martin Luther King Jr. mastered the art and craft of speaking truth to power through nonviolent civil disobedience only by learning from Mahatma Gandhi.

Likewise, Tony Dungy, former head coach of the Indianapolis Colts, who won Super Bowl XLI in 2006, credits his time under Steelers Coach Chuck Noll as invaluable in shaping both his personal life and professional philosophy. Upon his induction into the Hall of Fame in 2016, Dungy said,

> If I could speak to Coach Noll I'd tell him thank you for being
> such a role model for me. For not only teaching me the game,
> but showing me you could be successful in the NFL and still
> have a family life, still have your family important to you, still

give your assistant coaches time with their families, still do
things in a family friendly way and be successful. That you
could live out your faith and still lead a team. He showed me
all of those things and I never had to worry that you couldn't
do that.[2]

In that same acceptance speech, Dungy noted that he tried to
pass down what he had learned from Nolan to the players on his own
teams. That's exactly what happens in the phenomenon of mentoring. Mentoring is about a lifelong journey from youth to adulthood to
old age. In the early years, a boy is mostly learning how to become a
man and how to make his way in the world. But the day comes when
he starts influencing other men (again, wittingly or unwittingly,
positively or negatively). Over time, he becomes the mentor in the
majority of his mentoring relationships.

So, when I say, "We all grow," I'm describing what amounts to a
transfer of power—empowerment, agency, competence—essentially
a gift of life. That a man is designed to personally grow and develop
is God-ordained and the most natural thing in the world. And that
always happens primarily through a relationship with someone else
over time.

Small Men

What happens, then, if a man *doesn't* have that kind of relationship
with anyone? Quite simply, he doesn't grow. He certainly doesn't
thrive. He remains stunted as a person, diminished in some way. He
lacks depth and strength of character. He knows little if anything of
his gifts. He likely never finds work that fits him. He doesn't even
know that's possible! Worse, he never discovers his purpose.

Meanwhile, he has never been helped to confront his dark side.
That means he may well remain enslaved to his inner demons like
anger, fear, lust, sadness, self-doubt, or self-contempt. He remains a
stranger to himself and thereby suffers, and causes others to suffer

when he interacts with them. He likely doesn't know how to experience the joy of intimacy. And it goes without saying that he's not set up to mentor anyone effectively. So, when he does influence someone—as he inevitably will—it probably will not be for the better. Worst of all, he doesn't learn how to walk with Jesus or talk with Jesus.

On the outside, a man like that may become physically strong and virile during his prime—perhaps even successful, rich, and/or famous. But inside, he turns into what might be called a "small man," something of a dud, just a shell of the man he could have been and should have been, a man who is more existing than living.

Do you know any men like that? If so, pay attention! That's why men need mentoring—you and me included. We don't grow without it.

WE ALL LEARN

Don't growth, development, and learning amount to the same thing? Not exactly. Personal growth and development are the outcome or product of a learning process. In other words, in order to grow, we have to learn. So, it's worth taking a closer look at that part of the equation.

Since my dad and I wrote the first edition of this book, I've spent the better part of those twenty-five years focused on human giftedness. I specialize in helping people figure out what they were born to do and what God designed them to do. Usually, we apply that insight to finding work that fits the person and will prove both productive and fulfilling.

The process I use to do that involves a robust assessment tool that creates what amounts to an "owner's manual" on a person.[3] Among the "instructions" spelled out in that owner's manual are the environmental circumstances or conditions in which the person thrives. Just like a plant, a person only flourishes in certain conditions and merely survives in less favorable conditions. For example, one person thrives when they work in a structured, ordered environment, while someone else needs lots of freedom and latitude. Some people excel when they have a clear goal to pursue. Others function best when they have a problem to solve. There are countless circumstantial factors that condition motivated behavior.

A Modeling Individual

Among those possible factors is what we call a *modeling individual*, someone who knows more and/or is more experienced in whatever a person aspires to do. By observing that modeling individual and emulating them, the person begins to take steps toward learning and developing in a particular way. Sometimes a person won't be able to know their modeling individual personally. It's someone they read about or some famous individual they admire. But often there is a personal relationship, and the modeling individual becomes a guide, tutor, coach, or sponsor. The person then makes a great deal of progress as their modeling individual explains how things work; lets the novice try his hand; provides advice, critique, and feedback; and generally encourages his efforts forward.

So how common is it that a person requires a modeling individual in order to thrive? I estimate that in the time I've been doing this work, I've personally put about two thousand individuals through my process,[4] and I've looked at many times that many "owners' manuals" that my colleagues have produced. A modeling individual shows up in easily 65 to 75 percent of those manuals. In a word, it's an extremely common element.

Can you see the implications of that? I've got strong evidence showing that for 65 to 75 percent of people, a modeling individual is not just nice to have, but is a *requirement* to function at their best. With a modeling individual, they excel. Without one, they languish. For some, this need is so critical that when it comes to their career, I tell them, "You're not looking for a job; you're looking for a *person*— for a modeling individual."

No Coach, No Future

Among the most obvious examples of what I'm talking about are athletes who require a coach. Thank God for junior high and high school coaches! For countless young men, sports is the only part of school that makes sense, as many men reading this book know all too well. It's not because athletes are dumb or undisciplined or lack character or so many of the other flawed stereotypes people have about them. It's in large part because most of them *require* a modeling individual, and apparently the only place they find one is in their sport. (If you happen to be a coach, pay special attention to that. You may well hold the key to unlocking a young man's soul.)

I am not speculating or being overly dramatic. I see this reality all the time in my consulting practice. Perhaps one of the most pronounced cases I ever encountered was a former professional football player who had been a legend of the game. An acquaintance of mine had befriended him, and knowing that I specialize in career issues, he asked me to talk to him. So I met the man and his wife for lunch. He was every bit the imposing figure you would expect of an NFL star. But what stunned me as he told me his story, hardly picking at his food, was how he slumped over his plate, eyes down, voice low, and utterly listless. You'd never know he had rocked stadiums with his dynamic.

Every once in a while he threw a furtive glance my way, and as he did, I saw defeat and fear in his eyes. The defeat was the kind of defeat that football players exhibit toward the end of a losing game, when their last hope is quenched by a crushing takeaway or a knockout score. They just give up. This man looked like he had just about given up.

As for his fear, he made it plain that he had no vision of a future. And without that, he lacked purpose. Take away a man's purpose, and it's just a matter of time before he dies. In a real sense, this man was staring at the chilling prospect that nothing else of substance was awaiting him. All that remained was to die.

I'm sure many factors account for how a man ends up in a place like that. But when I looked at the stark contrast of where he had been just a few years before and where he was now, I couldn't help but run a simple analysis: *Okay, he left football, where he was spectacular, and now he's out on his own, where he's floundering. What changed? What's not there for him now that was there for him in football?* The most obvious answer is a coach, a modeling individual. I realized that since the time that man had been four years old, he'd had coaches telling him what to do, where to go, what time to show up, what to eat, what to memorize, what to focus on, what to think about, what to ignore, and so on. Take that modeling individual away, and that guy's life went right into the toilet.

What Do We Really Need?

Admittedly, that's an extreme case. But I have to wonder how many millions of men in our society who end up getting fired, going to prison, addicting themselves to substances, and otherwise just existing, just dragging themselves through life—a very broken life—get there largely because they don't have the modeling individual they require. And even a majority of men who are functional and holding down jobs are not exactly thriving. Gallup says that nearly 70 percent of American workers are not "engaged" at work, which means their heart isn't in it.[5] It's just a job, just a paycheck—and for some, a real curse.

Coincidentally, that 70 percent number does resemble the 65 to 75 percent estimate that I've given for how many people *require* a modeling individual. I can't help but think there's at least some correlation.

My point is, we all learn. So how does that happen? All the evidence shows that most men require learning from a guide. Instead, we are too often handed information, instructions, lectures, theories, platitudes, gushing praise for men who can do what we can't do, and withering shame when we look incompetent. If that's ever happened to you, then you know exactly why men need mentoring—you and me included.

WE ALL WORK

Nowhere is a man's personhood more expressed or repressed than in his work. And why not, since work is what dominates most men's lives. Sadly, all indications show that most men find their best stuff *repressed* when they're on the job. As the Gallup statics show, nearly 70 percent of American workers are not "engaged" with their work. That figure jumps to an astonishing 85 percent worldwide.[6] Clearly, for most men, work is, at best, just a means to a paycheck—and for many, it's a downright curse.

What a tragedy, because God gave humans work to be a blessing, not a curse.[7] The very first words that God spoke to human beings after creating them in His image have to do with our work: "Prosper! Reproduce! Fill Earth! Take charge! Be responsible . . . for every living thing" (Gen. 1:28 MSG). In other words: Make the earth fruitful. Cause it to flourish. The world on its own is not very fruitful. It just gives us raw resources. Only humans can add value to those resources that cause the world and its people to flourish.

And to every person God has given a particular means of adding value that can in some way cause the world and its people to flourish. That's what giftedness is. God has given everyone their own unique giftedness. One person has a knack for solving problems. Someone else is great at meeting a challenge. Another excels in influencing people. Someone else is at their best when planning a strategy. Yet another has a genius for creative storytelling. And another is the consummate team player.

I could go on and on describing the countless forms of giftedness that God has endowed humans with.[8] But here's the issue: It seems rather evident from the statistics on employee engagement that vast numbers of people are not doing work that they are designed by God to do. Instead, they are straining under the burden of job misfit, which is soul crushing. They're like hammers trying to drive screws or screwdrivers trying to cut wood, like a Ferrari just driving back and forth to the grocery store or a state-of-the-art computer serving as a doorstop.

So what does this have to do with mentoring? First, mentors can play a vital role in helping men discover their giftedness and use that insight to pursue meaningful job options. Second, mentors have become vital in today's work world. Let's take these in turn.

Discovering One's Giftedness

Giftedness is universal,[9] but, ironically, almost no one discovers their giftedness on their own. That's because each of us lives inside our own skin, with the result that when we're using our giftedness, we don't think about using it. We just use it. We wouldn't think of doing life any other way.

So how do we become aware of our gifts? (And by *gifts*, I mean our core strengths coupled with the unique motivational satisfaction that we seek through the exercise of our strengths.[10]) The most common way we gain a bit of insight is the feedback we get from other people who observe us in action—people like our parents, siblings, peers, teachers, coaches, coworkers, bosses, spouses, and children. They reflect back to us how they are experiencing us, and that input gives us clues as to what we're "good at" or "not good at," and where we please or disappoint. Over time, we gradually begin to get a sense for what we do well and not so well, and what activities we "like" and "don't like."

All of that is to be expected. But it's also highly subjective, and therefore suspect. Others assess you on the basis of what *they* perceive, but to a large extent their perceptions are *mis*perceptions because there is much of you they can't see. To make matters worse, their input invariably is affected by their *own* giftedness. That means they do life differently from how you do it. And that creates a problem, because when someone does things differently from how we do them—they make a decision differently from how we would or they go about a task a different way—it's just human nature to say (or think): "What's wrong with you?"

Given that reality, would it surprise you if I said that 90 percent of the people who come my way have been shamed for their real giftedness? For example, take the young adult who finds great joy in getting things exact and precise—right on the money, as in no margin for error. There's nothing wrong with that! Except that he's been told his whole life that he's a "perfectionist," that he's "OCD" (Obsessive-Compulsive Disorder), that he is "anal retentive" (a term from Freudian psychology). He's basically been told there's something wrong with him. Really? If I ever have brain surgery, that's the kind of person I want on the job! I don't want someone for whom "good enough" is good enough, who, halfway through the procedure says, "Oops!"

Of course, there's a whole industry devoted to assessing giftedness using a far more "objective" (supposedly), quantitative attempt at analyzing it.[11] You're probably familiar with personality tests, aptitude inventories, and the like, such as Myers-Briggs, Strengths-Finder, DISC, Johnson O'Connor, Strong Interest Inventory, the Wonderlic (used in the NFL), Caliper, and 16PF, to name but a few. Currently, the Enneagram is all the rage among some millennials. Literally thousands of such tests have been developed since the dawn of modern psychometrics in the early twentieth century.

Assessments like those have their place. But all they provide is information. Hopefully that information is somewhat accurate (and relevant). It may even be interesting. But it's still just information. It leaves the person looking at their scores, their "type," their themes, their letters, or whatever output the assessment yielded, and saying: "So what? What difference does this make? How do I use this?"

At that point, the person needs a coach. They need a mentor. They need someone to help them understand what they're looking at and the implications of what it says about them. Then they need guidance as they begin to apply those new insights to their work. They need someone to help them think through questions like: *Am I in the right job, given my bent? What would be my best use, career-wise? What does this say about how I learn, how I make decisions, how I relate to my coworkers, who I need around me to be effective, or how I need to be managed?*

Countless other questions could be asked. But in the absence of a coach, extremely few people will actually use what the test told them about themselves. And here's a simple way to test if that's true: If you've ever taken one of those assessments, where are your test results now? Do you have them on a laminated card in your wallet, or sitting on your desk, or close at hand in a drawer or on your computer where you can pull them out to consult on a regular basis? Or are they stashed away in a file drawer or a box somewhere? Or lost altogether?

Okay, maybe you're the rare type of man who looks at or thinks about your assessment frequently. But if 70 percent of the workforce is just working for the weekend, I think it's safe to say (a) most men have no idea what their giftedness is, and (b) even if they've had it formally assessed, clearly they haven't had much help to act on it.

We all have some form of giftedness, but on our own, most of us will never really discover what it is or what difference it makes for our work. That's another reason why men need mentoring—you and me included.

Later in the book, I'll show how you can not only gain greater insight into your own giftedness, but also become a "giftedness coach" for other men.

The New World of Work

Something unprecedented happened in the world about a hundred years ago: The nature of work began to change. Prior to the early twentieth century, most of the world's work took place on farms, in fields, and at factories. But after World War II came the rise of knowledge work,[12] which means work that is primarily driven by information. In other words, the workplace began to move from the land to the minds.

Most men reading this book are knowledge workers: real estate brokers, insurance agents, accountants and other financial services workers, doctors and nurses, pilots and air traffic control workers, EMTs, teachers, engineers, reporters, authors and publishers, pastors and church leaders, judges and lawyers, and more. Even guys who work in tool and die shops are now knowledge workers, because they use CAD/CAM and other technologies that are information-driven. Same with cops and fire fighters: they carry all kinds of gear that requires brainwork to operate. Most every kind of work today, including work that is said to be "with one's hands," such as auto maintenance, painting, plumbing, truck driving, towing, roofing, laying tile, or farming—almost all work involves a great deal more "knowledge work" than ever before in history.

So work has changed dramatically. But one thing that hasn't changed is the need for mentors in the workplace. If anything, that need has only *increased*. Unfortunately, however, we're having to relearn how mentoring works. That's because our culture largely abandoned mentoring when it shifted its public schools toward a classroom model designed to prepare large numbers of students to work in an industrial economy. As the Old World trades and crafts, which were inherently based on apprenticeships, gave way to the factories, we lost the art of mentoring.

Now we must recover it—because knowledge workers don't learn through the classroom lecture (a model of education that dates back to the fifteenth century). If they need information, they can just look it up online. Most of the real learning that knowledge workers engage in has to do with gaining competence in doing higher-level, more sophisticated tasks, such as sizing up a loan application, knowing what to feel for when examining a patient's neck for a tumor, determining what the data are telling you about where to drill a well, assessing the cost-to-benefits ratio of filing a lawsuit, and understanding how to reach the little person inside an autistic mind, so as to build a relationship.

Along with those kinds of nuanced capabilities are the countless "soft" skills required in today's workplace: communicating, thinking critically, hiring, leading, managing, running a meeting, making decisions, prioritizing, delegating, persuading, handling conflict, navigating organizational politics, working across cultural differences, and so on.

Nobody just shows up to the workplace at age twenty-two with a fully developed grasp of all that. It takes years to acquire such skills—and it takes mentoring. Because most of it confronts a young adult who is just starting out with a rather daunting reality: "I don't know what I'm doing." (To make matters worse, he also doesn't know what he doesn't know.)

Most knowledge workers of any age who come my way for "input" are really asking me a question that is sourced in the statement, "I don't know what to do." Maybe they're trying to find a better job. Maybe they're having trouble with their boss. Maybe they need to make a key hire or change up the roles of their team. Maybe they need to let someone go. Maybe they're just looking for some encouragement.

Whatever the issue, they're almost always facing a situation in which they don't exactly know what to do. Well, there's no shame in that! That's the human condition. It's also the nature of knowledge work. The truth is *no one* knows what to do in their particular situation! That's because no one has ever faced that situation before—not that exact situation, with those exact dynamics and those exact people, and this unique person in the middle of it all.

So what do we do? Well, I tell them, let's look at how other people have handled *similar* situations and try to learn what has worked and what hasn't. I tell them what I see when I look at their situation. I suggest a handful of questions that I would be asking if I were in their shoes. And then I invite them to brainstorm with me and see if we can generate some possible strategies for what they might do. Once we've worked up some sort of game plan, I then send the person off by essentially saying, "Okay, go figure out what you're going to do next, and I'll walk with you as you take care of this matter. Then we'll get back together and see what's happened and what we can learn from it."

In short, a knowledge worker doesn't learn by someone giving him the "right" answer. That takes the responsibility away from him and denies him from using his good mind. He'd rather experience the satisfaction and freedom of deciding how he's going to handle things. But to do that, he needs a coach. The coach doesn't tell him what to do. The coach arms him with the best possible wisdom he has to offer, along with whatever encouragement he can honestly convey that says, "I believe in you."

Have you ever faced a situation in your work where you honestly didn't know what to do? Maybe it had to do with the technical part of your job, but more likely it involved a people-problem and/or one of those "soft" skills I mentioned. Remember how frustrated you felt? How lost? Maybe even scared? And let's say you decided to try a course of action and things didn't end so well. How much did that misstep cost you? How defeated did you feel when you realized you'd chosen a losing strategy?

If you've ever ended up there, then you now know by personal experience why men—you and me included—need mentoring in their work.

WE ALL NEED AN IDENTITY AND A PURPOSE

I'm old enough to have witnessed four generations coming into their twenties: boomers (my generation), Gen-Xers, millennials, and now Gen Z.[13] In all four cases, the two most pressing questions at that stage of life were/are: *Who am I? What should I do with my life?*

Identity and purpose. Those seem to be two of the most basic building blocks that young adults want to lock into place once they come of age. The feeling is, "If I can answer those two questions, then I can really get on with my life."

I tend to agree. But alas, answering those core questions is much easier said than done. That's largely because there is absolutely no agreement on how to go about answering them. For at least sixty-five or seventy years, young adults have been offered a head-spinning buffet of countless options for "finding oneself." How many of those schemes actually work is anyone's guess. My own opinion is that most of them don't, and some are downright harmful.

Regardless, young adults spend a great deal of angst, energy, and money trying this, that, and the other during their twenties, wondering who they are and what path they should pursue.[14] By age thirty, however, most of them have given up on that project. They haven't gotten very far with it, and time is racing on. So they "settle down" (settle, unfortunately, being the operative word), "get practical," and take whatever job they can find that seems to split the difference between what they'd like to live on and what they're willing to give up in exchange for it. (Sadly, some also become completely disillusioned and drop out. Imagine that: dropped out of life at age twenty-five or twenty-eight!)

I could say a great deal about finding one's identity and purpose. But perhaps the most important thing to say is this: people are best understood through story.[15] Every person on this planet has a unique narrative in which they are cast as the leading character. Whether aware of it or not, they go through life living out a story that is still being told—because it's not yet finished—called The Story of Me.

And here's what I've discovered about that reality: until someone tells The Story of Me to another person, and that person actually pays attention to that story—not to "study" the storyteller but to understand him, to know him, to see him, to see the person through his story, in his own words—a sense of identity and purpose will prove elusive for him. I must admit, I don't totally understand how this works or why it is so. It's something of a mystery. But I've seen it happen so many thousands of times that I'm as certain of it as the fact that the sun will rise tomorrow.

If that's true, then it seems to me that mentoring could well be the answer to a very big problem in our world today. Our culture doesn't know how to get people from high school graduation into the adult world of work. As I've pointed out, the nature of work has changed, and our world is still trying to catch up with the implications of that change (we're only seventy-five years or so into the grand experiment called Knowledge Work).

But one thing we now know (and should have known all along). As young adults wonder and worry, explore and experiment, ponder and puzzle, dream and scream, hope and mope, get rejected and get selected, and otherwise hack their way through their twenties—*what most of them most need is an older adult to come alongside them and invite them into the adult world.* In my lifetime, I've seen a lucky few, relatively speaking, have the benefit of that mentor-figure, and it's made all the difference. Most, however, have not, with the result that many have ended up lost as lambs trying to figure out who they are and why they're here.

So what would happen if more of them had someone to sit down and listen to them tell *The Story of Me*? It sounds too simple and too idealistic to say it, but the truth is they would thrive. They would have more confidence about who they are because in listening to their story, the listener would validate *that* they are, *that* they matter, *that* their personhood is valued and belongs among us (I can't tell you who you are; in telling me your story, you will begin to reveal who you are, and thus to wake up to who you are and to embrace who you are). And if the listener wanted to, he could rather quickly help a young man determine what he was put here to do, and therefore what sorts of career options make sense for him.

How can I speak so confidently about all this? Because quite apart from the ever-growing research that now exists showing the over-whelming value of mentoring,[16] I have my own experience of the

45

past twenty-five years with (by now) thousands of people in their twenties—not through some TV show or podcast or blogpost or other one-off medium, mind you, but through firsthand, one-on-one, face-to-face, in-depth conversations and interviews.[17] I could cite hundreds of them in their exact words, but this man's story would be typical:

> Honestly, in high school, I really struggled with my identity. I mean, I was a popular kid all throughout that time. You know, I was a leader. I was the third in command in the (ROTC) brigade. You know, I was a four-year starter on the football team. So I had a lot of successful things. I had lots of friends. But I think the confidence—I was always trying to find who I was.

As you can tell, the man who told me that was by no means a loser. Quite the opposite! He'd been the starring quarterback on his school's championship football team. He attended a military prep school before entering the United States Naval Academy. Surely, one would think a guy like that would have a lot of confidence. Surely he would know himself pretty well and have a pretty good grasp on "who he is." But no. Despite all his strengths, all his obvious intelligence, all his achievements, "I struggled with my identity." I've heard that exact same thing from countless young adults during the past twenty-five years.

I also felt that way at age thirty. I was lost! I had been raised by great parents, no question about it. I had received an outstanding education: prep school, Harvard, a couple of master's degrees. I received numerous awards and made lots of accomplishments. People would tell me, "Bill, you can do anything you want with your life!" *That may be*, I thought, *but I have no clue as to what that should be. I don't even understand myself!*

Have you ever felt that way? If so, then you know in your gut why men—you and me included—need mentoring.

WE ALL DIE

One morning in February 2013, my cell phone woke me at about 5:15 in the morning. I took one glance at the caller ID and knew exactly what the call was about. It was my mom calling to tell me that my dad had finally died, having lingered with hospice for several days.

Our family gathered at my parents' home, and we stood around Dad's body to cry, sing, pray, hug, do what families do when someone they deeply love has passed away.

Eventually a couple of attendants from the funeral home pulled up in a van to remove Dad's body for burial preparations. I remember how they wrapped him in a shroud, which they then bound with straps before placing it on a gurney. As they lifted him from the bed, I was shocked at how small that shrouded bundle looked. Dad had not been a large man (he probably stood at 5´7˝ or 5´8˝), but in that moment he appeared so small, so reduced. And then the thought hit me: *This is where every man ends up, no matter who he is, whether great or insignificant—Socrates, Caesar, Mozart, Napoleon, Lincoln, King, my dad. All of us will end up in a shroud.*

I say that not to be morbid but to speak frankly. We do ourselves no good and much harm if we choose not to contemplate the end of our life on this earth. It's coming whether or not we pay attention to it.

And death is perhaps the ultimate reason why men need mentoring.

Passing the Baton

Earlier I described the cycle of generations. One generation is born, grows up, declines, and dies. As it travels that journey, another generation is born, begins to grow up, watches the earlier generation decline, and then takes over when they die. A generation comes, and another goes—on and on throughout time.

That pattern bears a striking resemblance to a relay race. In a relay, the objective is for runners to get a physical object—the baton—over the finish line before their competitors do.

What's the baton that one generation of men is supposed to pass on to the next? Wealth? Power? A system of government? Knowledge? An ideal? A cause? A message? A monument? A good memory?

My answer may surprise you. Many reading this book may expect me to say that the best legacy one can leave behind is to prepare men for the world to come by giving them the gospel. Well, I'm all for giving men the gospel. But let's not reduce the gospel to a fire insurance policy. Remember, God gave us an assignment way back at the beginning of history: "Cause the world and its people to flourish!" (Gen. 1:28, my paraphrase).

That was our mandate. How have we handled it? Not well. Thanks to our own foolishness and rebellion in buying into a lie, our relationship with God was severed, with the result that stewarding the earth became much more difficult. Instead of flourishing, the world and its people started dying.

Then, in an act of total grace, God became one of us and died on our behalf in order to restore our relationship with Him, and with it, our ability to serve Him as the stewards of this world and its people. In Christ, He is restoring us to our true humanity, and with it our capacity to exhibit love to our neighbor—which includes our work. He makes it possible for us to once again cause His kingdom to come and His will to be done *on earth* as it is in heaven.

In short, the only way to get ready for the world to come is to be saved by grace and then start living out the life of the world to come in this world at hand. As Jesus plainly said, "If you have not been trustworthy in handling worldly wealth, who will trust you with true riches?" (Luke 16:11 NIV).[18]

This concept of passing down a heritage that is a mixture of both actual, tangible assets as well as wisdom about and from God Almighty is right in line with the Old Testament pattern of the Israelites. God gave His people a land to possess, along with a Law to govern their stewardship of that land (and of each other). In Psalm 78, the singer Asaph implores the people of his day to pay attention while he utters "dark sayings of old, which we have heard and known, and our fathers have told us" (v. 2, notice the generational handoff). Rather than withhold those ancient truths from their children, the people are to "tell to the generation to come the praises of the LORD, and His strength and His wondrous works that He has done" (vv. 3–4). This generational transfer is not just a nice thing to do, or even just a wise thing to do. Asaph declares that it is commanded by God Himself: "For [the Lord] established a testimony in Jacob and appointed a law in Israel, which He *commanded* our fathers that they should teach them to their children, that the generation to come might know, even the children yet to be born, that they may arise and tell them to their children" (vv. 5–6, emphasis added).

From one generation to the next to the next, on and on to all generations. That's what God has told to do. For that reason alone, mentoring is a must! It's a matter of obedience.

And not surprisingly, God seems to have created men such that, as they get older, they discover a certain desire to pass along the lessons they have learned in life to younger men. The technical term for that impulse is *generativity*.

Getting Ready for the Game

My dad was fueled by a nitromethane-level of generativity. Nitromethane is what a top-fuel dragster burns to rocket down a drag strip. It's like a bomb going off, and my dad was the most explosive man I've ever known when it came to mentoring. He described it as "a ministry of multiplication." He implored men to pour their lives into other men, who could in turn build into other men coming behind them, just as 2 Timothy 2:2 says: "The things which you have heard from me in the presence of many witnesses, entrust these to faithful men who will be able to teach others also."

On the basis of that teaching, may I ask: what are you planning to leave behind? Remember, *this world is not the game.* It's the practice field where we're supposed to be preparing ourselves and one another for the game to come. The game is what makes everything matter, but that means we'd better practice just as well as we can. We don't get to practice forever, so as we face our inevitable death, we have to ask ourselves: "Am I ready to play in the real game? Have I prepared myself well? And have I helped other men get ready to play in that game by helping them learn how to practice well, too?"

The Story of Me: Final Chapter

There is one more role for mentoring to play in light of the certainty of death: mentoring can be a powerful means of getting men ready to die.

Mentoring tends to be portrayed as something that only younger men need. And of course, they do need it, for all the reasons I've given. But old men need it just as much. You see, as a man comes to stand on the edge of eternity, he tries to determine what his life has amounted to and whether it really mattered. He thinks about what went right and what went wrong, what he accomplished and what he failed to accomplish. He reflects on the people he was supposed to have had a relationship with, and where things stand with them. He may well think about his father more than at any other time in his life. He no doubt recalls his regrets—where he made mistakes through sins of commission and sins of omission. He may even have confessions to make in hopes of being released from guilt and shame.

And if his final days give him opportunity, a man may well begin a grieving process as he begins to feel the losses soon to come—perhaps of a beloved wife, a family, a place, the familiar sounds, the rhythms of the days and the seasons, the light, the air, and ultimately life itself.[19]

A man in the final days of his life is coming to the end of *The Story of Me*—at least, in this world. So with that thought, remember what I said earlier: a man must be able to tell *The Story of Me* to another man who really listens and pays attention to him in order to *see* that man through his story. Imagine doing that for an older man! I can hardly think of any greater gifts you could give him than (1) your presence and (2) your full attention. Those two simple gestures might well turn out to be extraordinarily powerful tools for helping that man gain a richer sense of who he has been and what his purpose was for living.

Would you like for someone to do that for you as you come into your senior years, and ultimately to the sunset of your life? If so, then you can see why even dying men—you and me included—need mentoring.

CHAPTER 3

WHAT IS MENTORING?

I need to begin this chapter on what we mean by mentoring by pointing out that the term *mentor* as we use it today doesn't exactly come from where most of us think it comes from—an epic Greek poem by Homer called *The Odyssey*.[1] If the ancient Greeks could listen to the way we talk about "mentors," they might scratch their heads wondering what we are talking about.

THE MYTH OF MENTOR AND THE MENTOR OF THE MYTH

The popular story about Mentor goes like this:

A man named Odysseus goes with his fellow Greek warriors to fight the Trojan War, and he's gone for twenty years. In his absence, he leaves a man named Mentor in charge of his household, whose duties include rearing Odysseus's son, Telemachus, from a boy into a man. Why does Odysseus entrust Mentor with that level of responsibility? Because Mentor has been Odysseus's beloved friend since childhood. When Odysseus finally comes home, he finds Telemachus all grown up and now capable of leading other men and fighting alongside his father—all thanks to Mentor.

That's what most people know about Mentor. And for that reason, Mentor is today viewed as the prototype of a father-figure, a wise, experienced, and trusted advisor who tutors a young man into adulthood.

But that concept is far from the actual Mentor of *The Odyssey*. The original Mentor is only a minor character in the story. And if he was supposed to guard Odysseus's household, he does a pretty lousy job of it. Things are in total disarray when Odysseus returns. Having given him up for dead, a group of unmarried men (called suitors) have been courting Odysseus's wife, Penelope. They've been at it for so long and with so much determination that they've moved into Odysseus's house, where they are drinking up his wine and squandering his wealth.

So where did we get the idea that a mentor is a guide, a sage, a guru, an instructor in wisdom? That notion came from François Fénelon (1651–1715), a French theologian, mystic, and tutor to the heir apparent of the French throne. In 1699, Fénelon anonymously published a treatise entitled *Les Aventures de Télémaque* (*The Adventures of Telemachus*) in which he purported to tell the untold story of Mentor's role in apprenticing Telemachus into adulthood.

Just as Odysseus went on an odyssey, so Telemachus and Mentor go on an odyssey of their own in *The Adventures*.[2] Through the twists and turns of that journey, Telemachus learns many lessons from the ever-wise Mentor, who ends up as the hero of the story.[3]

Les Aventures was a runaway success, and ever since, Fénelon's Mentor has become the model for what we mean by a mentor today. He imparts wisdom, support, and nurture to Telemachus, with the aim of grooming him into the ideal king.[4]

Without question, Fénelon's Mentor has enormous appeal. But Fénelon has created a myth—a clever myth, and a myth that dovetails perfectly with how you and I today like to think of ourselves.

But it's a myth nonetheless. By contrast, Homer's mythical Mentor is actually closer to the way things work in real-life mentoring. To understand how that works, let's go back and take a deeper look at how Telemachus is mentored in *The Odyssey*.

Instilling an Heroic Mindset[5]

When Odysseus sets sail for Troy, Telemachus is still an infant. He grows up with no memory of his father. Meanwhile, the suitors are spending down his inheritance. They are determined that one of them will have Penelope, and with her, Odysseus's kingdom (he rules the island of Ithaca). As the rightful heir of that kingdom, Telemachus's life is in danger.

So who comes to his rescue? It is not Mentor, but Athena, the goddess of wisdom, handicraft, and warfare, who intervenes to guide Telemachus. However, in typical fashion for the gods of Greek poetry, Athena does not appear to Telemachus directly, but rather disguises herself as Mentor. Throughout *The Odyssey*, Telemachus perceives that Mentor is advising him, but it is actually Athena.

Why does young Telemachus need Athena's help? Because, as Homer describes him, he is *napios*, the Greek word meaning "disconnected." He is disconnected from his father—and therefore his ancestors, his roots—which disconnects him from himself. He's also disconnected from knowing where or how he fits into Ithaca, into his world—and it's a dangerous world, thanks to the menacing band of suitors. Telemachus feels impotent in knowing how to confront them. He feels lost and afraid. In short, using today's language, we would say that Telemachus doesn't know who he is or what his purpose is, what his role in life is.

So how is Athena going to help him? Well, in Greek mythology, nothing happens on earth that the gods have not already discussed in the heavens. So, at a council of the gods, Athena declares that she's decided to give Telemachus *menos*. *Menos* means a kind of strength or might or force. But not just physical strength. *Menos* involves the mind. We might think of it as "strength of will" or "passion" or "spirit" or "pluck." *Menos* describes the heart of a champion. Certain athletes today are said to be able to "take over a game" and "will their team to win." In Greek thought, that's because they have *menos*. They "know how to win." That's what makes a hero.

Athena wants to impart *menos* into Telemachus. She wants to give him a heroic mind, a belief in himself that he has what it takes to prevail over the suitors and do what his father would do if he were there—protect his mother, and more importantly, steward the kingdom.

So the real "mentor" of *The Odyssey* is Athena. She brings him *menos* (a heroic mind). And it's easy to see that *menos* is only two letters removed from *mentor*. So guess what? *Mentor* means "he who connects mentally." Athena connects Telemachus mentally or inwardly to perceiving who he truly is and what he is destined to do.

Do I Have What It Takes?

So, there you have it, two different versions of Mentor: Homer's Mentor, through whom a goddess imparts wisdom, and Fénelon's Mentor, whose wisdom comes from himself. Fénelon's is the Smart Man, the man who knows, the man who has the answers.

Fénelon's Mentor remains the dominant model for mentoring to this day. The idea is that if you want to grow and develop, you need to hang around someone who knows more than you do and let him tell or show you what you need to know in order to do what he can do. It's a transfer, an exchange: your mentor hands off key knowledge and information to you.

That approach to mentoring makes a lot of sense, and I'm not totally opposed to it. But I think it misses the mark. Because here's what I've seen (and I'm far from the first or only person to have seen it). Every man is living out *The Story of Me*. And I have yet to meet a man who wouldn't love to be the hero in that story—if only he knew how to do it. But here's the catch: information alone can't turn him into a hero. Nor can technique. Nor can a strategic plan or a set of goals. Certainly no app can do it, either. Something has to take place *inside the man*—inside his heart and mind—that transforms him into acting as a hero would act. It's ultimately a matter of believing in himself.

Acting as a hero by no means has to involve life-and-death combat (though for some men it has and does). It could be as simple as a little boy wanting to learn to ride a bicycle so he can keep up with the older boys. It could be a teenager wondering whether he has what it takes to get into college. Or a college student whose head is spinning after a disastrous freshman year. Or a just-married husband wanting so much to please his new wife but sensing that he's fairly clueless as to how to do that. Or a new father driving mother and baby home from the hospital and realizing he's just been handed a whole new level of responsibility. Or a man whose wife has just learned she has breast cancer, and he's now confronted with the odious task of explaining that to their three young children.

I've been that man in every one of those scenarios, and I've met countless other men who have faced similar moments in their *Story of Me*. Sure, information can be a big help at such times. But quite apart from being told how one "should" respond to life's challenges and opportunities, such moments confront a man with deeper questions that he must ask himself (and continues to ask himself almost daily). One of the most pressing is: *Do I have what it takes?* It's the question of competence: *Am I adequate to do what's required of me in this situation?*

The research shows that the overwhelming majority of men answer that question, "Not really." In 2004, for example, Harvard-educated columnist and author Shaunti Feldhahn published research from a blind, random, nationwide survey she had conducted on four hundred men who answered two dozen questions about their lives: what they thought about, how they felt, and what they needed. Among the questions was the following:

Men who are taking risks and progressing in their careers will inevitably face many situations that are somewhat unfamiliar and challenging. Think back over several situations like that in your career. Which one of these feelings were you most likely to experience? [Choose One Answer]

- I can handle it, no problem.
- I'm somewhat out of my depth here, and I hope it doesn't show.
- I feel like a bit of an imposter; I'm not fully qualified to do this and I hope no one finds out.

How would you answer? When faced with a new and unfamiliar situation—which, of course, happens all the time, both at work and in life in general—are you prone to confidently think, *I can handle this, no problem*? The research showed that only 16 percent of men feel that way. More than four out of five admitted to feeling insecure—out of their depth (63 percent) or like an unqualified imposter (21 percent). That's how men feel. But they don't want to show it! As Feldhahn concludes, "The idea of someone thinking he can't cut it is humiliating—a feeling every man wants to avoid at all costs."[6]

That's absolutely true! *No* man wants to look incompetent. But most men *feel* incompetent when faced with something they've never done before. And it stands to reason that the younger a man is, the more insecure he's liable to feel. So, he has to conquer that inner demon first before he's ready to take on whatever external challenge the world may be throwing at him. He has to *believe* he can do it. Like Telemachus, he needs *menos*—a heroic mindset, a confidence that he has what it takes—in order to act as a hero would act.

The Heart of Mentoring

Information from a Smart Man does not impart a heroic mindset. Indeed, it may actually impede such a mindset, because the Smart Man is inherently intimidating. He's telling you what he knows precisely because you *don't* know it. And to most men, not knowing in and of itself contributes to feelings of incompetence. As the old saying goes, better to remain silent and be thought a fool than to open your mouth and remove all doubt.

This, then, brings us to the heart of mentoring. Quite apart from whatever "problem" a man is trying to solve—whether catching a bass, writing a paper for his history class, applying for a job, apologizing to his wife, figuring out what's wrong with the computer, walking with Christ—there is always a deeper transformation that is trying to take place. His soul is seeking to move from self-doubt to confidence. From not believing he can do it to believing he can.

No one can say exactly how that happens. But in telling the story of Telemachus, Homer shows that it always takes divine aid imparted through the person of Mentor. Here's an example: Early in his quest to find his father, Telemachus must speak with a king named Nestor but he's afraid to do that. He tells Mentor, "How . . . dare I go up to Nestor, and how am I to address him? I have never yet been used to holding long conversations with people, and am ashamed to begin questioning one who is so much older than myself." Telemachus is filled with insecurity and self-doubt. He's certain that he doesn't have what it takes to address the king.

But Athena (through Mentor) reassures him: "Some things, Telemachus, will be suggested to you by your own instinct, and heaven will prompt you further; for I am assured that the gods have been with you from the time of your birth until now." In effect, she tells him he indeed has what it takes, because the gods have been with him all through his life. And whatever he stills lacks will be supplied to him from above, as needed.

On the strength of her words, Telemachus and his party approach Nestor. After a meal, the king invites Telemachus to explain who he is and why he has come. The account then reads, *"Telemachus answered boldly."*[7] Something of a transformation has taken place inside him.

He is now able to act like a man with another man, like the hero he longs to be.

"Be Strong in the Grace"

The Greek gods and the God of the Bible are by no means the same. But Mentor's words to Telemachus are remarkably similar to the apostle Paul's words to his young apprentice, Timothy.[8] Paul appointed Timothy to pastor the church at Ephesus, and throughout 1 and 2 Timothy, Paul constantly reassures Timothy that he has what it takes to do that job—not so much by his own strength or smarts, but because of God: "This command I entrust to you, Timothy, my son, in accordance with the prophecies previously made concerning you, that by them you fight the good fight, keeping faith and a good conscience" (1 Tim. 1:18–19). "Prescribe and teach these things. Let no one look down on your youthfulness, but rather in speech, conduct, love, faith and purity, show yourself an example of those who believe" (1 Tim. 4:11–12). And most importantly: "You therefore, my son, be strong in the grace that is in Christ Jesus" (2 Tim. 2:1).

Mentoring has an aspect to it that goes beyond what humans can perceive. In mentoring, one man influences another man ("as iron sharpens iron"), but the deepest impact is not on the man's knowledge or skills, but on his own self-perception. He comes to see himself differently. Thanks to his mentor, he begins to believe in himself, which unleashes the strengths of his personhood and the man that God made him to be. The mentor is used to help him—quite literally—become a man.

And "used" is the operative word. Many men reading this description of mentoring will shrink back with the thought, "Oh, wow, this is way too deep for me! I could never do that! I don't have any training to get into someone's self-concept. I'm not a psychologist. Look, I just want to help somebody, not monkey with their soul!" (What was that about "I don't have what it takes"?)

If that describes you, think about this: It takes divine power to form and transform a man. No human or collection of humans is totally adequate to that task. The Odyssey is pure myth, of course, but even the Greeks recognized that something beyond human agency is at work in mentoring. Hence the presence of Athena, a mythical goddess, in the story. But in the New Testament, the true God with truly divine power speaks to Timothy through Paul in order to shape his life. The point is, by a process humans don't totally understand, God in His grace sovereignly uses men to sharpen other men. Sometimes a mentor is aware that God is using him that way, but probably most of the time he is not.

As I said in chapter 1, mentoring is a phenomenon. It's a fact of life. Men just have a way of rubbing off on one another. So, if we know that happens, then I think we can do things to make our interactions with other men as productive as possible. That's what the rest of the book is about.

WHAT'S THE DIFFERENCE BETWEEN MENTORING AND . . . ?

One last thing before we get down to business. In almost every book, article, lecture, or discussion I've ever encountered where the topic of mentoring comes up, people take pains to distinguish mentoring from countless other forms of influence: teaching, educating, tutoring, discipling, coaching, training, apprenticing, counseling, guiding, consulting, parenting, spiritually forming, spiritually directing, soul caring, and more.

In my opinion, trying to make hard-and-fast distinctions between terms like these has become somewhat pointless. In the first place, many of these terms are now commonly used so interchangeably that they've become synonyms. And even those who are paid to study the mentoring process have not yet settled on exactly what the term means. One paper reports that there are now more than fifty definitions of *mentoring* to pick from in the academic literature![9]

But the main reason I no longer worry too much about what qualifies as "mentoring" is that it's the person who benefits from a mentoring relationship who ultimately gets to say how that relationship helped him. I've heard countless men describe the decisive impact that a junior high teacher had on them. Or a coach in high school. Or a drill sergeant in basic training. Or a college professor. Or a manager. Or a therapist. Or a pastor. Or a grandparent. Or a friend.

Mind you, those men had other teachers, coaches, officers, professors, managers, counselors, pastors, relatives, and friends. But certain individuals stand out because they imparted something above and beyond and more than just the expectations of their role (occupational or otherwise). Those people helped the men become better men in some way, more confident in their own skin. To use Homer's term, they engendered *menos*—a heroic mindset.

In describing their mentors to me, men might actually say, "He was like a mentor to me." But they might just as easily use another term: "He taught me everything I know today about how to do that." "He kind of guided me through that crisis." "He was a true friend, really almost like an older brother." On the other hand, they may not use any term at all: "He really, really helped me." "He was a godsend." "What a wise man! I gained so much from being around him." "He was just a model for me of what a man ought to be like in a situation like that."

In light of that, here's how I would describe mentoring: **Mentoring** *is what happens when one man affects another man deeply enough to where he later declares, "I never would have become who I am were it not for that man's influence."*

A Divine Mystery

I'm not surprised that, to this day, no one has ever quite pinned down a precise definition of *mentoring*. That's because mentoring goes beyond a merely human process. There's also a divine mystery in play. Something happens in our souls, a shift that we experience but can't fully explain.

Even Telemachus could sense that. At the beginning of *The Odyssey*, Athena first visits him in the form of a stranger (named Mentes, interestingly enough). After urging him to go search for his father, the stranger then disappears when Athena "flew away like a bird into the air, but she had given Telemachus courage, and had made him think more than ever about his father. He felt the change, wondered at it, and knew that the stranger had been a god."[10]

PART I

FOR MEN WHO WANT TO BE MENTORED

CHAPTER 4

START WITH YOUR STORY

We've discussed what mentoring is and why it's needed. So where does your search for a mentor begin? Ironically, it begins with you. It begins with your own personal *Story of Me*.

I know that seems counterintuitive. It also goes against most of the advice that's out there on finding a mentor. But there are two simple reasons why that's where I would start, the first of which I'll give now, and the second at the end of the chapter.

YOU'RE ALREADY ON YOUR WAY

You can find tons of resources today offering guidance on developing yourself and doing something great with your life. But most of that advice is based on a myth. That myth says you can design your life more or less from scratch. You just decide where you want to end up and who you want to be, and with that end game in view you can chart a path to realize your dreams. You then go find mentors who can help you achieve those dreams.

That sounds very appealing! But that way of thinking ignores one incontrovertible fact: you are not starting with a blank slate. By now, you are well into *The Story of Me*. Quite a few chapters have already been written. And it would be a cataclysmic mistake to just throw away those chapters and try to "start over again." Life doesn't work that way. Yes, you're going to see new chapters added to your story as you go forward. But your story is already well in play, and what's already happened has huge implications for what's to come.

If I can do nothing else for you through this book, I most want to help you realize that your life is a story—and one that fits into a much larger story, as we'll see. The best way to understand yourself and discover your purpose is through your story. Sadly, most men have never paid much attention to their *Story of Me*, with very unfortunate results.

But you can—starting right now! Here's a simple exercise to help you with that[1]:

Go back to the very beginning and walk through your life in five-year increments from birth to the present: birth to five, five to ten, ten to fifteen, fifteen to twenty, and so on. For each period, answer the following questions (I suggest you record this on paper, or consider creating a simple spreadsheet to organize and capture your answers on your computer):

What were the highlights? That is, what were the main events that happened? Don't get too detailed; just a few words to summarize.

What were the high times? What things happened that left great memories? What were the best moments of that time period?

What were the hard times? What things happened that were difficult, sad, or even tragic?

Who were my heroes? Who were the people you most looked up to and admired?

What was the heritage from that period? In other words, what were the lessons you learned, whether good lessons or hard lessons?

WHAT DO YOU SEE?

When you've completed the exercise above, step back and take a look at your story as a whole, as if it were terrain that you are looking down on from a plane at thirty thousand feet. What do you see? What strikes you most about what's happened? What things loom large on the landscape of your journey so far?

For many men, there will often be one or two things that sort of dominate the whole picture. I have a friend who grew up on a farm in the Midwest. When he was maybe eight, a tractor engine exploded and he was severely burned, leaving permanent scars. The memory of that incident rises up like a mountain in his life to this day.

Likewise, a young man may think about the day he learned that his parents were getting divorced. Or when his dad had to ship out for the war, and that was the last time he saw him. Or when the girl he was madly in love with broke his heart.

On the other hand, the dominant thing may evoke fond memories: moving to a new school where, instead of being bullied like you were at your old school, you found some great friends and began to feel accepted and confident. Or when your coach chose to put you on the first string of the varsity team. Or when you got to college and someone told you about Jesus, and you discovered that you have a Savior.

Not all men, however, see anything that particularly looms large in their story. The terrain of their life seems fairly "flat" and unremarkable. The way they see it, they were born, they grew up with their mom and siblings ("Dad was out of the picture by the time I came along"), mom went to work every day, we kids went to school, everyone eventually graduated and went off to do their own thing, and that's pretty much it. Nothing really tragic, but nothing really exciting, either. Just kind of an uneventful, almost boring life so far.

No doubt there are other possibilities for how one might see one's life. But as you look at yours, toward which end of that spectrum do you find yourself: Has your life been dominated by one or two key events, or has it been fairly ordinary, with no great highs or lows?

WHAT DO YOU SEE IN YOUR STORY?

Looking at yourself the way I've just described will feel unfamiliar for many men. In truth, they've never spent much time reflecting on themselves or doing what they consider "navel-gazing." *What's the point?* is their attitude. *Where will it get me?*

I don't pretend to fully know the answer to that question, but I do know this: *self-awareness lies at the heart of becoming a healthy man.* It's not the only thing at the core, but it's definitely *one* of the things at the core. (By the way, it turns out that mentors are profoundly important in developing self-awareness.)

But let's return to your story and what you've seen so far. I want to ask you several questions about your reaction to what you're seeing in your story (and note: these are the kinds of questions for which there are no right or wrong answers):

- How would rate your satisfaction with your own *Story of Me* as it currently stands? Imagine a scale of minus-10 to plus-10, with minus-10 indicating "I hate my life," plus-10 indicating, "I can't think of a better life," and 0 indicating, "It's so-so." Where does your satisfaction level rank?

- What's the dominant emotion that you feel as you take a look at your story? There are countless words to use in describing what you feel, but a few to consider are: sadness, anger, frustration, self-pity, disappointment, guilt, grief, shame, apprehension, numbness, boredom, loneliness, resignation, hope, excitement, anticipation, determination, impatience, joy, gratitude. See if you can narrow things down to a single word.

- As you think about where your life seems to be headed, would you say you're mostly hopeful or mostly discouraged about the future?

- If you are mostly hopeful, what are your aspirations for the days ahead? Where do you desire to go?

- If you are somewhat discouraged about where you see things going, what are the main problems you think you're having to deal with?

There are countless other questions I could ask (and would ask if you and I got together and I listened to your story). But how you answer questions like these is all part of developing a narrative called *The Story of Me*. Whether you're aware of it, you tell yourself that story—and you tell others that story—all the time. But insofar as you're aware of that story, you can use it to help you identify potential mentors.

NEEDS AND WANTS

I described a "satisfaction scale" above by which you can gauge how happy you are with your life at this point. A similar way to assess things is to ask: When you look at your life story, is the glass half empty or half full?

Generally, guys who see their glass as half empty think a lot about what they need, whereas guys who see their glass as half full think more about what they want.

Whether your glass is half empty or half full is neither good nor bad. It simply is. Nor should you get hung up on the difference between needs and wants. Those are sometimes impossible to distinguish. That's one of the biggest advantages to having mentors: they can help you sort out what you really need and what you really want.

In *The Odyssey*, Telemachus needs to find his father, if he can, and figure out a way to fight off the suitors and save his family's legacy.

In *Star Wars*, Luke Skywalker wants to learn the ways of the Force and become a Jedi like his father.

Epic stories like these have appeal because they remind us that the lives of men are largely about seeking to have their needs met and seeking to get what they want. At the most basic level, we need to eat, and at the deepest level, we find a hunger in our souls for meaning and purpose. God has so made us that we are pushed and pulled, and driven and attracted toward a future that is unknown but inescapable.

So what about you? What do you think you need at this point in your life? And what do you think you want?

Your needs and wants may be very simple and straightforward: "Bill, I just need to find a job." "I need to start saving some money." "I need to learn what it means to be a dad." "I want to buy a house." "I want to get some experience in leadership." "I want to pay off my student loan debt."

Conversely, your needs and wants may be more complex: "I've got to figure out what to do with my life." "I really ought to decide whether I'm going to marry the woman I've been dating." "I just wish someone would give me a chance." "I'm not sure I can see much of a future for myself. I guess I'm just looking for some direction."

What if you have no clue about what you need or want? There's no shame in that. Many men find themselves in that boat. But they have a difficult time admitting it, because they don't want to look incompetent. If that describes you, don't sit on the sidelines and assume there's no hope for you. Instead, take heart that you've at least gotten clarity on the fact that you lack clarity! That's honest. You're going to gain more from mentoring than most because that degree of self-awareness—yes, ironically, the awareness that you *lack* self-awareness—already suggests that you're a teachable man. And no one is so appealing to a mentor as a teachable man.

WHAT ARE YOU LOOKING FOR?

And that brings us to the other reason why your search for potential mentor-figures should start with *The Story of Me*: that's where your mentors are going to start. Early on in your interaction with them, they're going to ask you what you're looking for at this point in your life, and how they might help you with that. They may ask that explicitly, or they may simply size you up to appraise what you're all about.

In reality, they're asking where they fit into your story, and what part you're asking them to play. You may or may not be sure. But because you've thought through your *Story of Me*, you're at least in a position to be as clear as you can about what you think you need or want, and what you are seeking. Now those men can be more helpful for you.

So now that you've taken that first vital step of looking back at your story, let's go deeper into sizing up potential mentors, and also look at what potential mentors are thinking about when they look at you.

CHAPTER 5

WHOM TO LOOK FOR, AND WHAT MENTORS LOOK FOR IN YOU

Remember the principle that underlies the whole mentoring process: you're going to be influenced by other men, just as iron sharpens iron (chapter 1). In other words, someone *is* going to mentor you. Someone *is* going to mark and shape the contours of your soul—how you think, what you value, how you live your life. That's inevitable. But knowing that, don't be passive about it. If anything, be a bit choosey as to whom you let speak into your life, and for what purposes.

In this chapter, I'll first offer my suggestions for assessing whether someone would make a good mentor for you. Then I'll look at the other side of the equation: what prospective mentors look at and look for in you as they weigh whether or not to invest in you.

SIZING UP PROSPECTIVE MENTORS

When I was in seventh grade, I wasn't looking for a mentor, but Mr. Gibson showed up anyway. Later, when I was a freshman in college

I was lost as a lamb and didn't even realize it. I desperately needed a mentor, and by the grace of God I met Steve, a graduate student who probably saved my sanity. By my thirties, I had had scores of men speak into my life in ways that I would now describe as mentoring. But I hadn't really looked for any of them. They just came along—now, I realize, because God brought them my way.

Sometime in my thirties, I finally began to figure out that I should be actively seeking mentors, that mentors were not just nice to have but essential to personal growth and development. As a result, I've been seeking out mentors ever since.

So what sort of man was I looking for in a prospective mentor? I'm not sure I had many well-defined criteria then. But by now, my experience suggests at least six qualities that I try to assess in sizing up such a man, and these are what I'd recommend to you as you search out your own mentors.

1. He Seems to Have What You Need

In the last chapter, I had you review and reflect on your *Story of Me* in order to identify what you feel you need and/or want at this point in your life. Whatever those objectives are, the person best suited to help you tackle them is someone who looks like he's already dealt with those kinds of concerns in his own life.

That should be self-evident. But for many men, I'm afraid it's not. For example, I've known young men who were looking to form a strategy or game plan for their life. That's outstanding! But then they end up talking to someone who doesn't think strategically. Nor does he have a well-conceived game plan for his own life.

As you look for mentors, find men who really know something about the area in which you want to grow. If you want to develop a prayer life, look for someone who demonstrates a consistent prayer life. If you want to become more responsible and generous with your money, look for someone who has been a good steward of the money God has entrusted to him and is also smart about how he donates it.

If you want to work on your marriage, find someone whose marriage is solid.

My dad frequently repeated a core principle that *you cannot impart what you do not possess.* So, look for men who actually have the goods, not just men who look good.

But let me dial this issue of competence up a notch. You can always find teachers, men who can teach you a skill or impart some basic working knowledge. Which is great! But remember that mentoring goes a step beyond the thing to be learned to the person learning it—namely, *you.* Ideally, you want to not only develop new skills and competencies in life, but also *become a better man in the process.* Some men have an extra gear by which they seem to be able to do that.

The Bible calls that extra gear *wisdom* (Hebrew, *chokmah*). Wisdom means skill in the way one lives life. It goes beyond knowledge to the smarts about how to apply that knowledge in real life.

So, let's take one of the examples I just gave. Say you want to understand the area of money—how to earn it, how to manage it, how to grow it, how to use it, and so on. (By the way, money turns out to be one of the most important areas in life for which you could seek out a mentor. I can't urge you enough to do so!)

Plenty of men can sit down with you for a couple of hours and give you a crash course in budgeting, saving, paying off debt, setting financial goals, investing, giving money away, and more.

That's fantastic! But somewhere along the way, I would be looking for someone who can press into what lies behind each of those financial-related activities. I'm talking about a man who has some insight into everything that lies behind money, which is *stewardship*: Who actually owns all your money? Who gave you the means to earn it? What are you given money for? What do we mean by "value"? What is wealth? How is it that so many men get into trouble with money? What's been your own experience with money (which includes how your family dealt with money)? If your money allows you to have a lot of things, how does that affect your soul?

Questions like that go beyond the topic at hand (in this case money) to the person learning about that topic (you). The result is that you not only learn a thing or two about money, but also gain some wisdom in the use of that knowledge. You've gained perspective. Your mentor—for that's who such a man would turn out to be—has helped to define the reality in which money operates. Money suddenly goes from a detached thing outside of you to a way of living, a way of relating to money that is healthy and life-giving. In short, by imparting wisdom, he helps you become a better man.

The book of Proverbs says, "He who walks with wise men will be wise" (13:20). As you evaluate men to pour into your life, ask yourself whether they look like they have some wisdom in addition to whatever intelligence, credentials, or track record they possess.

2. He's Had Some Proven Success

See whether he has proven to be successful. This might seem to contradict what I just said. But it doesn't. What I'm driving at is to look for some validation that the man knows what he's talking about. It's the issue of credibility.

Let's stick with our example of money. If you came to me and asked me to help you in the area of money, I would decline. I would send you to any of ten other men I could think of who know something about money ("know" in the sense of having real wisdom about it). Yes, hopefully I've got a little bit of wisdom about stewardship. And I understand basic money principles. But God has not entrusted significant money to me (I'm not complaining. He's given me other resources to steward, which is responsibility enough). In other words, I don't have a track record that says, "If you want input on money, go talk to Bill."

The point is, as you size up a man, ask yourself, *Is this guy effective in the thing that God has called him to?* For any and every issue, problem, opportunity, idea, desire, or situation you need input on, there's a man out there who has dealt with that same (or similar) area and acquitted himself well. That's the man you want to seek out.

3. He Seems Open to a Relationship

Life-on-life mentoring (as opposed to having a distant or "virtual" mentor[1]) involves a relationship. So, the ideal mentor would be a man who is willing to enter into a relationship with you. If he's really going to help you, then he needs to care about you at some level. He can't be self-absorbed and so focused on his own pursuits that he has no capacity to empathize with your concerns and no real desire to help you. If that's the case, you'll always have the feeling that you are "intruding" on his precious time.

This openness to a relationship is a tricky thing to gauge. Some men seem to become your new best friend the moment you meet them. But others don't appear to be relational. They have a rough, gruff affect that almost seems to communicate, "Stay away! Don't bother me!"

So how can you tell? Well, one clue is to assess whether the man in question has close friends. Is he even capable of having relationships? If not, I would automatically steer clear.

A related sign would be whether he appears to be a mentor-figure to anyone, especially younger men. Are you aware of any men who seek him out for advice, guidance, input, help, or feedback? If so, maybe you can become one of those men.

Closely correlated with mentoring others is the degree to which a man has been mentored himself. In chapter 2, I talked about the concept of a *modeling individual*—someone who serves as a model for what you would like to do. Mentors are a form of a modeling individual. I can say with some authority that about 75 to 80 percent of modeling individuals have had a modeling individual of their own somewhere along the way. I can also say that about 75 to 80 percent of those who benefit from a modeling individual tend to become a modeling individual for someone else at some point in their life.[2]

Do you see the connection? If someone has benefitted from a mentoring relationship earlier in their life, they are highly likely to be open to mentoring others. And that's as it should be. Mentoring is a matter of passing the baton to someone else. So, in a sense, you're looking around to ask: Who is running with a baton right now? Sooner or later they have to pass that baton off to someone else. There's no reason in the world that that someone can't be you.

When it comes to appraising a man's openness to a relationship, you'll have to be the judge of how deep you're hoping to go with him. But if you want a man who can pour into your soul, then you have to find a man capable of doing that. How would you know? Well, how deep does he appear to have looked into his own soul? Is he willing to talk about his own experiences, his feelings, and his struggles? Is he able to laugh at his own limitations and apologize when he's caused problems for others?

Relationships are about give and take—or better yet, about give and receive. You're hoping to receive something vital from this man. Is he capable of giving that? (Don't worry, it's not all one-way. You'll end up giving to him in ways you don't even realize.)

4. He Is Respected by Other Men

The idea here is that you want to check out a prospective mentor's character. How do other men see him, especially those who are seasoned in the faith? And for that matter, what is his reputation with those who are not (yet) Christians? It doesn't do any good for a man to be esteemed at church while people outside the church wouldn't trust him to take out their trash![3]

I'm suggesting that you conduct a kind of "background check" on your prospect, particularly if you don't know him personally or have not known him for very long. Your purpose is not to go digging for dirt, but rather to assess his reputation as a gauge of his character and integrity.

Ask around to find people who have known him well over time— perhaps a pastor, a friend, a coworker. What opinion do they seem to have of him? How do they react when you bring up his name, which you can easily do by saying something like, "Hey, I met Mr. So-and-So the other day. He seems like a pretty good guy. Do you know him?" How do those people talk about him? Do they speak highly of him? Or do you get the sense that they have reservations? How much do they trust and respect him?

It shouldn't take you long to get a sense for what the man's core values are—what a man values means everything when it comes to mentoring! Is he a workaholic, or does he put his work in perspective with the rest of his life? Where does his family fit into his priorities? Is he known for his integrity? Is he a man of his word? Does he speak honestly? Is he consistent in how he lives out his core convictions? Or is he in bondage to the fear of man?[4]

No man is perfect, except Jesus. But the point is that you're going to be influenced by the values, perspectives, and opinions of the man you allow to mentor you—again, as iron sharpens iron. So pay attention to whom that influential man is going to be. To the extent you can, you want to know up front what his limitations are and whether he's in touch with them and generally on top of them, or vice versa. A man whose character is flawed will likely reproduce those flaws in you—to an extent.

5. He Has Experienced Brokenness

The older I get, the more I appreciate the role that brokenness plays in a man's life. Brokenness means a situation in which one is taken all the way to the end of himself and left with absolutely no other recourse but to throw himself on the grace and mercy of God.

Brokenness invariably comes through significant adversity and/or suffering: the death of a spouse or child, a significant financial reversal, a tragic accident or life-threatening illness, a marriage-ending betrayal, a foolish choice that cost everything one had worked a lifetime to achieve.

Proverbs says, "The refining pot is for silver and the furnace for gold, but the LORD tests hearts" (17:3). The image is of a white-hot crucible in which a precious metal is melted to remove its impurities.

Similarly, God sometimes allows a man to be "melted down" so his heart is "tested." It's not the kind of test that includes right or wrong answers. It's more like a litmus test. God tests a man's heart to reveal what is in his heart.

In the Bible, God tested Abraham and found that Abraham would trust God's goodness and the reliability of His promises to Abraham, even if it meant giving up his own son. Abraham believed that somehow God would find a way to make good on His word. By contrast, God tested David to show him that his heart was as evil and wicked and as bloodthirsty as any of the pagan kings he had overthrown. Upon seeing that dark, evil reality, David was utterly undone and reduced to shame. He then begged God to purify his heart.[5]

Revealing what is in one's heart through extraordinarily difficult circumstances is a severe mercy. Through brokenness, a man comes to realize that his need for God is not partial but total. He throws away the ludicrous lie of self-reliance—that he is the captain of his soul, the master of his fate.[6] He comes to know in his heart, by experience, that he is what he is only by the grace of God. And he's confident that God's grace is really all he needs.

A man like that is worth gold as a mentor! I'm not saying that a man who hasn't experienced brokenness isn't worth considering as a mentor. But if you can find a man who's been through significant brokenness and has come out on the other side with a deeper trust in God and walk with Christ, I can almost guarantee he'll be willing to build some kind of relationship with you. That's just what brokenness does. It softens a man's heart and makes him much, much more compassionate and empathetic. And he almost always welcomes the opportunity to share with another man the wisdom he has gained through his trials.

6. He Seems to Take an Interest in You

In a way, this suggestion is an extension of number 3: Look for men who seem open to a relationship. But here I'm suggesting that you pay particular attention when someone seems not only open to a relationship, but genuinely *interested* in a relationship—with you!

I'll never forget the time my dad came home from a trip and told me about a businessman he had met. You'd have to know my dad to appreciate this, but just the way he was talking about the man, I realized he had to be a pretty amazing individual.

After singing his praises for a while, my dad then stunned me by saying, "Yes, and he says he wants to meet you." That stopped me in my tracks! "What did you say? Meet *me*?" I exclaimed. "Why in the world would he want to meet me?" Dad insisted it was so. He even gave me the guy's contact information.

So I decided not to question the man's intentions and called his office. To my shock, his assistant already knew who I was and why I was calling, and she put me on his calendar for just a few days later. I couldn't believe it.

A week later, I drove to the man's company (making sure to leave plenty of time to get there) and showed up at the appointed hour. I was greeted warmly by the man's assistant, and with absolutely no delay was ushered into his office. He greeted me with an enthusiastic handshake and invited me to have lunch with him at a table that was set for two. We spent a couple of hours or so just talking. Early on, I began asking him about his business, but he summed that part of his life up in about five sentences.

Then he began asking about me and my story (I was just getting started in my career). I found it quite reassuring that he seemed to take me seriously. And as he learned more about my aspirations and interests, he began telling me about his own aspirations and inter-ests. We ended up spending half of his afternoon in conversation before I left to head back home.

Now, I suppose there could have been any number of reasons why a man like that would devote that kind of time to me. Maybe he thought he was doing my dad a favor. Maybe he was sizing me up to work in his company. Maybe he was checking out my dad as a prospective mentor by seeking to get "the real story" on my dad from me.

Or maybe, just maybe, he was actually interested in me. Maybe my dad had said something to him about me that piqued his curiosity and caused him to say, "Your son sounds like an interesting person. I'd love to meet him. Would you mind asking him to contact me?"

I say that because a few days later, I received a note from him, attached to an article related to something we had talked about and inviting me to come back and see him sometime soon. Which I did. And quite apart from anything he had going with my dad, that man and I became friends over the years, and I regard him as one of my most cherished mentors. I can honestly say I would not be the man I am today were it not for his influence.

Sometimes younger men assume they have little to offer, with the result that they assume older men have little interest in spending time with them. Nothing could be further from the truth! Young adults have no idea how much leverage they have with older adults. When an older man sees something in a younger man—quite likely something that the younger man can't even see in himself—it's almost instinctive for the older man to do something to try and extract that potential. Usually, that starts with the older man trying to initiate some kind of relationship.

So if or whenever that happens for you, don't blow it off. Don't assume the older man is "just being a nice guy." Maybe he is a nice guy. But maybe he is seeing something of a younger version of himself in you, and he wants to help you become the best man you can be faster and better than he has. Check out the other criteria I've suggested, for sure. But if a man seems to enjoy your company and invites you to get together, by all means go until the light turns red. Sometimes, your mentor finds you before you find him!

HOW PROSPECTIVE MENTORS LOOK AT YOU

Believe it or not, you're not the only one looking for a mentoring relationship. There are actually men who are eager to play the role of a mentor in other men's lives. While there may not be many, relatively speaking, they are out there—and if I have my way through this book, hopefully there will be a lot more of them out there.

Mentors exist. But they don't just take on all comers. Mentors have to be picky, too. After all, they're going to make an investment in you—an investment of time, energy, emotion, trust, and other resources. That involves a measure of risk. If they devote the best of what they have to offer to you, what will you end up doing with it? Obviously, you want them to take a chance on you. But if they place that bet, are you worthy of it?

Here are a few factors I weigh as I assess those odds. You can use these criteria to do a little self-analysis and, where needed, make corrections.

1. Are You Ready?

This is an issue of timing and preparation. I've already said that mentoring involves not just skills and knowledge, but soul work. The process is aimed at making you a better man. Some men aren't quite ready for that.

It's not that they don't have potential. *Every* man has potential. But sometimes a man needs to do some demolition of old, worthless patterns or rid himself of a debilitating condition before he's ready to do the positive work of cultivating his soul with another man.

For example, mentors will tend to shy away from a man who is enslaved to an addiction. That's not a rejection but a concession to the fact that mentoring won't get very far as long as the man he's trying to influence is acting out. That man will do better to spend some serious time in an effective recovery process first so that he puts himself in a position to pursue positive growth.

Similar conditions would be psychological states such as

chronic/clinical depression, anxiety disorders, bipolar disorder, an eating disorder, schizophrenia, and the like. It's not that mentors don't care about the person who is struggling with a challenge like those. They care a great deal—so much so that they want the person to work with someone trained to help them with their challenge.

2. Are You Capable of a Relationship?

Just as you're going to gauge whether a prospective mentor is open to a relationship (suggestion number 3 above), so a mentor will ask the same thing about you. Fortunately, most mentor-types will give you the benefit of the doubt, at least initially. They're not too demanding. At minimum, they just want to see whether you can hold a conversation and respond somewhat meaningfully when they ask you a question. That's really not a very high bar!

Nevertheless, some men can't clear even that threshold. Again, that probably has to do with some damage that occurred in their upbringing. Four things will prove especially disruptive to having a productive relationship, and therefore will be off-putting to a prospective mentor:

- *Anger*. Mentors can usually deal with it when you show up frustrated over a setback at your job or mad at your girlfriend over a conflict in your relationship with her. But if a man senses—and it won't take him long to do so—that you're a volcano of seething rage and resentment inside, he's going to break off his relationship with you, unless he's a trained professional tasked with helping men with anger issues. At some point, that anger may be directed at him, and he wants none of that.

- *Fear*. Similar to anger, mentors generally have no problem empathizing with whatever insecurities you may be feeling as far as your competence, adequacy, self-esteem, and so on. Dealing with that stuff is a large part of what mentoring is about. But if you're unable to trust the man you want to mentor you, then a relationship with him is not really possible. It won't take him long to perceive that, and when he does, he may ask you about it. If he does, you should thank your lucky stars! He's giving you an opportunity to work on that debilitating part of yourself. But if he concludes you're afraid of him to the point of being incapable of trusting him, he'll back off.

- *Defensiveness.* Defensiveness can be driven by either anger or fear, or both. Regardless, only a rare man will tolerate getting his hand bitten off when he asks a simple question. Defensiveness indicates that you don't want to be vulnerable and transparent. If that's so, then you'll have a hard time finding a mentor.

- *Lying.* Relationships are based on trust, so a prospective mentor instinctively asks himself whether you look like someone who will be honest and shoot straight. He understands that you want to make a good impression and that you're going to put your best foot forward. There's nothing wrong with that. Nor is he expecting you to tell him all of your deepest, darkest secrets and sins the first time you meet him—or even the second or third time. But whatever you tell him—whether the first time you meet or the thirty-first time—tell him the truth, the whole truth and nothing but the truth. He can handle it. Can you? If not, he'll shut down the relationship because no one wants to waste his time on a liar.

3. Are You Teachable?

A world of difference exists between ability and teachability. I discovered that through my oldest daughter, Brittany. As a high school senior, she aspired to become a professional trumpet player, so she auditioned at a university renowned for its trumpet studio. Ninety-six other students were also competing for the three undergraduate slots available for the coming year. A few weeks after her audition, Brittany received a letter informing her that she had been awarded a spot in the studio. Needless to say, she was elated (as was I)!

So how did she do it? Well, she obviously has ability. But she by no means saw herself as the best trumpet player of the bunch—and she wasn't. But I learned that during an audition, the instructor will often stop a student and ask him/her to play the music in a different way—perhaps using a different technique or putting emphasis on a particular note. The instructor watches to see how the student will respond to direction.

Some students with outstanding talent balk at such interruptions. Doesn't the instructor realize how good they are? They already know what they're doing. Just let them show their stuff! But the instructor knows that he or she is going to put countless hours into each of the musicians in the studio over the next four years or more. So he or she watches to see how well a student takes instruction, and how responsive they are to it. The instructor doesn't want to waste time on someone who thinks they already have it all figured out. In that case, they don't need the instructor!

Like that instructor, a prospective mentor pays less attention to your ability than to your teachability, which should give you hope if you don't think you have much ability. In truth, you likely have far more ability than you realize. It's just that no one has ever helped you cultivate it. If you're eager to learn, humble enough to take instruction, and diligent enough to do what it takes, you're a mentor's dream! Who wouldn't want to invest in a man like that?

4. Are You Dependable?

Speaking of ability, I recently listened to a sports talk show in which the broadcasters were discussing various players on the Dallas Cowboys football team. One name sparked instant praise. "Why, he's the best in the league at his position!" one participant declared. Unfortunately, that player is injury-prone, and he'd been out with an injury for several games—a scenario that had happened in several previous seasons. Debate ensued over whether he was ready to come back. Could the team get by with his replacement for one more week? That player was also good, but not nearly as good as the star.

At that point, one of the other commentators spoke up with a dissenting opinion: "Guys, whenever he comes back, that's great. But this is a case where availability trumps ability. At some point it becomes more important that a guy can play, period, not whether he's the best player at his position."

A similar situation exists with mentoring. A prospective mentor is asking himself whether you seem like someone he can depend on. Are you reliable? If you agree to meet with him, will you show up? Will you show up on time? Will you show up prepared? In short, will you take the relationship seriously?

5. Can You Be Trusted with Confidences?

Mentoring is a privileged relationship. In mentoring, I have the high honor of listening to someone tell me his real thoughts and feelings, his hopes and desires, his fears and failures, his dreams and doubts. When he does, I feel so honored that he would take me into his confidence! I regard that level of vulnerability as a sacred trust, a responsibility that I take extremely seriously.

In turn, I let the man I'm working with in on what I've experienced and seen, and some of the lessons I've learned thereby. I may tell him stories I've shared with very few other people. I may voice opinions and ideas that I hope will prove helpful. And I may even take him into my confidence and talk about my own failures and what I would or could have done differently in times past—all in the interest of helping him grow. Naturally, I expect him to be discreet about what I've shared with him.

No mentoring relationship starts there. But because I know where it might go, I start out by sizing up the other man from the get-go as to what he will do when he hears things he maybe didn't expect to hear. Can I trust him to honor our relationship, as I will?

If you want a man to influence you, you have to expect that he's going to tell you things that are personal and private. That's the value of mentoring. It's not a transaction. It's personal. It's life on life. You're being invited into a man's world. And in that world, trust is the coin of the realm. So, the question you have to ask yourself is: Am I worthy of another man's trust?

6. Are You Someone I Would Trust with My Network?

Every mentor is a doorway into a network. As helpful as the mentor himself might be to you, he knows people who might be infinitely more helpful. That alone makes a mentor invaluable.

A few years ago, my friend Chris was just getting started in the world of development and raising funds for nonprofit work. Chris quickly realized that asking people for money is a rather sophisticated art. He needed help in learning that art from the standpoint of both the fundraiser and the donor.

So, Chris did something smart. He nosed around until he identified a man who has raised millions of dollars for Christian causes over the years and is regarded by many as a genius in that area. The two linked up, and that man began tutoring Chris in the finer points of philanthropy and donor development.

Consider the resources that man was able to offer Chris. He had a contacts list with thousands of names that Chris didn't have. He personally knew most of those people on a first-name basis. He knew where the affluent donor-types hang out and how to gain access to their exclusive venues. He knew who was giving and to which causes, how much they were giving, why they gave, and even what their potential for future gifts might be.

No amount of schooling, reading, research, or hard work on Chris's part could have ever equaled what he had by being connected to his mentor. One phone call or email of introduction, one important piece of information from that man, and Chris was already miles ahead of where he would otherwise have been.

You may have already realized that if you can find a mentor, you find a network. But consider this carefully: before anyone exports someone else's vCard to you, he has to have confidence that you're going to treat that contact list like the precious gift that it is. By putting you in touch with someone in his network, he's essentially putting his own reputation on the line for you. He's signaling to the other person, "Hey, here's someone I think you ought to know. I've checked him out. He's a good guy. He's worth your attention. You can trust me on this."

If he does that for you, will you be worthy of his generosity? That's what he's asking himself as he's getting to know you. He's reading you to see whether you're genuinely wanting to grow and develop, or whether you're just out to use him. If he suspects the latter, he'll at best throw you only a few crumbs from his contacts list—people you could probably access without his help. But if he sees that you're in earnest and that the people in his network will actually benefit by getting to know you—and vice versa—then he'll begin to open some doors for you. And that's when things get really exciting!

"CHEMISTRY"

So there you have it: six things to look for in prospective mentors, and six things they are sizing up in you. But what about the elusive element of "chemistry"? How do we account for the fact that two people just seem to "click," as we say? They experience an unexplainable connection to each other. They find it easy (or easier) to be with one another and communicate. In short, they "like" each other. This phenomenon is highly subjective, but universally present in relationships.

So what does it mean for mentoring? Two things, it seems to me. First, chemistry can't be forced. It either happens or it doesn't. That's one of the greatest challenges to organizations that set up programs for mentoring. They throw a mentor and a mentee (or protégé)[7] together and tell them to work with each other. Certainly, good things might result from that. But if there's no chemistry, the experience for one or both parties is liable to be mediocre at best.

The one caveat in saying that chemistry can't be forced is that chemistry may be delayed in happening. I can think of several of my mentors who initially underwhelmed me. Some of them I felt I had little in common with and felt no compelling interest in knowing them. But later, as circumstances changed—more importantly, as I changed—those men came to have a new appeal, and I found myself drawn toward them.

Which brings up a second reality: chemistry doesn't have to go both ways. If either person feels an attraction, an interest, a pull toward the other person, that can be enough. Remember, iron sharpens iron: an iron mallet strikes an iron blade and bends it back into shape. If I have an odd feeling that another man could "sharpen" me if I just hang around him, then he may well turn out to be a mentor for me. Conversely, if I see something in a man and feel a strange impulse to try and "sharpen" him in some way, I may well turn out to be a mentor for him.

I think we would see a lot more mentoring taking place if men would trust their instincts and explore beneficial relationships with one another. Are you ready to do that? In the next chapter we'll talk about how to get things started.

CHAPTER 6

PUTTING YOURSELF IN OPPORTUNITY'S PATH

Most mentoring happens unintentionally and unexpectedly. But we know it does happen. It's like lightning. No one can predict where or when lightning is going to strike. Nevertheless, we know that it *will* strike. That being the case, if one wants to increase the odds of a lightning strike, he should find a thunderstorm, get under it with a metal rod, and stick the rod up in the sky. Sooner or later, lightning is bound to strike!

In this chapter, I want to offer some strategies for increasing the odds that lightning will strike in your search for a mentor.

START BY PRAYING FOR A MENTOR

Do you think God wants you to find mentors? Let me ask it differently: Do you think God wants you to grow into the man He intends you to be? I don't think there's any question about that. The New Testament says, "It is God who works in you to will and to act in order to fulfill his good purpose" (Phil. 2:13 NIV) So, if God wants you to grow into a mature, whole man (like Christ), and mentors are a vital means of bringing that about, then God has more of an interest in you finding mentors than you do!

But you might ask: If God already knows I need a mentor, why do I need to pray to find one? For the same reason Jesus told us to pray and ask God to meet all our other needs: "Ask, and it will be given to you; seek, and you will find; knock, and it will be opened to you. For everyone who asks receives, and he who seeks finds, and to him who knocks it will be opened" (Matt. 7:7–8). "For your Father knows what you need before you ask Him" (6:8).

Again, why would Jesus instruct us to ask God for what He already knows we need? As Richard Foster explains, "The most straightfor-ward answer to this question is simply that God likes to be asked. We like our children to ask us for things that we already know they need because the very asking enhances and deepens the relationship."[1]

The question here is not whether God knows what you need, but whether you realize you are totally dependent on God to meet your needs. Are you sincerely eager to find a mentor? Then by all means, start praying about that! Pray earnestly. Pray intentionally. Praying intentionally for a mentor indicates you are intentional about finding one. In God's good timing, you will. And when you do, your trust in a good God will increase.

PLACES TO LOOK FOR A MENTOR

The *where* of finding a mentor is deceptively obvious: potential men-tors are all around you. So why don't you see them? It may be that you're looking for all the wrong things. You may have the idea that a mentor has to be someone who is unusually successful, prominent, brilliant, or outstanding in some other way. But the truth is many men who would make the best mentors are not spectacular but just solid. They may not stand out in a crowd, but they stand tall in terms of the criteria I laid out in the previous chapter.

With that in mind, two hunting grounds seem the most obvious. The first is your work. The workplace is, by far, the most obvious source of mentors in our society today. That's where most of us spend most of our time. Indeed, for many of us, the people at work become like a second family—for better or worse. So, think through your coworkers, your supervisors, your vendors, and others in your field or industry. Think through your union or your professional association. Flip through your contacts list. Does anybody strike you as a possible mentor?

A second obvious place that can be a gold mine for finding a mentor is your church. That's because churches are intended to be centers of human development (the technical term is "discipleship").[2] I'd be amazed if you couldn't find at least one or two seasoned men at your church who have something to offer you and are willing to get together to tell you what they know. If your church has absolutely *no* men like that, then I'm not sure you're at the right church, because that's the pattern of healthy, biblically based churches: to raise up godly men who in turn raise up godly men.

What if you don't go to church? Well, you should start looking for a church *today*! I'm well aware that many millennials (among others) see church as optional. Some of them have had bad experiences with churches, and they can see all kinds of problems with churches.

Well, guess what? No millennial has more experience with churches than I do, because I've been going to church since nine months before I was born, and I've been part of a church somewhere my entire life. Believe me, I've seen it a lot—the good, the bad, and the ugly.[3] But if I'm going to follow Christ, then I must love what Christ loves. And if Christ loves anything, He loves churches. Not only *the* church as a whole, but also all the local expressions of it worldwide.

Both Scripture (see Acts 2:44–47; Heb. 10:24-25) and history show that it is well-nigh impossible to make much progress in following Jesus apart from a community of God's people. Regardless of whatever reasons you may have for not being part of a church, your spiritual health and vitality actually depend on committing yourself to a local, physical expression of God's people somewhere (even if much of your participation takes place online).

WHAT ABOUT MEN WHO ARE NOT CHRISTIANS?

It would be a mistake to assume that only men who are followers of Christ can make a substantial, positive impact on your life. In all likelihood, you've already experienced the positive benefits of hanging around someone who by no means was a man of faith but had real wisdom to impart to you[4]—perhaps a coach in high school, a sergeant in the military, a boss at work, or a neighbor up the street.

In my own experience, I'll never forget the time as a teenager when I was driving our family's 1967 metallic-green Ford Mustang (that was a classic!), and it broke down in traffic. Fortunately, there was a filling station nearby, and I pushed the car into its driveway and asked for help. The owner was a crusty old man who was puffing on a fat cigar and looked like he didn't care one whit about me or my car. But with a grunt, he jacked up the hood and started looking things over.

While he did, I glanced around his shop. The walls were adorned with scandalous calendars, and it was evident that this was no shrine of faith. The man poked and prodded, spat and swore, until finally he said, "Here's your problem," and held up a spark plug wire. "Sometimes they get a short in 'em," he explained, "and it sure knocks the [expletive] out of the engine."

After he replaced the wire, I followed him into the office to pay up. I had two dollars and change on me. The bill came to a little more than five bucks. "Can I write you a check?" I asked (I can't believe I used to carry a checkbook with me!)

The mechanic nodded, and I made out the check. After handing it over, I reached for my license, but the owner waived me off. "I don't need to see that," he growled. "If you're gonna stiff me on a five-dollar check, then you're really not worth a [expletive]!"

A salty observation, yes. But it was a basic lesson in honesty, and from a most unexpected source. As you can see, I never forgot that man or that lesson. I doubt he knew Jesus, but he clearly knew something about trust and honesty.

In the ideal, you should look for mentors among those who are vibrant Christ-followers who can speak to you from a biblical foundation. But when someone comes along who doesn't fit that category, don't automatically rule him out just because he's not a follower of Jesus. He may actually invigorate your faith through the way he sees things and lives his life. You may even find that your relationship with him causes him to consider (or reconsider) his own spiritual needs.

However, be aware of the stream from which you are drinking. As Paul wrote, "Examine everything carefully; hold fast to that which is good; abstain from every form of evil" (1 Thess. 5:21–22).

MAKING AN INITIAL CONNECTION

Okay, let's say you've identified a man that you think might be a candidate to become one of your mentors. What do you do next? That all depends on your relationship to him. How well you know him determines your initial approach.

There are three possibilities: (1) you already know the man, and he knows you; (2) you do not know each other personally, only by name; or (3) you have no relationship whatsoever. Yet think of these possibilities as overlapping and existing along a continuum.

Generally speaking, the better you know the man, the more you can rely on your relationship with him as a basis for asking for his help. Conversely, the less you know the man in question, the more you'll have to approach him on some other basis than a prior relationship. So let's look at how to approach a man depending on these three possibilities:

1. You Already Know the Man Reasonably Well
If you and the man already have a relationship, then asking for his input shouldn't be difficult. You may have already done that before.

Of course, just because you ask for his input doesn't immediately make him your mentor. But at least you know that the next time you've got an issue, you can probably turn to him again. And he now knows that you are serious about your life. That's the sort of positive, productive interaction that can turn into a mentoring relationship.

2. You Know Each Other by Name Only

Whether at work, at church, in your community, or wherever, you likely have various acquaintances, men whom you perhaps know by name but have never really interacted with.

With that pool of men in mind, let's say you encounter a serious problem. For example, one of your children is diagnosed with a life-threatening illness. That's not something to walk through by yourself. You would be well served to invite another man to come alongside you and give you moral support, guidance, and wisdom, because you're now sailing in uncharted waters.

So, let's say one of your close friends or perhaps a pastor at your church mentions that a guy named Pete faced a similar situation when his kids were little. You know Pete in passing, but you don't know him well. But if he's gone through what you're going through, he could be a Fort Knox of input at this point.

There are two possibilities, then, for approaching Pete. First, you could just contact him directly and ask if he'd mind getting together. But you may feel that would be too awkward or too forward. In that case, contact Pete and remind him of how you know him. Then briefly describe your situation and ask him if he knows of any resources that would help. Presenting the matter in those terms allows Pete to choose how much he wants to get involved. But there is a strong possibility that he will talk about his own experience with his child's illness. At the very least, he will have been offered a chance to help—and people who have been through tough times usually like to help someone else walking that same difficult journey, to the extent they can.

The other possibility is to ask the person who mentioned Pete to you whether they would mind contacting Pete and gauging his willingness to give you some help.

So, if Pete agrees to help you, does that qualify as a mentoring relationship? No, it doesn't start out there, but it could turn into that. The point is that your initial approach would be determined more by the problem at hand than by the relationship. Quite possibly, a deeper relationship could grow out of that initial conversation. In fact, you would want to ask Pete if you could call him from time to time, which leaves the door open to future possibilities.

3. You Are Strangers to Each Other

Just because you don't know someone doesn't mean there's no possibility for initiating a relationship. There are several strategies for making yourself known to a man who looks like he might be a potential mentor.

The first is to approach him on the basis of his expertise. However, you have to be smart about how you do that. You can't just call George Lucas and say, "Mr. Lucas, I'm a huge *Star Wars* fan, and I've decided I want to make movies like you do. Would you mentor me?" First, you'll never get to George Lucas—at least, not that way. And even if you did, he would almost certainly be put off by that approach. It's not only too forward, but also too self-centered. It's only considering what you want, not what might be in his interests.

But let's stick with the example. Let's say you do, in fact, aspire to be a filmmaker, a storyteller who uses film as your medium. Don't start with George Lucas. Start with somebody local, somebody more at hand, and somebody more accessible—somebody who might return your call or email. Perhaps a professor of film at a college in your town or state, or a man who produces TV commercials.

Approach him *first* to ask for information.[5] For example:

Hello, Mr. Smith,

My name is Bill Hendricks. I'm a sophomore in college at Local University, and I am thinking through my career options in preparation for selecting a major. Among the options I'm considering is filmmaking, which has always fascinated me. But before I commit to that path, I thought it would be helpful to talk to people who are already pursuing similar careers.

I know that you make films and similar media in your work. Would it be possible for me to get together with you for a half-hour or so sometime in the near future, to learn firsthand a bit more about what filmmaking actually entails? Please understand, I am not looking for a job, I'm just looking for information.

Thanks for any help you can offer.

Bill Hendricks

Framing things that way leaves the man in control. He can say yes or no. In my experience, unless it's just a bad time for him, 90 percent of the time he will say yes.[6] Why? Because older, experienced people seem to have a heart for younger, less experienced people who care about what they care about. They just do.

Will a thirty-minute meeting lead to a mentoring relationship? I don't know. Will throwing a baited hook in a lake lead to catching a fish? I don't know that either. But I know you won't catch any fish otherwise.

Potential mentors are all around you. But they can't tell whether you're looking for a mentor until you exhibit the behaviors of someone looking for a mentor. Asking for information about a potential career option is often perceived as one of those behaviors.

You may feel hesitant to approach a complete stranger, no matter how much you think he might have to offer you. In that case, nose around in your network to see whether you know anyone who knows the man in question and would be willing to put you in touch with him. Failing that, see whether you know anyone who knows someone who knows the man in question, and ask whether they will put you in touch with that person so you can ask them if they would put you in touch with that man. Using that strategy, you'd be surprised at how closely related you are to most anyone you'd ever want to meet.

MORE IDEAS FOR INITIATING A MENTORING RELATIONSHIP

There are endless possibilities for making an initial contact with someone who might be a potential mentor. This is an area where creativity and initiative count for a lot. Obviously, some men are better than others at initiating relationships. But here's a list of ideas to stimulate your creative juices. Remember, we're talking about attracting the attention of a prospective mentor and signaling that you'd like to get to know him better.

1. *Bring him information in which he might be interested.* I just suggested a strategy of information-gathering as a way to meet and initiate a relationship with a potential mentor. The same principle works in reverse. If you can bring a man something he needs to know about or that benefits what he is working on, you will likely have his ear. You'll at least have his interest.

For example, suppose your prospect is interested in a particular cause, such as helping troubled youth. You come across a write-up of a novel approach to that problem that is being tried in another community, with considerable success. Why not send that to him with a note: "Al, you may already know about this, but when I saw this article I thought of your concern for kids. I would love to discuss it with you sometime. Let me know."

2. *Bring him an interesting opportunity that you have.* By an "interesting opportunity," I mean interesting to *him*. It needs to be worthy of his attention. For instance, when I was just starting out in my

career, I had high regard for a man in our community who was a creative genius in the display of information. I had actually studied that man's work to gain clues about his unique approach to communication. Then one day I was asked to serve on the board of a museum that was just getting started. Guess whom I immediately contacted about participating in that project? As I predicted, the man for whom I had such great admiration quickly became interested in the project, and before long he was heavily involved in it. I then had an opportunity to observe him up close and in action.

3. *Respond to something he has done.* Keep an eye out for the activities and accomplishments of your prospective mentor. Pay attention when he completes a project, writes a book or article, gives a speech, or wins an award. Those achievements provide you with opportunities to send him a note telling him not only that you've noticed what he's done, but that you've thought about what it means. He may well invite you to get together to talk about it some more.

4. *Ask him to look at and react to something that you have written or produced.* This is the reverse of the previous idea. If you've created something you think he might be interested in—a paper, a blog post, a report, or perhaps an artistic expression like a poem, a song, a painting, or a photograph—send him a copy for his review and feedback. Do this especially if he was an inspiration or help to you in producing it. Thank him for his assistance.

If the thing you've created can't be mailed or emailed, invite your prospect to come see it firsthand and give you an evaluation. Examples could include: You have a knack for laying tile, and you want him to see the walkway you've put in. You have a group of young people you've been working with and you want him to see that your efforts are succeeding. You're an actor and you'd like him to watch you in a play. You've been asked to give a speech at a community organization, and you'd like to invite him to come hear you.

Any and all of these scenarios open the door to follow-up interaction.

5. Offer to solve a problem for him. Prospective mentors are like the rest of us: they don't want people to bring them problems nearly as much as they want them to bring solutions. That's certainly true for me. Recently I was developing materials in connection with what I call giftedness coaching.[7] A man who had already been through some of that training brought me several models he had developed for ways to creatively summarize and apply the insights that people gain from a giftedness discovery process. I was thrilled! Needless to say, I've made time for that man ever since.

6. Interview him in connection with a project you are working on. This strategy is particularly useful if you've never met the man. The purpose of the interview needs to relate to something the man is already working on or interested in, but the interview format provides a specific reason for getting together. Thus, it minimizes the awkwardness that naturally arises when meeting a stranger. It breaks the ice in making an initial contact. And later, you may be able to follow up with subsequent visits based on that experience.

7. Praise the person on his expertise, then ask him to use it to help you develop yours. I once read about a young man named Andy who wanted to meet an expert in a particular field. The expert had written numerous journal and magazine articles (those were the days before the internet and blog posts), and he received quite a bit of criticism for his views. Andy wrote a letter defending the expert's position and sent it to the editor of one critical newspaper. The paper printed Andy's critique in its Letters to the Editor section, and Andy sent a copy of that to the man. In his cover letter, he asked the gentleman whether he would be willing to meet in person. Under the circumstances, the prospective mentor could hardly say no, and his office phoned Andy to schedule an appointment.[8]

You can use the same principle to initiate with your prospect. For example, "Ed, I was really impressed with your analysis of what worked and didn't work with the recent project we completed. Could I buy you lunch to find out more about how you went about putting all that together?" "John, I've never heard anyone talk about praying before going into a sales presentation, the way you did at our Bible study this morning. That's a new thought to me. Could I talk with you about how I could learn to pray like that?"

8. *Honor him publicly—or privately, as the case may be.* If you think highly of someone, let other people know, and why. Don't embarrass him by how you do that, but make it plain that you have high regard for him. For instance, if you win an award, consider honoring him when you're asked to say a few words (again, if it wouldn't embarrass him). If your team has had a big win and he's been a large part of that, then speak up when everyone is high-fiving and celebrating the victory by saying something like, "Hey, everybody, we all know that the guy we need to say a big thanks to is Jason, for all that he contributed to this achievement!"

You may be hesitant to do that, lest anyone think you are "sucking up" to a particular leader. In that case, never hesitate to write a private, personal note of thanks when someone has done something extraordinarily helpful or praiseworthy. People in today's workplace are particularly starved for affirmation. Even peak performers often wonder whether anyone really notices what they've done to achieve success. A brief, handwritten note from you will stand out like a clarion trumpet in a silent room.

9. *Take advantage of any structured opportunities for interaction that he offers.* If he teaches somewhere, show up. If he holds seminars, enroll in one. If he's going to make a presentation at your company, find a way to get a seat in the room. If he's going to facilitate a meeting, ask if you can be a participant. Scenarios like these are golden opportunities, because the whole point of such venues is to allow the man to influence people with his ideas and presence. There's not a reason in the world why you can't be one of those people.

I can think of two men I know right now who are rock stars when it comes to pursuing potential mentors through structured settings. I've watched both of them on numerous occasions approach a presenter after he's concluded his remarks and strike up a conversation. Invariably, they ask for a card, and, invariably, he hands them one with an invitation to follow up. That's all they need! They indeed follow up, with the result that they've developed some mentoring relationships with some of the key people in their respective fields.

10. *If he has ever told you to look him up sometime, take him up on his offer.* Obviously, this springboards off the example I just gave. But we've all had someone close a conversation or an email with the words, "Let's get together sometime."[9] If the man you're trying to get to know has ever used that line, then by all means follow up on it. Contact him and remind him of his offer, and give him some options for possible times to meet. I would suggest that you set forth a reason for why you're following up, even something as simple as, "You'll recall that we briefly talked about the challenges of corporate politics. I'd love to get more of your thoughts on that." However you do it, let him know that you are genuinely interested in *him*.

11. *Enlist the man's support even before you need it.* They say that the best time to look for a job is when you already have one. A similar principle applies to finding a mentor. As odd as it sounds, the best time to approach a potential mentor is long before you need his help. Why? Because you're probably more relaxed and the situation is less threatening when you don't need to ask for any favors.

I wish more young men in high school, vocational school, college, or graduate school could be helped to realize that many of the older men they know only casually will someday be the men they need to help them grow into manhood and get launched as adults. When you're trying to pick a major, trying to buy a used car, trying to understand your girlfriend, trying to figure out how you're going to pay for your education—those are relatively "low stress" issues that you should take to an older man to ask for his input. In doing so, you build relational capital with him that may come back to pay hefty dividends later.

"Later" means when you're in your late twenties or early thirties and you're starting a career, starting a family, buying a house, taking on real responsibility. Then you'll *really* need a mentor—only you won't have to look very far because you'll have that history with those older guys that you reached out to when you were a bit younger.

Potential mentors are all around you. But you may not need their help today. No matter. Get to know older men *today* because the time is coming when those older guys *will* be the guys you look to as mentors.

12. *Give him periodic updates on yourself.* Every man you meet should become part of your network. You'll have greater chemistry with some than with others, and some will more naturally fit with your own aspirations and needs. But if a man proves helpful to you once, there's a good chance he may prove helpful again in the future—quite likely even more helpful.

That being the case, stay in touch with men whose input you've found valuable, just to let them know what you're up to, what you're working on, and where you seem to be headed. An occasional email or phone call will signal to that man, "I'm still out here. I'm still in the game. I'm still growing. And I'm still interested in staying in touch." When the time is right, your relationship with him may take a whole new turn toward mentoring.

I have numerous men who drop me a note every time they are coming up to a job change. Others keep me posted on new projects they are working on or new opportunities that have come their way. And of course, some let me know about sadder news: job losses, illnesses, divorces, and setbacks. Either way, I appreciate that these men keep me informed. It renews the relationship. It reminds me to pray for them and tells me how to pray more intelligently. And it leaves the door open to future interaction.

ONE THING NOT TO DO

Let me offer a word of caution before we leave this chapter. If I were you, I would avoid using the terms *mentor* or *mentoring* as you approach the man. I know that sounds utterly ludicrous, since I use those terms repeatedly throughout this book. But that's this book. Things are different in everyday life.

Think about it through your prospective mentor's eyes. Imagine that you show up in front of him, and after some casual conversation to break the ice, he asks you how he can be of help. So you clear your throat and say, "Well, the truth of the matter is, I'm looking for a mentor. Will you mentor me?"

You're liable to get one of two reactions. On one hand, he may get a puzzled look and ask, "Huh? What do you mean a mentor? I'm not sure I know what you're talking about!" I doubt that will instill much confidence in you.

But the more likely scenario is that he will give you a deer-in-the-headlights look and turn a bit pale before he holds up his hands and says, "Oh, buddy, you've got the wrong guy! I mean, I'm not . . . I can't . . . I wouldn't know the first thing about that. A mentor? No way!" Somehow, I don't think you'd want that reaction, either.

But why would he react that way? Because men don't see themselves as potential mentors. It doesn't matter whether they actually have that capacity (most do). They simply don't see themselves that way.

That's because many men have unrealistic expectations of what a mentor is and does. Others are afraid of sounding pretentious. You see, in our culture, it's okay for someone to perceive *me* as his mentor; it's not okay for me to see *myself* as his mentor. Make of it what you will, but that's the reality. So you have to pay attention to it.

Fortunately, you don't need to talk about a "mentor" or "mentoring" to establish the relationship you want. It doesn't matter how you describe it. What matters is that you develop it. So just pay attention to the relationship.

Are you willing to glean from another man's wisdom, experience, and expertise? Are you willing to seek him out for advice? Are you willing, when it becomes appropriate, to shoot straight and let him know what you're really thinking and feeling? Are you willing to ask him for help in troubleshooting problems, recommending resources, introducing you to people, and otherwise opening doors to the world and windows to the mind? If so, *that's* what we're talking about.

CHAPTER 7

MAKING THE RELATIONSHIP WORK

Okay, so you've initiated a relationship with a prospective mentor. Now what? Do you just let your proposed mentor take the lead and set a course for working together?

I'm afraid not. With one exception—which I'll cover in a moment—you can't assume that any man automatically comes pre-programmed to know exactly what he's supposed to do as a "mentor." It just doesn't work that way.

STEPPING UP TO YOUR RESPONSIBILITY

That being the case, the ball remains in your court to, believe it or not, guide your mentor in how he can best guide you. That may sound like a contradiction, but it's not. It's really no different from going to your doctor, a lawyer, or an auto mechanic and explaining how you think he or she could help you. You don't just passively show up and let them try to figure out what they can do for you.

What I'm describing here is a basic fact of life: whether it's mentoring, your health, your education, your finances, your marriage, your relationships, or whatever, *you* have to take responsibility for your life. No one can do that for you. When you were a baby—and I suppose as a little boy growing up into your adolescent years—your parents bore the lion's share of responsibility for what happened to you. Maybe they did a good job; maybe not. Regardless, once you finally turned eighteen—which, in United States culture, is the threshold of adult independence—you were handed responsibility for your own life. That's how it works.

I'm not talking down to you. I'm talking to you man to man. If you're eighteen, you're an adult now. You're not a kid anymore.[1] You may be a "young adult," but you're an adult nonetheless. That's exciting, because the world needs what you were put here to offer!

In truth, taking control of your life is actually what you've wanted to do since you were about twelve or thirteen. That's how God makes human beings. That's normal, natural, and healthy. So, taking responsibility in a mentoring relationship translates into thinking meaningfully about how the man you'd like to mentor you can be most helpful to you. You can then communicate that to him so he has direction for what you're hoping (expecting) from him.

A RELATIONSHIP WITH A PURPOSE

What I'm describing here is a relationship with a *purpose*. Many relationships aren't really governed by a purpose per se. Take your friends, for example. You hang out with them because you like them and they like you. Or consider your neighbors. They live close by, and hopefully everyone tries to keep things reasonably livable. But you couldn't really say that there's a "reason" they are your neighbors.

But a mentoring relationship is different. No man looks for a mentor just because he thinks it's a good idea to have a mentor. He looks for a mentor because he has some sort of notion for how a mentor could be helpful to him.

Maybe he thinks having a mentor will advance his career, teach him a new skill, help him sort out a problem, or point him in the right direction. Even men who are assigned mentors by their company submit to mentoring because that's a condition for working at that company.

Knowing your purpose in getting together with your mentor helps you set expectations and establish an agenda, meaning the things you intend to work on—your goals, issues, problems, needs. Establishing an agenda is key because it informs what you'll actually do when you and your mentor get together.

However, as you and your mentor work out an agenda, a lot depends on whether you're operating under a formal or an informal mentoring arrangement.

FORMAL VERSUS INFORMAL MENTORING

There are two basic kinds of mentoring. One is structured, facilitated, and formal. The other is nonstructured, spontaneous, and informal. We could view these as two ends of a spectrum, and in fact we often find the two combined: formal mentoring programs that involve informal activities, and informal mentoring relationships that make use of more formal strategies for development.

Formal Programs

Formal programs for mentoring are now common in schools and workplaces. Many churches and parachurch ministries have also developed mentoring programs in recent years[2] (see Appendix A: Formal Mentoring Programs). In a formal program, a younger or junior participant (often called a "mentee" or "protégé") is paired up with an older, more seasoned mentor whose job is to take the mentee under his or her wing and guide them through some form of training or orientation process. In some cases, the program is structured by an established set of guidelines for how often to meet, what to cover, how to mark progress, and so on.

Even a casual survey of the many formal mentoring programs that now exist shows a wide variety of models being used. They range from the relative few that are extremely well designed and executed, to the many that are somewhat perfunctory. Not surprisingly, where quality is high, results are impressive (when evaluated over the long term). Conversely, formal programs that are mere formalities are rarely given high marks by those who participate in them.

Without question, formal mentoring programs can be difficult to execute. As I noted earlier, one of the hardest things is to get the match right, the "chemistry" between the mentee and mentor. But that aside, the number one factor that determines whether a mentoring program takes hold and makes a difference is whether people-development—for which mentoring is a strategy—is a core value of the organization. That means that mentoring is not so much a program as it is "the way we do things around here."

Informal Mentoring

By far, the most common form of mentoring is the informal approach. It is rarely called mentoring and tends to be overlooked. Nevertheless, you can find the principles of informal mentoring being practiced everywhere. For example:

- A manager at a company invites an up-and-coming employee who shows promise as a leader to sit down and help him plan an upcoming meeting. In addition to setting the agenda and talking points for the meeting, they discuss the nature of meetings and how to make them effective. The manager then lets the junior leader run part of the meeting they've planned together. Then they debrief afterward on what happened. Through these interactions, the manager informally mentors the employee.

- A man invites a teenage neighbor to help him with some home landscaping. He shows him how to move dirt using a mini-Cat, place stones for a walkway, plant shrubs and small trees, and lay sod. At the end of the day, he hands the young man three twenty-dollar bills and tells him he's a quick learner and a hard worker, and he's welcome to come back and help him anytime. That's an informal type of mentoring.

- A student pursues a particular major because he is drawn to one of the professors. He takes all of the professor's courses, makes regular use of the man's office hours, and does special projects that the professor suggests. Nothing requires the student or the professor to develop that kind of relationship. It just emerges naturally. It's a form of informal mentoring.

- A man in his late twenties becomes friends with a man who is in his forties. They attend the same church and see each other around town. They periodically get together for lunch and over the next fifteen years build a close friendship. In the process, the older man has a profound influence on the younger man as he observes his older friend's Christ-centered life and outlook. If asked, the younger man would say that he regards the older man as one of his mentors.

Can you see some of the differences between formal and informal mentoring? Neither one is better. They just start out with different expectations. With formal mentoring, there's usually a stated objective that your mentor is supposed to help you achieve. For instance, say you're an apprentice on a construction site and the company pairs you with an experienced man. The agenda would be structured along work lines, and your task would be to shadow the veteran as he shows you how to do things and try your hand while he observes.

By contrast, if you ask to have coffee with someone, the two of you have to develop your own agenda, since no one from the outside is imposing one on you. That's why knowing what you want or need makes it a lot easier for the man you're meeting with to help you. You're giving him something to work with.

But let's not lose sight of the heart of mentoring. Whether formal or informal, clearly defined or not so much, a mentoring relationship almost always starts with someone's external concern. To use one of the examples just mentioned, it may be to learn the ropes in the construction industry. But to end up as true *mentoring*, the relationship has to ultimately affect the *person* behind the concern—the man who is the apprentice.

Remember, mentoring is not transactional; it's transformational. A man comes to see himself differently and actually behave differently—because he indeed *becomes* different in some positive way—as a result of the mentoring process.

SOME SUGGESTED ACTIVITIES

If you're participating in a formal mentoring program, that program probably gives you some pretty specific guidelines as to what you should do and what your mentor should be doing to satisfy the requirements of the program. But whether the mentoring process you're engaged is formal or informal, no one ever said that personal growth has to be boring! You and your mentor can and should be as imaginative as you want to be in thinking up ways to promote your development.

What follows are a handful of ideas for projects and exercises that my dad and I have seen and/or used over the years (especially in informal mentoring). This list is not exhaustive, just suggestive, in hopes of sparking your own brainstorming and creativity.

1. *Get on your mentor's turf.* If the main angle of your mentoring is vocational, visit your mentor at his workplace to see him in his natural habitat. If the two of you are working on your marriage or family life, see if you can get invited to his home. The point is to get on-site to the places where he hangs out. If he travels, maybe you

can go on a trip with him. The idea is to see him in action. As you do, play the part of an observer. See what you can learn just by watching him "do his thing," especially when he's in his own element. As they say, when it comes to learning, more is usually caught than taught.

2. *Invite him onto your turf.* This is the reverse of the previous suggestion. Depending on the nature of your work together—and also on the nature of your relationship with your mentor—invite him to come visit your workplace or your home or whatever venue seems appropriate. Let him observe you. If he's a perceptive man, he'll pick up on things you never even noticed.

3. *Take on a responsibility.* Organize a project. Help out in a program. Take responsibility for a purchase. Tackle a problem. Deliver a package. Your mentor may or may not supervise you in the activity, but let him observe you in action. Then, debrief with him so he can critique your performance—and character.

4. *Go through a process together over time.* A process involves a series of events or steps that take place over a period of time. Examples could include: a course of study, a counseling situation, a family or personal illness, a relocation. Anything that plays out over time offers a great opportunity to make use of your mentor. Let him act as your sounding board to provide critique and feedback as you're going through the process. As he observes you in action, he can bring invaluable input regarding your discipline and work ethic, your commitment and determination, your problem-solving ability, your response to unforeseen developments, your ability to size up people and situations, your learning style, your leadership gifts, and more.

5. *Give a speech or presentation in front of a group and then debrief with him.* This suggestion will appeal to some but intimidate others. Research has consistently shown that the number one fear people have is the fear of public speaking—even more than losing their job! So why include it as an idea for mentoring? Because one of the most valuable things you can do for your personal growth is to develop your ability to communicate well.

You may or may not have gifts in teaching, persuasion, or other communication arts. It doesn't matter. Sooner or later you're going to find yourself in a situation where you need to express yourself in front of a group of people—even if it's just a small group of two or three. Your mentor will be doing you an invaluable service if he instills in you the confidence to say what you have to say clearly and effectively.

6. *Do a "nonmentoring" activity together.* This may seem counterintuitive, but you stand to gain a lot by doing something with your mentor that has nothing to do with the primary purpose for why you get together. That's because mentoring is more than just a transfer of information, as I pointed out again just before launching this section. You're a person, and you bring your personhood to everything you do. Ultimately, it's *you as a person* that should benefit the most from mentoring. By doing something "off script" with your mentor, you stand a good chance of learning something you might never have learned otherwise.

So go to a ball game. Hike a trail together. Play a game of chess. Go see a movie. Read a book and discuss it. Take a trip. Attend a concert. Have a backyard barbecue with your wives or families. Work on a car or motorcycle together. Help him build a deck in his backyard.

It's in moments like those, when your guard tends to be down, that some of the best teachable moments come along.

7. *Involve him in a significant decision you are making.* Are you buying a house or car? Planning your life insurance? Trying to figure out where to send your kids to school? Changing jobs or considering a promotion? Taking on a new role or assignment at your church? Major choices like these call for wisdom. Your mentor should be able to supply some of that.

Remember that decisions are always values-driven. They reveal what matters to you. So, allowing your mentor to help you think through things will surface your fundamental beliefs and commitments—whether positive or negative. That creates opportunities for insight and growth. Ultimately you must make the decision, but your mentor can help make it an informed decision.

8. *Pray together.* I'd like to think that this would be a given, but that's not always the case. Men will work together and play together, but not always pray together. So, let me challenge you to ask your mentor to join you in prayer. It's not the words that matter, but the worship that counts.

One great aspect of prayer is that it reveals a man's heart. Think what that means for your mentoring relationship. When your mentor prays, you get a front-row seat in watching him relate to God. What an awesome privilege! There have been times when I've listened to godly men with a solid walk with Christ pray, and I've learned more about faith from those prayers than from any book or sermon. They didn't just talk about praying to God, they talked to Him! Those experiences have transformed my own prayer life.

It's also the case that when men pray together, they bond. They've come together, man with man, before our triune God—the ever-good, ever-loving, ever-gracious Father; our Older Brother and Savior, Jesus; and the source of our life and the power by which we live, the Holy Spirit. "Where two or three have gathered together in My name, I am there in their midst," Jesus promised (Matt. 18:20). So, when we pray with another man, we are—among other things—returning to our oneness with and in Christ, and bringing Him into our deliberations. I can't think of a better person to have in the mix!

CHAPTER 8

WHAT SHOULD YOU WORK ON?

I concluded the previous chapter by listing a few ideas for activities that you can do with your mentor. You'll obviously want to organize those experiences around whatever agenda the two of you have established.

In this chapter, I want to dig a bit deeper into five broader areas of inquiry that you would do well to explore with a mentor at some point. You may or may not get into any of these issues with a mentor you've been assigned through a formal mentoring program. And even if you have an informal mentor right now, he may or may not be the person who should speak into any of these areas.

Regardless, somewhere along the way you should seek out another man (or men) who can help you with the following matters. These are just a handful of the things that could be worked on, based on my own experience with men under forty (I have suggested others in the section of the book written for prospective mentors).

THE STORY OF ME

In my perfect world, you would tell your *Story of Me* to just about any man who is willing to listen. It's that valuable! But of course, the reality is that few men are willing to listen to it. In fact, very few. That's because we're all too busy—too busy to tell our own stories and too busy to listen to other men's stories.

No wonder most men today remain a closed book—with the result that at some core level, they feel a bit worthless. And why not? A book contains a story, but a closed book remains an untold story. If a story remains untold, was it worth being written in the first place?

I have been told that the Italians have a saying, "I can't know you until I have dined with you." I happen to agree with that. But I would add, "I can't know you until I have heard your story." If I'm going to pay attention to you—and I have yet to meet a man who doesn't want someone at some point to slow down and pay attention to him, to *attend* to him, to see him, to listen to him, to deal with him as a person, not just an item to check off a to-do list—I have to hear from your own lips about your journey so far in this world.

Upon reading that, you may be thinking, "Oh, Bill, you wouldn't want to hear my story. It's really not that interesting." So you're saying *you* are not very interesting? I very seriously doubt that. In fact, I know it cannot be true, because you are made to image God. He fashioned you to show the rest of us a tiny, finite picture of Himself in human form. What could be more interesting than that?[1]

Your story is the best and most direct means of discovering what the image of God looks like in your case. That's one reason why there's so much value in telling your story. You'll need to tell it many times, and to different people. Just in the telling of it, something good will happen. Your humanity will become more alive, more present. I can't explain that; it's a mystery that seems to happen between people. But it's real.

What you're looking for and hoping for—and trusting God to bring about if, as I've challenged you to do, you've been praying about it—is that one of those people will be a man who slows down long enough to actually hear you, and in the process to *see* you, to *attend* to you, and to *notice* things in your story, things you haven't seen before or things you've always seen a certain way, but he sees rather differently. And the way he sees them proves rather helpful, like a light suddenly turning on, or a big weight falling away.

From my own life experience and the lives of others, I've observed that men like that become men of whom someone says, "I never would have become who I am were it not for that man."

YOUR WORK AND CALLING

For many young adults right now, career and calling issues are the number one reason they are seeking out mentors. After all, who doesn't want an answer to the question, "What should I do with my life?" I myself spend a great deal of my time helping people with that very issue.

But I think it's important to point out that that question never goes away. Our culture perpetuates a myth that by the time you are twenty-two or twenty-four years old, you "figure out what to do when you grow up" and then you go do that. But in reality, things don't work that way.

What actually happens is that having figured out what to do when you grow up, you start doing it—or you at least do something. And then things change! Your company gets sold. You get laid off. New technology comes along and changes your job or your industry. New opportunities come along that you hadn't bargained on. You're doing the thing you decided you were "supposed" to do when you grew up, only now that you're grown up you've learned a lot more about that thing. And the main thing you've learned is that you don't, in fact, want to do it anymore. Now what?

I've discovered that even people who become quite successful in life, who maybe even love what they do for work, often walk around with a nagging voice in their head asking, "Yeah, but what *should* I have done with my life?" Successful as they are, they still wonder whether they somehow missed out.

Mentors can prove invaluable as you navigate your work life. They can help you reflect on the kinds of work that fit you and then steer you in the direction of where to find those kinds of work. They can offer perspective in dealing with the day-in-day-out and year-in-year-out nature of work, so you don't get lost in the trees and forget about the bigger forest. They can open doors to new and better opportunities. And they can walk alongside you as you make key decisions that affect your job and career prospects.

Most importantly, mentors can help you think meaningfully about the larger concept of your *calling*. As my dad used to put it, your job is what you're paid to do, while you're calling is what you're made to do. What are you made to do? God designed you a unique way. He did so because He has a unique purpose for you, a unique set of "good works" that He prepared specifically for you to do.

I believe that many of those good works can be found in one's day-to-day work. But calling is never limited to a job or even a career. It extends to the whole of your life—which means your life as a whole can be lived with a sense of meaning and purpose, not randomness. Mentors can offer wisdom and objectivity in helping you discover that larger, lifelong purpose.

MONEY

I mentioned this in passing in chapter 5. Money is one of the most important categories of life, so it makes sense that a man would flag money as a key area to examine, reflect on, and pray about. A man needs to search his soul as to where money fits in his life.

He will need help in doing that. I have no idea what kind of background you've come from. But if we look at the United States as a whole, we discover that one of the most—if not the most—affluent nations that has ever existed appears to do an utterly abysmal job of raising its young to handle money. Nearly three-quarters of Americans leave debt behind when they die, averaging $61,554.[2] Is it any wonder, then, that millennials who are twenty-five to thirty-four have an average of $42,000 in debt each, only 16 percent of which is student loan debt?[3] Meanwhile, most young millennials (eighteen to twenty-four) have less than $1,000 in savings accounts, and nearly half have no savings whatsoever.[4]

With numbers like that, I'm not sure that a few blog posts or seminars on budgeting, paying off credit cards, and finding some good mutual funds and IRAs to invest in are going to do much to transform the way a person raised in our culture thinks about money. It seems a whole new mindset, a whole new relationship toward money, is required.

You would do well to seek out anyone who has an in-depth understanding and practice of the biblical concept of *stewardship*. That may be a new word for you, or at least a new idea. But it undergirds *everything* that God has told humans about money. If you can get under a man who "gets" the principle of stewardship—in his money, his assets, his ownership of his property, his investments, his giving, his use of his energy, time, and attention—you will be far better off than the richest fool who's never heard of that term.

AUTHORITY

Another watershed issue that men spend their lives coming to grips with is the question of who is in charge. This is all about the exercise of authority and power, and the ways they get confused, abused, and misused.

Obviously, a boy's first taste of authority comes from whatever home in which he is raised. And right there we can see that in American culture, many if not most boys are somewhat doomed from the start. Think of all the homes in which the parents are in constant conflict, and where abuse—whether emotional or physical—runs rampant (often both ways). That's not a safe home for a child, and it seems hard to imagine such a child will walk out of that home with a positive or healthy concept of authority.

Then there are all the homes torn apart by divorce. Whatever the various causes and whatever else one could say about it, divorce throws a monkey wrench into a boy's sense of who is in charge.

And then there are the boys whose fathers are missing—perhaps simply gone, perhaps in jail, perhaps killed, or perhaps the victim of an accident or terminal illness. While it's certainly possible for a boy raised without a father to avoid the most negative outcomes—and if that happens, we most often have a supremely devoted and tenacious single mom to thank for it, and/or some deeply committed and self-sacrificing grandparents—there's no question that a void has been left by someone who, by rights, should have been a key authority figure in the boy's life.

And even boys from so-called "normal" backgrounds have grown up in a culture in which *authority* has tended to be synonymous with *privilege* and *advantage*. That's kind of been the American Way. Jesus observed a similar tendency in His day. He noted that the way people knew who was in charge was by how someone exercised power. If you had power, you used it to "lord it over" those without power—to dominate and control them (see Matt. 20:25). Things haven't changed in two thousand years. Powering up, power grabs, power politics, power plays—boys grow up with the idea that authority is all about power.

If that's the legacy you've received from your background, you might be surprised to learn that the overarching metaphor for leadership—dating as far back as recorded history can take us—is the shepherd. Most of us living in the developed West, where work has moved from the land to the computer, have no clue as to what it means to be a shepherd. But historically, "shepherd" was the symbol for "leader." The gods were regarded as shepherds, and rulers were seen as their undershepherds. Their primary duties boiled down to two responsibilities: protect and provide for the sheep.[5]

What does this have to do with you finding mentors? Everything, because whatever else mentoring does, it tends to develop *leaders*. Mentoring helps men know who they are and what their purpose is, and those kind of men just have a way of ending up in leadership. That's because when someone knows what he's about and where he's going, people instinctively follow him.

So when you end up in leadership, what kind of leader will you be? That all depends on your model of leadership, which is why I urge you to find men who understand that *leaders are servants first* (see Matt. 20:26–28). Their leadership begins with God as the Chief Shepherd, and every human authority is an undershepherd who follows the lead Shepherd and is accountable to Him.

This brings us back to the notion of *stewardship*, which I just mentioned in connection with money (money and power often seem to go together). Viewed through the lens of stewardship, authority means having the power to cause people and the world to thrive and flourish. In that model, the leader's interests and needs are among the last to be considered. He is a servant first and foremost. In the words of Jesus, "[He] lays down his life for the sheep" (see John 10:11).[6]

TROUBLE

One of the best questions I've ever heard for putting a team together is: Who do you want to get in trouble with? The idea is that it's a certainty that troubles are going to come.[7] Therefore, find people who won't fall apart when things start falling apart.

That same reality will apply to you. As you go through life, you can expect that troubles are going to come your way, and that when they do, your heart and soul will be tested (recall that earlier I talked about brokenness and the experience of the crucible, in which God tests a man's heart).

Most troubles are the garden-variety type: a broken-down car, a child with the flu, a neighbor who's mad because your dog barks too much, or someone swipes your wallet. Those are hassles, for sure, and everyone has to deal with them. But they pale in comparison to what might be called "crucible experiences" that have the potential of completely melting you down: losing your job unexpectedly, going through infertility with your wife, losing your apartment or house in a fire, hearing the doctor say you have cancer. It's a safe bet that something like these will come along sooner or later.[8] And when it does, it will rock your world.

So let me ask: If one of those giant rogue waves washed over you right now, to whom would you turn for help and input? I don't mean your family. Obviously, you would probably let them know what's going on—assuming you are close. But whose wisdom would you seek out for how to handle such overwhelming circumstances? If you've cultivated some mentoring relationships, you'll have the benefit of seasoned guides who can walk alongside you as you weather the storm.

Bobb Biehl has been mentoring men for as long as I've known him, and he probably knows as much about mentoring as anybody. He points out that mentoring is like a group of men scaling a mountain. If a guy is linked to another guy above him, and that man in turn is linked to other men farther up the cliff, then together they have safety, stability, and strength. If a man slips and begins to fall, fifteen or twenty climbers absorb the impact and pull him back from disaster.

But imagine a man climbing alone, with no support system. He may achieve great heights. But one wrong move, one slipped rock, one unforeseen contingency, and he can fall thousands of feet to his death without so much as anyone hearing his cry. That's why Scripture says, "Two are better than one because they have a good return for their labor. For if either of them falls, the one will lift up his companion. But woe to the one who falls when there is not another to lift him up" (Eccl. 4:9–10).

Sadly, we're seeing too many men today traveling through life as Lone Rangers. They are placing less and less value on their relationships, with the result that when the rain starts falling and quickly turns into a flood, they have nowhere to take shelter in the storm. Caught out in the wild without any experienced guide, they are at peril for drowning and drifting away.

That need not happen for you. Decide now, before the storm hits, to befriend some mentors, men who are committed to helping you grow into the man God intends you to be. Refuse to believe the lie of the evil one that says only weak men need help. The truth is, it is men who secure the help of godly men who end up becoming strong.

CHAPTER 9

WHAT SHOULD YOU WATCH OUT FOR?

Many men reading this book are likely familiar with church youth groups. If so, you may be able to relate to the following true story:

> Michael wore the expression of a basset hound as he sat in the car with Will, his high school buddy.
>
> "C'mon, man, let's go in and get a burger," Will said, nodding toward the restaurant nearby.
>
> "I'm not hungry," mumbled Michael. He made no move to open the door.
>
> "Look, he's gone, and that's that," Will replied, starting to sound a bit exasperated.
>
> "Yeah, I know." Michael shook his head. "I know. But that's what I mean. He's gone! He's not coming back. And the worst of it is he didn't even say good-bye!" There was genuine bitterness in his voice, and he was staring out the window as if the world had suddenly taken on an entirely different look.

"You spend all that time with a guy," he continued, "and then one day—poof! He vaporizes."

Michael then assumed a different voice. "'We're brothers, Michael—you and me. We're brothers in Christ, man!' 'I'm with you all the way, man!' 'You can count on me, man!' Yeah, right!"

Michael kept shaking his head. "What a lousy thing to do!" Finally he sighed and opened the car door. As he shifted his legs to get out, he muttered, "Well, that's the last time I trust one of these bozo youth leaders that the church keeps bringing in!"

WARNING: ROAD HAZARDS AHEAD!

This story is tragic—but all too familiar. A bright, enthusiastic, energetic young man takes on a leadership role for the youth group at a church. He pours his time and talent into working with those teens, firing them up, challenging them in the faith, encouraging them in their friendships, helping them with their problems—until they think he's just the greatest. They invest all of their young, inexperienced loyalty in him. If he says it, they figure it's got to be right. If he does it, it's got to be cool. If he condemns it, it's got to be bad. In their eyes, he's the leader. He's the pacesetter. He's the man to follow.

Then one day, he's suddenly gone. Maybe he's found a new job. Maybe he's graduated from college or seminary. Maybe he's newly married and moves away. But he makes a catastrophic mistake: He forgets to put closure on his time with the youth group. He walks out and leaves a giant hole in the hearts of his teenage troops. And for some of them, like Michael, it's a really bad blow. They will never forget that their role model took off and never even bothered to say good-bye. Between my dad and me, we've seen that scenario play out scores of times.

Experiences like that often give mentoring a bad rap. "Don't bother me with all this talk about finding a mentor," a guy will say in reaction to the call for men to form vital relationships. "Sorry! Been there, done that! I tried it once, and it didn't work out. It sounds good, but it doesn't happen that way. People let you down. They flake out. I can't take that again. So count me out!"

That kind of disillusionment makes me want to plant a warning sign at the front end of every mentoring relationship that reads, "Caution! Men at Work!"

You know what a construction project looks like. It's really messy, with lots of dirt and debris everywhere. That's what relationships can be like, too. Why? Because all of us are still under construction—you and your mentor included. None of us will be fully complete until the Lord takes us home. So when you interact with a mentor, his flaws will cause problems for you, and your flaws will cause problems for him. That's just the nature of human relationships.

That being the case, it's best to proceed with a bit of caution. To this point, I've described the benefits of mentoring relationships. But now let me now warn you about a handful of potential breakdowns—some barriers to surmount and some potholes to avoid. By anticipating these trouble spots, you stand a far greater chance of having a positive, productive journey with your mentor.

UNREALISTIC EXPECTATIONS

In chapter 7, we talked about setting expectations with your mentor. That's the best way to avoid frustration and disappointment later on. But even after you've done that, you may discover that you've set unrealistic expectations. And that can work both ways: you can expect more of your mentor than he is capable of delivering, and he may demand more of you than you are capable of doing.

My dad promoted mentoring like no one else, as far as I can tell, and one day a man who had bought into the concept hook, line, and sinker asked to come by and see him for some help. "Howie," he said, "I've been pouring my life into this young man for the past year, and I'm just worn out. I don't like this mentoring thing anymore."

So Dad asked him to tell him about the relationship. He described a scenario in which he had been getting together at least once a week with the young man and talking on the phone with him about every other day. "It's gotten to the point where I'm not even getting my own work done!" the man said.

That much interaction was an incredible investment of time and energy! In fact, it was far more than should have been necessary, because those two men were not in a structured mentoring program. They were meeting together on a strictly volunteer basis.

Dad asked him why he thought he needed to put in that amount of effort. The man explained, "Because when we started out, I wanted this fellow to know I was committed to him. So I told him I'd always be there for him. I just had no idea that he would interpret 'always' as *always!*"

Both of those men were operating from an unrealistic perspective. They needed to cut way back on the number of times they were meeting, and they needed to define their objectives more clearly. They especially needed to see that the purpose of mentoring was not for the older man to carry the younger, but for the older man to help the younger man learn to walk on his own.

The crazy thing about expectations, though, is that many times they are insidious. You remain unaware of them—until they are unmet. Then you suddenly feel ripped off.

So what can you do? Well, first of all, realize that it's impossible to not bring at least some expectations to the mentoring relationship. That's just a reality. Some of them you will be aware of and will be able to articulate to your mentor, and vice versa. In doing so, you allow each other to respond and determine together whether those expectations are realistic. But other expectations you may be unaware of, and when those go unmet, one or both of you will feel disappointment.

If you start feeling that way toward your mentor (or vice versa), that's a good time to stop and ask a few diagnostic questions:

- What did we expect to happen that hasn't happened?
- On what grounds did we base our expectations in the first place? Where did they come from?
- Did we communicate to the other man what we wanted? Did the other man agree to that?
- In general, what are we hoping that this relationship will accomplish? Is that hope realistic?

The best way to avoid disappointments is to clarify as much as you can up front. Again, that's why I talked about setting an agenda earlier. If the two of you can reach an agreement, especially in terms of goals and frequency of interaction, you won't be making assumptions that will come back to bite you later on.

This point leads right into . . .

UNFULFILLED EXPECTATIONS

Even when your expectations are thoroughly realistic and mutually agreeable, sooner or later you are bound to be disappointed—or to disappoint. No matter how perfect he may seem, your mentor will probably let you down at some point. He will space out an appointment, fail to make a phone call that he promised, neglect to send a letter of recommendation that you asked him for, or give you less input on a decision than you had hoped for.

I remember all too well—and with lingering pain and embarrassment—how a man I had been working with decided to write a book. Knowing that I've authored a number of books, he asked me for my input in his project, including tips about getting it published. Among the points I stressed was that he needed to get plenty of endorsements. He went to work on my suggestions and not long afterward asked if I would mind being one of his endorsers. I was honored and immediately said yes.

I should have penned my words of praise for his book right away, but I didn't. And then I got busy. Imagine how I felt, then, when a gift copy of the book arrived in my mailbox several months later—with no endorsement from me. I was so happy for him, that he had gotten his first book published. But I felt sick that I had let him down.

Your mentor is only human—just as you are. In fact, the longer you hang around him, the more the clay in his feet will become evident. As happened with me in the case of the endorsement, your mentor may make commitments that he doesn't keep. He may promise you more than he delivers. He may violate some of the very principles that he has held up to you. When it happens, don't be wiped out by it.

But don't excuse it either. When he fails to fulfill what the two of you had agreed upon, you're going to have to do a brave thing: call him on it. Not in a nasty way, but in a straightforward way: "Hey, I thought we were supposed to get together? I really missed the time with you. It's important to me." Or, "Don't forget, you said you were going to send an email introducing me to So-and-So. Can you take care of that by this weekend?"

The beauty of mentoring is that you have someone to look up to. But the risk and the inevitable reality is that the man you think so highly of is also going to let you down at some point. When he does, deal with it in a Christlike way and move forward.

WHEN A MENTOR FAILS

Mentors are human, so occasionally they drop the ball. And being human means being fallen, so it's always possible for your mentor to go beyond just a mistake to committing an outright sin. For example, he might violate his marriage vows by having an affair. He might do something unethical in his work, like falsify a report or defraud a customer. He might be discovered in a lie. He might fly into an uncharacteristic, and unexpected, fit of anger, using vile, hurtful, and malicious language. He might betray someone who has long trusted him in the interest of political expediency. It might come out that in his role as a leader he has covered up a matter that should have been brought to the authorities.

What should you do when something like that happens? There are no easy answers to that question. Every case is unique. But a few general principles apply across the board. The first is to pray. Pray for your mentor, for God to work in his life to bring about repentance, forgiveness, and restoration. Also pray for yourself—for wisdom, sensitivity, and a sense of direction for what to do. Pray for patience, too, that God would keep you from just reacting, instead of responding. And pray for the grace to forgive him—especially if his sin has directly wronged you.[1]

It's also a good idea to pull back from the agenda you and your mentor have established. I'm not necessarily suggesting that you abandon the relationship. But if your man is struggling through deep waters of his own, how much of a resource can he be to you?

A third piece of advice is to learn from his failure. Sometimes when a man sees his hero wiped out right in front of his eyes, it's actually one of the best things that could happen to him. That's because he's elevated his mentor to such a high pedestal that only a catastrophic fall could have corrected his distorted perspective and redirected his focus on the Lord. It's a tough way to learn, but the lesson will stick with him permanently: no man is invincible.

The idea of a mentor failing begs the question: If a mentor fails, does that nullify everything he's ever contributed to your life? By no means! It may well undercut his credibility. I mean, if someone's been telling you from day one that your word is your bond, and then it's discovered that he's skipped out on numerous debt obligations, it's going to be hard to trust him going forward. And yet, even if he was unable to live up to his own stated standard, it's still true that your word must be your bond. Ironically, his failure actually supports the need for having integrity in business dealings.

In Hebrews 11, you'll find a lengthy list of people whom God used to accomplish His purposes. Many of those people are remembered as much for their failures as for their faith. For example, Moses led the Israelites out of Egypt, crossed the Red Sea, delivered the Ten Commandments, and led the people for forty years. But at a key moment he disobeyed God, which cost him entrance into the Promised Land (see Num. 20:1–13). Did that cause Joshua, his successor, to dismiss everything that Moses had said and done? Not at all.

Likewise, David committed adultery with Bathsheba and then arranged for the death of her husband, Uriah (see 2 Sam. 11:1–12:15). Those were egregious sins, to be sure. But did they nullify David's accomplishments as Israel's king? Did they invalidate his many psalms? No.

Learning from someone else's sin means paying attention to your own vulnerability in that same area (see Gal. 6:1). It also requires that you guard against becoming disillusioned with the faith or with the mentoring process. If your mentor has failed, that's a tragedy. But his lapse doesn't nullify the truth of God's Word or the value of life-on-life relationships. If anything, it underscores the need for men to keep short accounts with God, and to hold themselves accountable to other men.

PROBLEMS OF CONTROL

Mentoring is all about influence—one man influencing another. But influence, by its very nature, is rooted in the issue of power. If I influence you, it's because you are granting me the power to influence you. When you let someone mentor you, you are granting him the power to affect your life.

That kind of influence is necessary if you want to grow. But can you see the inherent danger in that setup? As long as your mentor respects your sovereignty as an individual and takes the Christlike posture of a servant-leader, you're okay. But what happens if he usurps control of your life and starts using you to accomplish his own agenda? What happens if you abdicate responsibility and become a puppet in his hands and a parrot of his words?

What happens is that someone else starts running your life. And you don't want that! Taken to an extreme, you could end up as the pawn of a cult leader, like a Jim Jones or David Koresh.[2]

Jesus Christ is the only person to whom one should ever cede total control of one's life. And yet we can't escape the fact that we need to let others also influence and shape us, as the Bible itself explains: "Remember your leaders," Hebrews says, referring to leaders in the faith. "Consider the outcome of their way of life, and imitate their faith. . . . Obey your leaders and submit to them, for they are keeping watch over your souls, as those who will have to give an account. Let them do this with joy and not with groaning, for that would be of no advantage to you" (Heb. 13:7, 17 ESV). Scripture is clear: the Lord wants us to place ourselves under the spiritual authority of godly leaders, for our own good.

So how can we do that without handing over too much control? Answering that question is itself a key part of the learning process. As boys grow into men, they have to establish their boundaries and learn to protect them. That comes by experience—often in the school of hard knocks. But here are some principles that may help.

No Unlimited Commitments

First, whatever authority you relinquish to someone else should be limited and temporary. Recently, I had to visit the doctor for a procedure that called for complete anesthesia. Before they put me under, I signed several consent forms giving the doctor and other medical personnel permission to treat me. But that consent was limited. I wasn't signing my life away. I was merely allowing them to sedate me for an hour or so to perform the necessary work. It was a limited procedure.

In a similar way, as you place yourself under another man's influence, focus on a few limited objectives for a certain period of time. You may be aware of additional things that could and maybe should be worked on. Likewise, your mentor will no doubt see plenty of areas that you really ought to address. But try to stay focused on just a few key issues at a time. You may never get around to working on everything with that man, but hopefully over time you'll have made a few measurable gains.

An Outsider's Perspective

A second principle comes from Paul's relationship with Timothy. Remember the apostle's charge to his young protégé? "The things which you have heard from me in the presence of many witnesses, entrust these to faithful men who will be able to teach others also" (2 Tim. 2:2). Notice that the context in which Paul gave his instruction to Timothy was *in the presence of many witnesses*. In other words, Paul and Timothy's interaction did not occur in secret. There were other people around observing what was being said and what was taking place.

Other people can be one of your best defenses against someone gaining too much control over your life. That's one reason I encourage mentoring to take place in groups, as well as one on one. It's a lot harder for an overly domineering mentor to force his will on a group than on an individual.

Never be afraid to check out anything your mentor says or does by consulting another trustworthy person. If you have doubts about what is going on, compare notes with someone whose judgment you respect. And pay special attention if someone tells you, "Hey, I think you're letting So-and-So rub off on you just a little too much."

I might add that you should always compare anything you hear— from your mentor or anyone else—with Scripture and the testimony of the Holy Spirit. If someone is telling you something that does not resonate with what the Bible and the Spirit teach, it's off-base, no matter how good it may sound.

Whose Life Is It, Anyway?

One final way to test whether your mentor is exerting too much control over you is to ask yourself whether you can regain control whenever you wish. If you can, you're okay. If you can't, you need to reevaluate the relationship.

When I was in college, I had a friend who was participating in a group sponsored by a particular parachurch ministry. One spring break, this group decided to hold an event designed for evangelistic outreach. As the holiday approached, I asked my friend what his plans were for spring break. "Well, I'd like to go home," he told me. "In fact, I need to go home." He then described a serious situation that had come up in his family.

"Yeah, it sounds like you need to be there," I said.

"But I don't know whether I can," he replied, much to my surprise. He then explained that one of the leaders in the parachurch group, a man who had spent quite a bit of time working with him, was urging him to stick around and participate in the outreach event. "He says that staying around for this event is kind of a test of my commitment to Christ. If I go home, it's like I'm making my family more important than Christ."

In my judgment, that's too much control for one man to exert over another. That guy had essentially lost his freedom. He was no longer being given the right to choose his priorities and make his plans. They were being made for him. I told my friend as much and warned him to rethink his relationship with both that man and the group he was with.

Maybe the best way to avoid problems with control is to evaluate your prospective mentor before you ever initiate a relationship. Look to see whether he is encouraging people to go out from him, as well as inviting them to come to him. Are they "graduating" from his program, or merely enrolling in it? Is he a useful transfer station along the way, or a warehouse for an ever-expanding collection of dysfunctional people?

In my experience, the people who run into the most problems with control are the ones who fail to take responsibility for their own development (see chapter 7). When Paul said to the Corinthians, "Follow my example, as I follow the example of Christ" (1 Cor. 11:1 NIV), he was shining a light on the footsteps of faith, so that the Corinthians would know where to walk. Notice: Paul intended the Corinthians to *walk* in Jesus' footsteps, not for someone else to carry them in His footsteps.

Your walk through this world is *your* walk. No one else can or should walk that journey for you. Jesus has offered to guide you, and sometimes He provides that guidance through other men who have walked the trail a few steps ahead of you. So pay attention to what they have to say from their wisdom and experience. But always, always follow Jesus.

CHAPTER 10

WHERE WILL THIS PROCESS END UP?

I've already told you how my dad was a great communicator. He was also a master teacher. So, you can imagine that when it came to teaching his students how to communicate, he was a force to be reckoned with!

One time, one of those students, who had graduated and become a pastor, invited Dad to come to his church and preach. Dad loved to do that sort of thing, since it gave him a chance to see how his apprentices were doing, and also to stay current with the realities facing pastors and churches.

On the appointed Sunday, Dad showed up with his A-game and delivered a classic Hendricks sermon, complete with gripping illustrations, laugh-out-loud humor, on-fire passion for the Word, and spot-on practical applications of biblical truth. By the time he finished and sat down, he felt confident he had done exactly what his student had asked of him.

When the service ended, people began lining up at the back door to greet the preacher, as was the custom at the time—a ritual that Dad humorously derided as "the Glorification of the Worm Ceremony." Most of the people gave him a simple handshake and, "Thank you." "Thanks so much, Reverend." "Thanks for that word." "Great message, sir."

Then along came one old boy who grabbed his hand warmly and blurted out, "That wasn't bad preachin', son. But I gotta tell you, you'll need to come up with some different illustrations, 'cause our pastor already uses the ones you used today. You could learn a lot from him. I'll tell you what, you should come back and hear him sometime. He's the best!"

I have no idea how Dad felt upon hearing that. But I have a pretty good idea that in time he became delighted to know that his student's congregation thought more highly of his preaching than they thought of Dad's. After all, that was the point of Dad's teaching: prepare men to preach the Word. What did he care whether they thought Dad was a big deal? So long as their pastor (his student) was getting the job done, that's what mattered to my dad.

GAINING COMPETENCE

Jesus said something similar when He told His disciples, "A pupil is not above his teacher; but everyone, after he has been fully trained, will be like his teacher" (Luke 6:40). The Lord was pointing out a basic lesson of teaching: *the teacher has not taught until the student has learned.*[1] Something like that should happen for you as a result of time spent with your mentor. Sooner or later you should be able to do what he does.

I mean, that was the point in the first place, right? Back in chapter 5, the first thing we said about sizing up a prospective mentor is to see whether he seems to have what you need. Then find a way to work with him so as to meet that need. If that happens, his influence has been effective.

But let me clarify what I mean by "being able to do what he does." Jesus said that the student would be "like" his teacher. That sets up a comparison between student and teacher, which leads to three possibilities. One would be that you get to the point where you are able to do something just as well as your mentor.

We see that a lot with what I've called "top level" skills. For instance, a bricklayer apprentices a younger man in the craft of laying bricks, and if he does his job right, the day comes when the younger man can lay bricks as well as his mentor. Or a seasoned fly fisherman schools a novice on how to spot trout in brooks and streams. It takes a while, but the day comes when the novice is no longer a novice but can easily spot trout as well as his mentor.

A second possibility, however, is that in learning whatever you're learning from your mentor, you actually get to the point where you can do the thing even better than he can do it. That happened with my daughter, Brittany, the trumpet player, as I mentioned earlier. She began playing the trumpet in fifth grade and practiced diligently under an instructor who worked with her all the way through eighth grade. Then one day he explained to her, and to me and her mother, "You really need to find another instructor. I've taught you everything I can, and you've got talent that needs things I'm not really able to give you." With that, we found a professional who was playing at the highest levels of the trumpet guild, and he took things from there.

That could happen for you, as well. I know you may be hesitant to believe that. Many men are. They assume they'll never surpass their mentor, because he's always been something of a hero to them, as well as a model. But one of the beautiful things about mentoring is that it enables a man's real talent to blossom and thrive. Thanks to the mentor, a man finds encouragement, instruction, guidance, wisdom, opportunity, correction, and accountability. As a result, in time his talent will rise to its proper level—which may just surpass his mentor's talent.

If that happens, you should pray that your mentor is a man of humility and grace. Brittany's trumpet instructor was such a man. He was one of the nicest, most decent people I've ever known. But he also had the humility to say, in effect, "Brittany, you will surpass me. You will become a better trumpet player than I'll ever be. So, go and do that by finding someone at a higher level of the trumpet world than I am." By "releasing" her in that way, he did her a tremendous favor. And in truth, something of him and his tutelage lives on in Brittany's trumpet playing to this day.

Unfortunately, things don't always end that well. Mentors are human, and one of the besetting sins of competent humans is jealousy of someone who has greater competence than they have. Sadly, if it turns out that you have greater potential than your mentor in the area in which he is helping you, he will likely know it long before you do (because he has more experience and more familiarity with what the upper limits of competency are). If he's the jealous type, you may begin to experience symptoms of that envy such as:

- Increasingly critical comments about your performance
- Increasing conflict, often over petty matters
- Sarcastic remarks about you, your performance, your attitude, your future, and so on
- Denial of opportunities he promised to give you
- Cancelling meetings with you
- Sudden preferment over you of others he is working with
- Sabotaging something you are working on so as to hinder your performance of the task
- Saying disparaging things (or even lies) about you to other leaders

Needless to say, developments like that can be pretty unsettling! No one likes to feel estranged from someone who has been so helpful to them. But if your relationship with your mentor seems to be souring, you might consider whether things have run their course and it's time to move on. Obviously, that would not be the best outcome of your relationship with your mentor. But it can and does happen. So be aware that it can happen for you.

NOT LIKE MY TEACHER!

The third possibility, of course, is that, in fact, you never do become as good as your mentor in the thing you are trying to learn. Hundreds of men claim legendary basketball coach John Wooden as their mentor. He made an indelible impression on them—not only on how they played basketball, but how they live life. Not one of those men has ever been said to have surpassed Wooden as either a coach or a mentor. Does that mean Wooden failed as a mentor?

Hardly! Some men are simply the masters of their craft—so much that they essentially define the craft. They simply are not normal. For whatever reason, God has so endowed them with a gift or a talent that they set the standard for doing that thing. No one will ever really surpass them. Yes, at some point (probably once in a generation) someone will come along who rises to the level of doing that same thing with greatness of their own. But at that level, comparisons are not made in terms of who is or was "better," but in the unique ways in which either man does the same thing with greatness.

If you are fortunate enough to be mentored by such a man, count your blessings! Who better to learn from than the best of the best? Take what he gives you and apply it to your own talents, to develop your assets to be the best *you* can be.

Which brings us to your own humility and grace. Just as mentors can be tempted by jealousy, so can men being mentored. Beware of coveting your mentor's gifts! It's fine to admire his strengths, and it's fine to desire that your own strengths be refined and developed by observing him use his. But don't let the comparison between you and your mentor spill over into jealousy—especially if it seems that you'll probably never have the ability he has. Rather, get a sober, accurate appraisal of what God has given you to work with: "For through the grace given to me I say to everyone among you not to think more highly of himself than he ought to think; *but to think [of yourself] so as to have sound judgment*, as God has allotted to each a measure of faith" (Rom. 12:3, emphasis added).

One of the best ways to get a "sober, accurate appraisal of what God has given you to work with" is to ask your mentor to help you begin to identify your giftedness (see chapter 14). I can't stress enough how important that is! Your giftedness is what God designed *you* to do. You will always function best when you are using your giftedness. You will always struggle—at least motivationally—when you are operating outside of your giftedness.

Which leads to the observation that if you're not able to do something anywhere near as well as your mentor, it may be because God hasn't given you the same giftedness that your mentor has. (I say "may be"—I'm personally inclined to think that's almost always the case.) If you don't have the giftedness for it, you can try your hardest and your mentor can do his best to help you, but it's just not going to happen. It's not a matter of intelligence, character, discipline, or desire. It's a matter of *design*. A screwdriver is designed to drive screws. It can mentor under a hammer in order to learn how to drive nails, but it's never going to drive nails like the hammer, because it wasn't designed to drive nails. Put that screwdriver with another screwdriver, however, and now you've got something!

BUILDING CONFIDENCE AND CHARACTER

Whether you end up being able to do something as well as your mentor, better than your mentor, or not as well as your mentor, we're talking about "top level" matters of skill and competence. But the best mentoring happens at the deeper levels of confidence and character. In a way, the ultimate question of how effective your work with your mentor has been is: Are you a better man for having been with him?

Looked at from that perspective, Jesus' observation that after a man has been "fully trained," he will be "like" his teacher means that your heart will have taken on some of the same qualities that characterize your mentor's heart. For example, if your mentor is a man of great patience, you begin to display a greater degree of patience. If he is generous, a spirit of generosity begins to mark your own life. If he excels in helping people in conflict settle down and listen to each other and resolve their differences, you become something of a peacemaker. If he is a man of prayer, prayer becomes a higher priority and practice for you.

When that happens, we say that your mentor has "rubbed off" on you—which is exactly what is supposed to happen. Iron is supposed to sharpen iron. By placing yourself in relationship with a man of character, you begin to develop your own character.

Not passively! Not unintentionally! Parking yourself in a garage will not turn you into a car. Nor will hanging around a man of integrity automatically make you a man of integrity. Conceivably, it might only reveal how much you lack integrity. But if you hang around a godly man with the intention (the "agenda," if you will)—and therefore the effort—to learn from him and emulate his ways, his godly character will begin to shape your character. That's because you'll start to see the world—and God—through his eyes. You'll be drawn toward the desires and aspirations that drive him. You'll begin thinking about things by asking similar questions to the ones he asks. You'll explore your inner life and what is really inside you the way he has looked into his own soul and brought both the best and the worst of himself before God, for God to do with as He wills.

By that means, your soul will be more conformed to what God intends for it to be. That's what I would call the sweet spot of mentoring. And to be honest, I'm not sure that can ever really happen apart from mentoring. It certainly can't happen on one's own, by oneself. God seems to have designed men to be shaped by men, one on one, life on life. No wonder Jesus left His followers with the mission to "make disciples." Literally, make learners. Make apprentices. Make followers of Jesus by inviting men to follow us as we follow Jesus.

That's Jesus' life rubbing off on us, and we in turn rubbing off on other men.

SAYING THANK YOU

Let's say that happens. Let's say that God appoints a man—hopefully a number of men—to build into your life, such that you look back and say, "I never would have become who I am were it not for that man's influence." When the day comes that you realize that fact, I hope you'll do something that rarely happens: track down that man and express your appreciation to him.

One reason that rarely happens is that by the time someone realizes what an influence a man has been on him, that influencing man has passed away. But too often it happens because men just don't think about it. I learned that from a man named Gene, who fondly remembers my dad as one of his mentors.

Dad had helped Gene with some significant career opportunities. So, late in my dad's life, Gene decided to thank him by taking my folks out to dinner with his wife, and expressing his gratitude for all that Dad had done for him. The two couples had a lovely meal as Dad and Gene reminisced over things they had done together.

Then, as the evening began to draw to a conclusion, my dad surprised Gene by turning to him and saying, "Thank you! Thank you so much for this evening. You know, I rarely hear thanks from most of the people I've worked with. So this means a great deal."

Gene was stunned. How could that be? In the days following that special dinner, Gene reflected on why men don't come back to say thank you to the men who have made such an impact on them. Finally, he concluded that it's because we somehow think that those men, with all of their competence, all of their gifts, and all of their wisdom, somehow don't need our feedback and encouragement.

But that's precisely wrong! As I said earlier, mentors are as human as you and I are. And if a human needs anything, he needs affirmation and encouragement. He needs to know when his efforts have yielded results. So, as you get older and begin to realize that certain men have made a particular contribution to your life—especially in terms of helping you become who you are as a man—I implore you to do what Gene did with my dad. Call them up. Write them a letter. Invite them to have a meal with you. Go visit them in their home (or nursing home). Tell them what they have meant to you and express your appreciation. By doing so, you will complete the circle. And when they are gone from this life, you will have the satisfaction of knowing that you gave honor to whom honor was due, while they were able to receive it (see Rom. 13:7).

THE CYCLE OF MENTORING

We now live in a time of radical individualism. People in our culture are obsessed with *my* identity, *my* rights, *my* future, and what *I* get out of life. One result of that self-absorbed way of thinking has been a loss of regard for the natural flow and rhythms of successive generations: a generation comes, lives, and dies off, even as another generation rises up and succeeds it. This turnover has been going on for as long as humans have existed, but many young adults in the West seem oblivious to it.

That's about to change. We boomers thought we were a big deal when we showed up. And we were, from about the 1960s through the end of the twentieth century.[2] Then, the millennials came along and supplanted the boomers. Today, millennials dominate the culture: in movies, music, entertainment, the economy, education, and, increasingly, the work world. In some ways, that's as it should be. A generation comes, and a generation goes.

But right on the heels of the millennials is Gen Z, which is an even larger demographic.[3] Soon, they will be making their presence felt. And as they rise up, and as boomers begin dying off, millennials will gradually realize that they, too, are subject to aging—and eventually to passing from the scene. As hard as it is to believe when one is young, millennials, too, will be confronted with the question of legacy: *What are you going to leave behind? What will you be remembered for?*

In talking this way about generations, I'm not at all intending to foment generational envy or acrimony. Nobody gets to choose when they will be born. No, I'm simply highlighting a fact of life: that none of us will be around forever, and that others will come after us.

This cycle of the generations gives rise to a cycle of mentoring. Mentoring is a lifelong process, as well as a multigenerational process. When a man is relatively young, he mostly learns from men older than he is. But with each passing year and decade, he finds that other men—especially younger men—begin looking to him for input and guidance. If he pays attention to that and takes advantage of the opportunities, he can become a skilled mentor by the time he is in his sixties. (I suppose the alternative is to just grow old and become irrelevant.)

In my case, my particular giftedness predisposed me to try and have an influence on other men. I can remember as far back as when I was in seventh and eighth grade creating clubs for boys in fifth grade who looked up to me as an older kid. A few years later, I served as a camp counselor one summer, and when I got back to the city in the fall, a group of guys who had been in one of my cabins asked me to meet with them every week over the next year to talk about life. That pattern of getting together with men who were slightly younger than I continued throughout my twenties, thirties, and forties. Neither I nor anyone else ever really called it "mentoring," but that's essentially what was taking place.

Then I turned fifty. And the only way I can describe what happened is that suddenly people started taking me seriously. I mean, I would say something, and someone would reply, "Wow, that's good! That's so helpful!" Sometimes they even wrote down whatever I'd said. Meanwhile, I'd be thinking, "Wait a minute! What's the big deal? I've been saying that for twenty-five years. Why is that suddenly worth writing down?"

GET READY TO BE A MENTOR

What I didn't realize is that somewhere around age fifty, a man becomes old enough to be perceived as having something to say—if indeed the things he says have merit, otherwise he's just ignored. That's when I began to appreciate the power and the potential of mentoring. I realized that men were paying attention, not because of me, but because of *them*: they were actually eager to learn and grow and talk to someone who was just a little further down the trail than they were. I realized that I could serve them well by just telling them what I knew—basically telling my *Story of Me*. To my surprise, they found that rather helpful in coming to grips with their own *Story of Me*.

So why am I telling you this if you're still just in your twenties or thirties or early forties? Because I want you to realize that the day is coming when that will happen for you. Someday, another man will come your way, seeking your help—for instruction, for guidance, for insight, for a listening ear, whatever. So start preparing for that day now!

I know it seems like a long way off, but that's an illusion. As my mother-in-law, Carol Turpin, perceptively says, the days are long, but the years go quickly. You're so busy now that you don't have time to think about when you'll be fifty. But tomorrow you'll wake up at fifty and wonder, *Where did the years go?*

How can you get ready to be a mentor? First, by proactively seeking out mentors of your own. And I stress mentors *plural*. Sure, you may find one man in particular who proves invaluable as a trusted advisor. But learn from any and every man you can, wherever you find him. Different areas of your life call for different kinds of input: your work, your family, your spiritual life, your emotional life, your relationships, your character, your purpose.

Another preparation for mentoring is to read widely. The practice of reading has fallen on hard times nowadays, but the fact remains that leaders are readers, as the saying goes. Men of depth invariably read deeply. That is, they expose their minds to other men's thoughts in order to stretch their thinking.

Reading is a different activity from listening or watching—though those forms of learning have their place. Reading has a way of forcing the mind to think logically and comprehensively. It also exposes the reader to the most important ideas and issues of the human condition: right and wrong, beauty, truth, courage, love, death, the good life, and so on. Obviously, I'm talking about reading real literature and "serious" books, not fantasy novels or sci-fi or fiction written for pure entertainment value—although there is nothing wrong with those. In our culture, certain books are consistently regarded as the Great Books of Western Civilization, and that would be a good place to start.[4]

One other practice that will help you in becoming a mentor—which is to say, to help you grow personally—is to keep a journal. Writing down your thoughts helps you think. That's one of the real problems of our age—people are so busy that they're too busy to think, with the result that they become thoughtless, mindless, purely reactive, never reflective. By taking twenty minutes or a half hour each day to *pause* and *attend* and actually *put into words* what you are thinking about will center you, meaning that you can reconnect with what matters to you, what you believe, and what is on your heart. And having that record of your thoughts over time becomes a great way to mark your trail, so that you have something to look back over and see where you've come and how you've developed.

A TREE OF LIFE

A few years ago, my family was invited to join several other families for an afternoon at a farm that belonged to a friend and her family. It was a gorgeous late fall day, and the highlight of our time together was a hayride we all took to a stand of massive pecan trees. They were easily a hundred feet tall or more, with limbs that created a dense canopy under each tree.

When we jumped off the wagon and began walking around, we found enormous pecans lying on the ground everywhere. As a native Texan, I'm used to seeing large, healthy pecans (the pecan tree is the state tree of Texas). But these were oversized! We all had grocery bags to collect as many pecans as we wanted, and it took no time at all to fill up several bags. We could hardly lift them, they contained so many.

Back at home, we enjoyed those pecans for months afterwards. But why were we able to do that? Because the trees those pecans had come from had been planted about forty-five years earlier, when our friend was a little girl. She told us how, at the time, that area was just a field. She and her family spent weeks digging holes and placing pecan seedlings across it. Then they waited while nature went to work.

I like to think of mentoring as a form of planting some seedlings in another man and then letting nature go to work. As a mentor, I don't really cause any growth. I just deposit the germ of something that has the potential to grow and take root and flourish inside another man. It's God who then causes the man to grow.

What I'm getting at here is that personal and spiritual growth is a lifelong process that never ends until you die. If it ever does end, you die. Whether a tree is young or old, it's either growing or dying—or dead.

That means when you're young, your main task should be to put down roots so that (1) you are firmly established, and (2) you are taking in good nutrients and water for your soul. That's the purpose of finding mentors. Mentors can help you get grounded, and they can also feed your soul.

But as you mature, your calling is to start putting out more and more fruit that's worth harvesting. That's what we expect of mature trees—fruit. When I was a kid, my family also planted a pecan tree in our backyard. But that tree never did produce any fruit. Eventually it died, and we cut it down.

What good is a fruit tree that bears no fruit? Jesus actually told a story about that very matter: "A man had a fig tree which had been planted in his vineyard; and he came looking for fruit on it and did not find any. And he said to the vineyard-keeper, 'Behold, for three years I have come looking for fruit on this fig tree without finding any. Cut it down! Why does it even use up the ground?'" (Luke 13:6–7).

We expect mature trees to produce fruit. So does God. But whereas trees produce figs or pecans or oranges or coconuts, the fruit that men produce is other men. In other words, I believe that God will evaluate our "success" as men—really our effectiveness—not only by how we've used the gifts and resources He has invested in us and with us, but also by the influence we've had on other men, for better or for worse.[5]

A LIFE WORTH LIVING

As you get older, my hope is that the second half of this book will become increasingly useful to you. With each passing decade, you'll move closer to the end of your life, and the day will eventually come when you'll watch your parents and their generation pass away. At that point, thoughts of a legacy will begin to loom much larger. But right now, while you're younger, your thoughts are mostly about what your life is going to become and what you should do with it. At your age, calling and purpose are not as much about what you're willing to die for, but rather what is worth living for.

So this is a fair question: What *are* you living for? My friend Grant Skeldon says that young adults today want to change the world.[6] I think that's fantastic! Our world has a lot wrong with it, and every generation has an opportunity to change it for the better.

But can I offer my two cents about devoting one's life to bringing change? First, change itself can often be accomplished fairly easily and in relatively short order, but fundamentally changing the world itself for the better tends to be hard and takes a while.

For example, ever since the Age of Technology was born, popular opinion has held that "technology changes everything." Anyone under forty has never known a time when there wasn't technology, so that tends to translate into thinking that technology is the answer to everything. With technology, we can change the world, right?

Well, I was alive when the Age of Technology was born. And yes, technology has brought profound changes to the world, and it's done so with increasing speed. Steve Jobs alone is said to have changed six industries (personal computers, animated movies, music, phones, tablet computing, and digital publishing),[7] and he did all that in one, brief, thirty-five-year career. Other innovators and their gadgets could be mentioned as well.

But let me ask: Given that we now have marvelous new technologies, has that really changed human nature? And has it changed it for the better? Changing the human heart is not for the faint at heart. Historically, the people who have made any headway in doing that have been people of deeply committed faith in God who devoted their lives to things they knew would not come about until the time of their grandchildren, if then. I'm thinking of a William Wilberforce or a Charles Loring Brace or a Florence Nightingale or a Martin Luther King Jr.[8]

Changing humans is difficult work and it takes time. Which leads to my second point: people change one person at a time.[9] If you stop and think about that, you can see why "changing the world" is a daunting task—some would say an impossible task. Look how hard it is for an individual to change his lifestyle—to quit smoking or drinking, to stop eating junk food, to exercise and pay attention to his body, to get proper sleep and rest. Even harder are changes of character: to learn to tell the truth, to control one's anger, to be patient, to remain civil in difficult conversations, to refuse to give way to cynicism, to show mercy and extend forgiveness, to be generous, to be filled with a spirit of gratitude.

In short, we all can agree that the world needs changing. And I have no problem with anyone devoting his life to doing what he can to promote positive change. But I happen to believe that real change and lasting change is a life-on-life proposition. Which of course comes back to mentoring.

You've been handed a set of gifts and certain realities and opportunities by a God who has your highest good in view. He's given you those assets precisely so you can do real good in this world. He wants you to cause the world and its people to flourish. But whatever that purpose ends up looking like for you—whatever your vocation, whatever your marital and family status, whatever your station in life—be certain that you *are* going to have an influence on other men. My challenge to you, then, and my purpose for writing this book, is that you do it intentionally, and you do it well.

PART 2

FOR MEN WILLING TO
SERVE AS MENTORS

CHAPTER 11

ARE YOU WILLING TO CARE?

Tony Burton pastors the Church of the Incarnation in Dallas. He served numerous churches in his native Canada before coming to Incarnation. As a bishop during those years, he ordained to the priesthood an eighty-five-year-old Native American named James Settee. (Can you imagine a man of that age seeking ordination? With that kind of spunk, he reminds me of a modern-day Caleb! See Joshua 14:6–12.) Tony relates James's story:

> James was tall and lanky and upright, and when he came to town he wore rubber galoshes over his moccasins. He looked like Gregory Peck, if Gregory Peck were an eighty-five-year-old Indian. He was good and holy, a man of few words. After I ordained him, he went on to revive his parish, built a new church, and taught the youngsters of his community to speak the language of their ancestors. When he died six years later, they put up a big picture of him in the new church's sanctuary.
>
> James was locally famous as a woodsman, and years before there had been a renowned incident when a little Cree boy had gone missing in the woods for three days. They organized a

mass search, but nobody could find the child, and they were desperately worried that he might not make it through a third cold night.

Finally, the authorities went to get James, who set out on his own and walked for two hours through the woods, directly to the place where the youngster was. James was a big man and the child was terrified of him, so James just gently sat down beside the boy for a while and offered him something to eat and drink. After a while, the little fellow let James pick him up and carry him out of the woods.

I asked James about this story, wondering how he did it. "Did you look for tracks or broken plants or disturbed moss?" I asked him.

"No," he said. "I was a little boy once, and I just thought about what I would do if I were he."

Tony has often reflected on that response. When James found that Cree child, what was it that the boy really needed? A map? Answers to life's questions? Advice about what he should do? No, he needed a guide, a person who knew the way home.[1]

That's it! That sums up the spirit of mentoring in a nutshell. We men tend to get stuck in life when we don't exactly know what we're doing. When we don't know how, don't know what, don't know why, don't know the way. In moments like that, what do we most need? A guide, someone who once didn't know either but now that he's more experienced and wiser, he knows the way forward when we're trying to learn, and he knows the way back when we're lost. A guide doesn't just tell us; he *shows* us. Then he walks with us and talks with us as we make our way forward. By that means, we grow and develop and become men.

Just like James, the longer you live, the more guidance you have to offer other men. The question is, will you offer it?

THE HEART OF A MENTOR

In chapter 5, I listed half a dozen things that men should look for in evaluating prospective mentors. You're welcome to read through that list and see how you stack up. But there's one characteristic of a mentor that only you can know whether or not you possess: *Do you care?*

In truth, I've had mentors (of a sort) who probably didn't care. At least, I couldn't tell if they did. I recall a professor in graduate school who was rather cynical, highly opinionated, and not at all afraid to let everyone know exactly what his opinions were. Undergraduates were terrified of him, and most of my peers steered clear of him. But somehow he took a shine to me—at least, in sort of a snarky, backhanded way. And while we never became close, I still managed to squeeze out of him some invaluable insights into print design— which was my interest in working with him.

That man definitely left a positive impression on my life, but I would never have turned to him for help at a deeper, more personal level. He gave no indication that he cared about that stuff. My own hunch is that he just wasn't wired to help other people in that way. That didn't make him a bad man, just not the right man for in-depth mentoring.

Not every mentoring relationship goes deep. Many, perhaps most, remain at what might be called the "top level" of engagement. By that I mean someone comes your way because you have some particular skill or expertise, and you can help that man develop his own competence in that area. That's great! He benefits, he grows, he gets what he needs. And at that point, the relationship has more or less run its course. There's absolutely nothing wrong with that. Men need that, without question.

But then there's the "deeper level" of mentoring. The deeper level has to do with the man himself. Quite apart from the thing to be learned is the learner. That learner is a person, a man with a soul and a *Story of Me* (see chapter 2). That man may acquire vast amounts of knowledge, skill, and experience in life. But if he never discovers who he is and what his purpose is, his soul will remain stunted and his story will go untold. *You* have the opportunity—should you choose to pursue it—to help him with that deeper need for self-awareness.

The question is: *Are you willing to care?*

In my experience, there are two categories of men, generally speaking, who seem willing to care enough to extend themselves as mentors to other men. One is men who themselves have benefitted from in-depth mentoring. They know by experience how invaluable mentors can be, so they tend to have an impulse to "pass it on." The other is men who didn't have mentors but wish they had, and have come to realize what they missed out on. They don't want that to happen to other men, so they look for opportunities to come alongside other men and do what they can.

If you fall into either of those categories, this section of the book is for you. (By the way, I'm assuming that most men reading this section of the book are over thirty.)

TURNING BACK THE CLOCK

When I was a junior in college, I earned money by waiting tables at an upscale steakhouse on the waterfront of Boston's harbor. On weekend nights, the place was packed, but on weeknights, things were much slower—especially if it was winter and the temperatures were in the low twenties or teens, or lower.

On one such wintry evening, it was my luck to work the closing shift. Closing time was 10:00 p.m., but wouldn't you know a couple came in at 9:55. So, I went into action. They ordered drinks and an appetizer, and then told me to come back later when they were ready to order. That left me with time to kill.

Right then, a busboy burst into the kitchen to tell me about a fire nearby. I walked out on the loading dock, and sure enough, an abandoned warehouse about ten blocks away was going up in flames. It was a spectacular sight!

Without thinking, I began walking toward the fire. A half block into my walk, a fire truck pulled by, lights flashing but no siren. It was obviously headed toward the fire, but it was crawling along the street. I noticed that no one was riding on the back. So, rather impulsively, I jumped aboard. I mean, why walk when you can ride, right?

No sooner had I hopped on than the engine roared and the transmission shifted into a higher gear, and the truck began speeding up. That's when I remembered I still had customers at the restaurant! What was I thinking?

I needed to get off, and fast. By now we were doing maybe eight to ten miles an hour. I stupidly thought that if I could jump and run, maybe I would be okay. Bad decision! One foot hit the ground, the second followed, and with that I began to roll. Pens, tickets, and whatever else was in my apron pockets started flying every which way. I flipped four or five times and skidded to a stop on my elbow. I was lucky I hadn't bashed my head in!

Quickly picking up what belongings I could find, I limped back to the restaurant, right trouser knee ripped open and shirt torn, blood oozing from a nasty scrape on my right arm. After a quick visit to the men's room to survey the damage and administer a little first aid, I somehow managed to finish my shift—taking care to approach the remaining party on my left side, so as to conceal what had happened over on the right. (Believe it or not, I got about a 25 percent tip because the couple felt bad for keeping me late!)

YOUTH IS WASTED ON THE YOUNG

Now why do I tell that story? Because it perfectly illustrates what men are liable to do when they are young, impetuous, lack judgment, are still somewhat irresponsible, think they are bulletproof, and—if I can put it kindly—are stupid.

Not every man is or was as foolish as I was at that age—or at least on that night. Some are or were far more so! But boneheaded high jinks like that are the least of it. The real regret that I and countless other men I've talked to feel as we look back on our adolescence and early young adult years is over the golden opportunities squandered at that age, the priceless options we were too blind or stubborn to exercise, the once-in-a-lifetime experiences we failed to take advantage of, and, most importantly, the key men we were too blind to bother building a relationship with.

Be honest, unless you're a very unusual man, you have some of those regrets, don't you? Somewhere in looking back over your younger years, you think, *What was I thinking? How could I have missed that? Why did I let that pass me by?* By now, we realize what we didn't realize then. No wonder we say that youth is wasted on the young!

But here's what I find most ominous about that waste: The same immature mindset that would impulsively choose to jump on the back of a fire truck is the mindset by which that young man was making far more consequential choices. Like what to do with his life, what woman he should marry, whose leadership he should follow, what sources he should consult to gain understanding of the world, how he should handle his money, how he should think about himself, how he should think about God, what really matters in life, and so many other vital issues.

THE HANDOFF

If one is not careful, one can easily get cynical about the younger generations and just write them off. I see a lot of baby boomers doing precisely that nowadays. Many of them complain about how millennials are overly idealistic, entitled, self-absorbed, lacking any sense of a work ethic, overly sensitive, unreliable, addicted to their phones, disrespectful, and on and on—all the usual stereotypes.

But as I pointed out in chapter 2, writing off younger generations is *not* an option God has given us or ever does. Has God written off the boomers? Certainly not! Despite our generation's many failures—our materialism and self-indulgence, our narcissistic preoccupation with self and the Cult of Me, our sexual promiscuity coupled with our widespread failure to honor our marriage vows, our greed that led to the Great Recession of 2008, our failure to address racism, our misuse of the earth, to name but a few[2]—God has remained faithful. Boomers for the most part haven't even been grateful for God's mercies. Nonetheless, every morning when the sun comes up, God continues to show new compassion to us (see Lam. 3:22–23).

Well, that same faithfulness, what Scripture calls God's "loving-kindness"—His passionate, virtually irrational heart-commitment to faithfully, mercifully, and devotedly bring about His good on our behalf, in ways that vindicate us over evil—is said to be everlasting and a love that extends *to all generations*.[3] So, if God is unreservedly pledged to our children and grandchildren and great-grandchildren and beyond, there can be no such thing as "writing them off." Quite the opposite: we are called to get on board with what God is doing in the rising generation that He is raising up.

So, I return to my earlier image of a relay race. In an Olympic relay (the 4x100- and 4x400-meter events), each of three runners must run his distance and then hand off a baton to the next runner, until the fourth runner, or anchor, races around the track to get the baton across the finish line. The baton must be handed off within what is called the "exchange zone," an overlap in the course of twenty meters. Boomers are now in the exchange zone with millennials and, increasingly, with Gen Z. The time has come for us to hand off the baton.

We can do that well or we can do that poorly. If we do it well, we significantly advantage the man who must run the next leg of the course. If we do it poorly—and God forbid we drop the baton—we destine our successors to play catch-up the rest of their lives.

In this section of the book, I want to explore how we can acquit ourselves well as we finish up our leg of the race and make a solid hand off to the men just starting theirs.

CHAPTER 12

DO YOU REALIZE WHAT YOU HAVE TO OFFER?

One of my most cherished mentors was a guy named Pete Hammond (1936–2008). Pete spent his career with InterVarsity Christian Fellowship–USA in a variety of roles. I knew him best during the years he ran something called Marketplace Networks (eventually called Ministry in Daily Life). His passion was to help people integrate their faith into their day-to-day work, and he regarded mentoring as a primary strategy toward that end.

One time, Pete and I were invited to speak to a group of guys in their twenties. As was his custom, Pete challenged those younger men to seek out older men as guides and mentors.

But one young man challenged Pete with a perplexing problem: "I've been trying to find an older man for a long time," he said with some exasperation, "but it just doesn't seem to happen! It's like every time I try to get something going with someone, the guy finds an excuse to shut it down. You're saying, 'Find a mentor,' but I'm wondering, where are they!"

As I had often seen happen, a twinkle blazed up in Pete's eye, and he leaned forward, his head scanning the group. "Let me let you in on a little secret," he told them. "You guys sometimes scare the pants off us older men!" he chuckled.

The group looked somewhat disbelieving.

"I'm serious! I mean, look at you! You're young. You're strong. You're healthy. You're virile. You're handsome—most of you, anyway." Nervous laughter broke the tension. "You dress well. You've got all this energy and all these opportunities. An older guy looks at all that and he thinks, *Man, there's no way I can keep up with those guys! What do I have to offer?*"

Pete let that sink in for a second before he delivered the punch line: "Somehow, you've got to convince him that you value his input."

SUPERSTARS NEED NOT APPLY

Does Pete's description apply to you? You may feel totally inadequate to serve as a guide or a role model. As you read this book and contemplate the task of mentoring, you may be feeling pretty intimidated. You're perceiving that with the mentoring role come a whole lot of expectations you have to live up to, and you're convinced there's no way you could ever do all that.

You are far from alone in feeling that way. Most men in our culture do not see themselves as mentor material. They are persuaded they don't have what it takes: "I don't know anything." "I don't have any training." "I can't teach." "I'm not very good at relationships."

I've heard all such excuses. But most all those excuses are based on misguided perceptions and unrealistic expectations about the mentoring process. They are a holdover from the Smart Man model of mentoring that I mentioned in chapter 3—the all-wise, all-knowing, omnicompetent mentor-figure who has all the answers and is brilliantly adequate to every moment.

If you ever find that fellow, send him my way, please! Because as far as I'm concerned, he's out there somewhere in the woods with

Sasquatch. You know, Bigfoot, the mythical white-haired cousin to Chewbacca, who roams the North American wilderness.

Where I live, there are no Gandalfs or Yodas or Dumbledores. No man carries a magic wand. There are only everyday men like you and me, men facing the same set of realities every other man has to deal with—from earning a living to changing diapers to fighting the common cold. Indeed, if there's one characteristic my mentors have had in common, it's how remarkably normal and human they turned out to be.

And why not? If a man is such a superstar that he's not only never failed, but never even *felt* afraid of failure, then he's too far beyond anyone else to be of help. He's too intimidating. Whereas when a guy who seems just "average" acquits himself well in working through the challenges of life, we feel more hopeful, even inspired: "If he can do it, maybe I can too."

ABILITY VS. AVAILABILITY

That's exactly what Scripture shows us. The Bible tells story after story of God accomplishing His purposes. And in most of those stories, He chooses to use a human—an average, everyday Joe. Not a Super Man. Not an All-Star. Usually not even the "best and the brightest." Indeed, oftentimes He uses an unknown, a dark horse, a *Who?* Occasionally even a loser.

Into these "earthen vessels" (2 Cor. 4:7), He channels His grace and power, and seemingly out of the blue they end up vanquishing kings, enacting justice, bringing to pass divine promises, shutting the mouths of lions, walking through fire, escaping the sword, exercising unusual physical strength, excelling in battle, putting armies to flight—even raising the dead! And some, by virtue of their assignment, were given the faith to endure torture, withstand mocking, hold up under beatings, hold out in prison, and even accept martyrdom or exile (see Heb. 11:32–38).

This all sounds dramatic, I know. But if God has already used everyday people—men and women "with a nature like ours" (see James 5:17)—to do amazing things like that, then why could He not use the likes of you and me to help other men grow and develop into men?

Right here is precisely why mentoring turns out to be so effective, because the power to transform the life of another man does not come from us, but from God. In mentoring, we can trust that God is already at work in the other man. Yes, we need to show up and do our part. But we're not the main actor; God is. Whatever our ability may be to serve as a mentor, of far more importance is *our availability for God to use us as a mentor.*

WHAT GOD USES

Seen from that perspective, the man who says, "I have nothing to offer," is a bit like Andrew standing in front of Jesus, with a hungry crowd sitting behind them. Andrew's got five loaves of bread and two fish to work with, and upon doing the math he can only ask, "What are these for so many people?" The answer is: not much in the hands of men; but more than enough in the hands of God (see John 6:1–14).

So, let's assess what your "five loaves and two fish" might be. In my experience, the older a man gets, the more loaves and fish he has to offer—if only he would see them. I'm thinking of things such as:

Experience. At some point, you began to understand how the world works. Not totally, but substantially. Through the school of hard knocks you've come to learn what works and what doesn't work. You've also been through some adventures—some of them exciting, some hair-raising, some rather difficult, and perhaps some that were utterly devastating. Can you appreciate how valuable those experiences might be for another man? If I were going to climb Mount Everest, you can bet that I'd go talk to men who have already done it. I'd be a fool not to! Well, your Everests could be the difference between wisdom and folly for another man who is embarking on a similar quest.

Knowledge. Certainly, you've developed knowledge in your particular vocation—whether in law, medicine, finance, business, construction, sales, retail, law enforcement, plumbing, teaching, you name it. You owe it to your field to cultivate the talents of younger, up-and-coming leaders.

But you also possess knowledge about the world and life in general. I've known men who had in-depth knowledge of the history of a country or city or company, and how things have come to be as they are. Or knowledge about people and organizations and what makes humans tick. Or knowledge of an ecosystem and what animals live there, and how humans affect that environment.

And what about knowledge of Scripture? Or knowledge of other kinds of literature? It tends to be older men who can ask, "Have you read such-and-such a book? It's got the answer you're looking for."

Access. Your network may be the most valuable asset you have in regard to another man (see chapter 5). You know people he doesn't know. More importantly, you've earned a reputation, and your phone calls and emails will get returned by those people. That means you can open doors that will instantly accelerate his progress. Obviously, you have to be discerning about whom to put him in touch with. But your reputation and your role as gatekeeper could prove invaluable to his development.

Money. Jesus challenged us to use our wealth to populate heaven (see Luke 16:9), which forces us to ask: How much are we investing in people? Even buying lunch for a younger man in order to have a conversation with him can be powerful. Did it ever occur to you that unless you pay, such a lunch might never happen, since he may not be able to afford it?

Other ways to use money as a mentor might include paying for a man to get training and development, or to gain more education. You might send him on an adventure or learning odyssey—maybe to go check out something that you're interested in but are too busy to visit yourself. Maybe you buy him a book to read or a tool to use.

What about investing in another man's project? That's perfectly acceptable—as long as you're wise about it and the money part makes sense. Any investment comes with risks, so you have to weigh those risks and decide whether you're willing to accept them. But putting money into a venture usually gains you the right to bring other resources to bear, such as your experience and wisdom, along with your networks and contacts. In my experience—yours may differ—people never invest in a deal but in people. By putting money into something that a man you're working with believes in and is committed to making work, you're granting him a huge vote of confidence.

Resources. Over time, you've probably acquired more resources than you realize—in most cases, certainly, more than the man you're working with. By "resources," I mean useful assets such as a home, a car, an office or workspace, tools, personal property, books, collections, a swimming pool, a hunting lease, a membership at a health club, and so on. Many of those things you may use once or twice a year. Otherwise, they just sit there. Imagine inviting another man to enjoy the benefit of one of your possessions. Doing so might help him grow in ways you can't even imagine. And that kind of generosity is one of the best ways I know to be a faithful steward of what God has given you.

I recall how our family used to take an annual vacation to Colorado when I was a boy. I could tell you endless stories of Jeep rides in the mountains, horseback rides through virgin wilderness, trout fishing with my dad at a little pond called Presbyterian Lake, and trips to Buena Vista to get chocolate dip top cones at the Dairy Queen. So many memories! But only later did I learn that the cabin we stayed at was gifted to us by an accountant in Dallas who thought the world of my dad and wanted to bless him and our family through his resources. By doing that, he enriched my life in ways he could never have imagined.

Friendship. If nothing else, you can offer companionship. The journey from boyhood to manhood can be ever so lonely, which is why we often hear disillusioned young men say, "All I ever wanted was for someone to be there."

Being there. I cannot overemphasize the importance of those words! They speak directly to the power of presence. Brothers, whatever else we do with other men, by far the most important thing we can ever do is to just *be there.* Show up. Be present.

It sounds too simple, I know, but I will tell you that the power of presence is a real phenomenon. Somehow, most of us completely overlook it. I don't know why. We all seem to remember those little league games we played in, the high school sports we were part of, the band concerts we performed in, or our graduation ceremonies. And what do we most remember about them? Whether our dad was present! If he was, we may or may not remember a word of anything he said. But we always will remember whether he was there.

There's something about our presence that makes us indelible in someone's memory—especially someone we've developed a close relationship with. I admit, it's something of a mystery to me, how that works. But I've come to trust the power of presence enough to just show up when I need to, whether I think I have anything significant to say or do. If by doing so I communicate to another man that I'm for him, that I believe in him, that he's going to make it, that he can trust me—that's enough for me.

This discussion about being there leads to . . .

Time. The older you get, the busier you get. As one person put it, "I don't know what I do anymore, but it sure takes up all my time!" That's all too true. But it's also true that the older you get, the more *control* you tend to have over your time. You can be more selective as to where and how you spend your time. That's especially the case if you're nearing retirement or are already retired.[1]

I must say, when I consider how many young men I'm aware of who are desperately looking for mentors—there are literally millions of them—I wince as I observe the way our culture tends to segregate the elderly from the young. That seems like a profound disconnect to me: rising generations screaming for guidance as they lay hold of adulthood and the responsibility for stewarding the world, while retiring generations are cordoned off to live separate lives—the afflu-ent and able-bodied to pursue their little hobbies and amusements, the less well-off and disabled to sit around playing bingo and watch-ing TV (and feel rather useless).

If you have any time and means whatsoever, may I appeal to you to make yourself available to a younger man?

Yourself. This asset goes hand in hand with the power of presence. Here, I'm talking about your unique personhood that you bring to everything you do. You bring your special slant on life, your unique bent and style. No one else is exactly like you. No one else can match your unique contribution. No one else can ever tell your unique *Story of Me*.

So the question is, are you willing to just "be yourself" with an-other man, and by doing so help him discover and tell his own *Story of Me*?

I could add other items to this list. The point is to stop looking at what you don't have and start looking at what you do have—and, therefore, what you can place in God's hands to be used as He chooses in the life of another men.

YOUR ACHILLES' HEEL

Despite anything I may have said to make the case for mentoring, many men believe there's a trump card in their past, an Achilles' heel that ultimately disqualifies them as a mentor. Somewhere back there, they made a terrible mistake. They may have committed a grave sin (are there any other kinds?) or had been ensnared by a terrible habit. Whatever the specifics, they made a mess of their life, and now they feel they have no business trying to guide others.

If that describes you, I have to ask: What is your understanding of *grace*? And for that matter, what has been your experience of God's *forgiveness*? Rather than give you answers, I suggest you go spend some time reading and reflecting on what Jesus said to Peter just hours before His number-one disciple would deny even knowing Him

(Luke 22:31–34). Pay special attention to the words, "When once you have turned again, strengthen your brothers" (v. 32; see also John 21:15–17).

Your particular Achilles' heel may have to do with your family. Perhaps you have a wayward son or daughter. Or maybe you're divorced and completely estranged from your ex-wife and children. Whatever the failures on your part—perceived or actual—you may now feel unqualified to step in and help any other young adult. If so, consider that the painful lessons you've learned may actually be the greatest things you have to offer.

Imagine if we could talk to some of the "fathers of failures" in the Bible, such as Manoah, the father of Samson (Judg. 13:2); Eli, the father of Hophni and Phinehas (1 Sam. 2:12–17, 22–25, 34); Samuel, the father of the corrupt judges Joel and Abijah (1 Sam. 8:1–3); or David, the father of immoral Amnon and rebellious Absalom (2 Sam. 13:1–14; 15:1–16). Do you think any of those fathers might have something to teach us? The same could hold true for you.

UNDISCOVERED TREASURE

I'll close this chapter with the true story of a close friend of mine who became the pastor of a small church in New England. For several years, he faithfully shepherded the congregation, and by God's grace it began to grow into a sizable group of people. Before long, it became obvious that a new building was needed. But the expense of that seemed out of the question.

While trying to decide what to do, the leadership decided they could at least repair the church's bell, which had been out of use for as long as anyone could recall. When the workmen went up into the bell tower to get started on that project, they discovered an old painting wrapped in newsprint. Someone had apparently stored it up there long before, and there it sat all those years, forgotten.

The painting seemed unremarkable. But just to be sure, the church had it appraised by a professional in Boston. To their shock, news came back that it was a priceless original by an Italian Renaissance master, worth a fortune. Overjoyed, the church eventually auctioned off the painting and put the proceeds toward its building project.

I think about that painting as I reflect on what men have to offer other men. I'm satisfied that we have countless treasures around us everywhere, sitting inside men: their knowledge, their wisdom, their memories and stories, and all the many other assets stored inside of them. If only we would engage with other men! So many things we've forgotten and so many things we've come to take for granted would turn out to be priceless treasures!

CHAPTER 13

WHAT ARE THE QUESTIONS MEN ASK?

How do informal mentoring relationships get started? About the same way most any other relationship gets started. Two men meet—perhaps at work, at church, in the context of a school, at a social gathering, at a luncheon, at a conference or convention, in a coffee shop, or on a plane. However they meet, they begin to interact. Neither one is thinking about mentoring. They're just two men interacting.

Circumstances may then start putting them in contact on a regular basis, perhaps through their jobs or in a course that one of them is teaching and the other is taking. Or they may just decide to get together again and resume the conversation, perhaps based on some need one of them has or a topic that surfaced the first time around and needs more discussion.

At that point, nothing says that the relationship has to or will turn into a mentoring relationship. But nothing says it can't or won't. The potential is always there, waiting in the background.

So should either man try to "make something happen"? I wouldn't advise it. I would just treat it as a friendship. The best friendships seem to grow organically out of two people wanting to get together. Yes, there may be something of an "agenda" they're working on, but the relationship grows out of that, not because they are "working" on the relationship itself.

TOP LEVEL MATTERS

Recently, I listened to an interview with a successful entrepreneur describing the beginnings of his very initial venture, a line of clothing. His first big break came when he and his partners managed to book $300,000 in orders. But they had zero capital with which to fulfill those orders.

"I didn't know what I didn't know," the man recalls. "I went to all the banks that I could, and I got turned down by twenty-seven of them." Having grown up in the inner city, he had absolutely no financial background. "I didn't know how to fill out a loan application."[1]

If ever a man needed someone to help him, it was that man at that moment. "I didn't know what I didn't know." That pretty much sums up the need for mentoring. So now imagine that you work in finance and that young man runs into you. You listen to his story and you can hear the frustration in his voice as he tells you, "Man, I've got the orders, but I don't know how to get a loan!"

So, you decide to help him. You get together and you explain what a loan is and the different kinds of loans there are and the different places you can get them. You introduce him to concepts like collateral and credit risk and interest and amortization. You give him insight into what loan officers are thinking and how they size up an application and the person making it. In short, you give him a crash course in getting a loan, and hopefully that bit of timely input helps that young man surmount a hurdle and get launched on his way.

That's an example of what I call a "top-level" issue. Top-level issues tend to revolve around learning activities that have an immediate practical concern, sort of a need-to-know basis. Probably most mentoring starts off with top-level matters, and often that's where it remains.

Other examples of top-level concerns might be:

- how to buy a car or a house
- learning to read a financial statement
- how to go about finding a job
- getting pointers on rebluing an old rifle
- learning a new language
- learning to operate a sailboat
- discussing what to do about a conflict with one's boss
- how to size up an offer at another employer
- when to know it's time to get engaged
- what to do when your parents have told you they're getting divorced after twenty-eight years of marriage
- where to find a good counselor to work through some personal issues

FOUR LEVELS OF HELP

Given the practical nature of top-level issues, there are four possibilities, generally speaking, for how you might be able to help another man.

1. You've faced the exact same scenario. Sometimes, someone turns to you for help because you're the perfect person to ask for help, because you have lots of experience in the area in which they need help. So, to stick with the example given above, if you've filled out numerous loan applications or, better yet, you routinely work with loans at a bank or a mortgage company, your experience and/or expertise can prove invaluable to a man who knows nothing about loans.

As you grow older and gain experience in your occupation or career, you should expect people to turn to you for help in the area of your expertise. And, of course, you can always take the initiative and offer to help someone who appears to be struggling in an area that you know well.

The one caveat here is that you should never assume that just because your area of specialization is easy for you to understand, it will be easy for the other person. Human giftedness predisposes each person to have a unique bent, a unique set of abilities and interests, and those gifts may or may not favor the person's functioning when he finds himself operating in your area. As a loan guy, you may be extremely comfortable with numbers, equations, ratios, and money matters. But the man you're working with may not "get" that stuff. That doesn't make him dumb; it just makes him different from you. So, be sensitive to men who are wired in other ways than you are, and do your best to "put the cookies on the lower shelf" in explaining the basics of what he needs to know.

2. You've faced a similar scenario. Consider the example I gave above about a young adult coming to you for input after learning that his parents are splitting up after twenty-eight years of marriage. Let's say you and your wife have been married for forty-three years and you both came from stable home backgrounds. So, it's hard to directly relate to what he's going through.

But let's say you have a daughter whose marriage ended in divorce after six years. Or maybe you and your wife are friends with a couple whose marriage ended in divorce. Because of those experiences, you at least have some familiarity with what that young man is facing. On the basis of that, you can offer empathy, support, and perhaps some practical thoughts about what he might expect, how he might respond, and what he should be aware of.

3. You've never faced his scenario, but you have some ideas. Sometimes a man will tell you about something you've never encountered personally. I once interacted with a young man whose father had made a fortune in business and had set up trust funds for him and each of his siblings. In short, before he had even graduated from high school, this young man had been made independently wealthy.

But he didn't want to just "cruise" on his good fortune. He wanted to earn his own way, so as to feel legitimate in his accomplishments. "Is there some way I can give it back?" he asked me, with great sincerity.

We were already out of my depth when he told me about his trust fund! That was a long way away from my background, for sure. Nevertheless, because I knew his father, and because I had experience with children from other affluent families, a few ideas were occurring to me as I realized what he was dealing with. So, I suggested a few things I would be thinking about and some questions I would be asking, were I in his situation. I also mentioned some possibilities for others he might want to talk with to get their input. My main objective was to let him know that I understood his concerns and was willing to be helpful in any way I could, even if it was just to provide moral support.

4. You don't know how to help him, but you're willing to walk with him as he learns. Occasionally, another man will ask you about something that is totally unknown to you, and you have no idea how to help him. In that case, it's best to say early on, "I really don't know anything about that subject. I'm not sure I can help you." No need to waste his time.

That said, if the man I'm talking to is someone I've grown to regard as a friend, I'm reluctant to just say, "I don't know anything about that. Go away." As his friend, I want to see him get some help. So, obviously the first thing I'd do is start thinking about people I know who *could* be helpful to him, or who might know someone who could be helpful to him. That's an example of using my network on his behalf.

Regardless of whether I can lead him to any helpful resources, I always feel compelled to let him know I'm willing to walk alongside him as he works through whatever he's dealing with. That's what friendships are for, it seems to me. Yes, he has to do his homework and make contacts and think through things and make decisions and take responsibility for his situation. But I want him to know that he's not alone in doing all that. If he needs input from me, I want him to know I'm available to give it, if I am able. If I'm not able, I need to let him know that. Frankly, as he's learning, I end up learning, too. What I experience with him may prove helpful to someone else later.

And even if that man is working on something totally outside my wheelhouse, the one thing I can always do is pray for him. For many men, that alone is worth everything, because they've never had anyone pray for them. They themselves may be inexperienced in praying, so to have another man exercising faith on their behalf is tremendously supportive and encouraging. And that just might lead to a deeper relationship.

THE DEEPER LEVEL OF MENTORING

Most mentoring relationships don't go very far beyond top-level issues, and that's not bad. It simply is. Nor does it mean that the relationship between the two men remains shallow. They may become good friends and come to know each other fairly well over time.

But as I stated earlier, the potential is always there for something deeper to take place. And that "something deeper" has to do with the soul of the man being mentored. He ends up changing in some core way—particularly in how he sees himself and the world.

Imagine an apprentice on a job site. The company assigns him to a veteran, or "mentor," which makes this a somewhat formal sort of mentoring relationship. By shadowing his mentor, the apprentice learns a variety of skills and knowledge over time that he'll need in order to become an effective construction worker. He learns to use certain tools. He comes to understand certain processes and physical laws that govern construction. He becomes familiar with the codes and standards of his industry.

If the mentor does his job right and the apprentice applies himself, at some point the apprentice becomes a fully certified workman who can be assigned projects independent of his mentor. He becomes a full-fledged member of the crew.

Now from one point of view, the mentor has helped his apprentice learn a construction trade. He's trained him. So, he now knows how to do construction, right?

Yes, but does he *know* construction? I'm willing to bet that nine out of ten veteran construction workers would answer that question, "Not really." Sure, he's professionally certified. Nevertheless, they would describe him as "green." Green doesn't just mean inexperienced. It means lacking in self-awareness. That's really what experience brings—evaluated experience, that is.

In the case of construction, it means discovering how construction interacts with who one is—how it tests you, what it demands of you, why it matters to you (or not), what it means to you.

For countless men, construction is "just a job," "just a paycheck." But to real construction workers—the ones who take pride in their work and do it with excellence—it's a way of life, a set of values, a craft, an expression of who they are.

That's what has to be mentored into a new man. Not just a set of competencies, but a mindset, a way of thinking, not only about construction, but about *oneself* and the way one engages in construction. The man is changed in some way, such that he looks back and reflects on the men who guided him along as he learned the trade and says, "I never would have become who I am, and I never could have done my work the way that I do it, were it not for the influence of those men."

SOUL QUESTIONS

Men always operate at two levels. There's the task at hand, and then there's the man doing the task. Most of the time, we focus on the task and forget the man, unless we've become accustomed to doing otherwise. Countless Bible passages speak to this dual reality:

"You shall love the Lord your God with all your heart and with all your soul and with all your might" (Deut. 6:5). "Your might" indicates the task, "your heart and . . . soul," indicates the man.

"Man looks at the outward appearance, but the LORD looks at the heart" (1 Sam. 16:7). "The outward appearance" points to the task, "the heart" points to the man.

"For what will it profit a man if he gains the whole world and forfeits his soul?" (Matt. 16:26). "The whole world" is the sphere of tasks, "his soul" describes the man.

"Do not work for the food which perishes, but for the food which endures to eternal life" (John 6:27). "The food which perishes" is within the realm of tasks, "the food which endures to eternal life" pertains to the man.

"Therefore we do not lose heart, but though our outer man is decaying, yet our inner man is being renewed day by day" (2 Cor. 4:16). "Our outer man" relates to tasks, "our inner man" relates to who we are as a person.

Passages like these show that we tend to ignore the inner realities of our heart as we get caught up in the day-to-day demands of life—the top-level issues. That's why the Bible implores us to "watch over your heart with all diligence, for from it flow the springs of life" (Prov. 4:23) The word-picture here is of a stronghold that is to be guarded as tightly as Fort Knox. To paraphrase, "Whatever you do, be exceptionally cautious about who and what you allow to have access to your heart, because that's the wellspring of your life."

You can see why that's true when you consider the soul matters that every man must contend with:

- Issues of self-worth and self-doubt: Who am I? Where did I come from? Am I good enough? Do I have what it takes?

- The whole problem of making money and paying the bills: Can I provide for myself? Can I support a wife and family?

- Where to allocate his time and energy: What really matters? I can't do everything, so what is worth doing? What do I give priority to?

- How to make his mark in life: What should I do with my life? What was I born to do? What is my purpose?

- What to do about his sin and brokenness—and by extension, the generational sin of his family: Why do I do things I know I shouldn't do and neglect things I know I should do? What do I do about my guilt and shame? How do I live with my regrets? Am I good enough for God?

- How to come to grips with his body and its mortality: I may be strong now, but it won't always be that way. What then? What if I get sick along the way? How will I manage in old age?

- How to think about eternity, and trying to determine whether his life really matters: What happens when I die? Where will I spend eternity? Is this it, or is there something beyond this life? Is there a God?

GOD IS AT WORK

I grant you that most men spend very little time consciously thinking about the matters I've just listed (which is why Scriptures like the ones I've just cited warn us as they do). But thoughts like these are there in the soul, nonetheless, conscious or not. As Ecclesiastes says, God has "set eternity in [our] heart" (3:11), and He makes Himself known to every person in every culture (see Ps. 8:1–2; Rom. 1:20–21).

Which means that God is already at work in any man you meet. God loves that man infinitely more than you ever can or will. So, you can prayerfully look to see where God might be working in his life, and then try to get on board with that, if you so choose. It might be through a top-level concern, and the main point of God bringing him your way might be that for maybe the first time in his life he experiences someone who treats him like Jesus would—like a person, like a man with dignity and value, like a creature who bears the image of God. By helping him develop his capacities and gain some competence, you implicitly communicate that he matters, that he has a purpose and a contribution to make. You also show him that you care. For many, that's the first step in discovering that there is a God who cares about him, too.

But it's also possible that through your interaction with him over time, you begin to speak into one or more of his deeper soul issues. And when I say "speak into," I by no means am thinking of cognitive, rational arguments in answer to the various questions I've listed above. Others have done that far more brilliantly than you or I probably can, so if you want to put him on to some of those resources, great.

But "speaking into" a soul issue has far more to do with how he sees you handling that issue in the way you live and the way you do life. For example, a man—even a man who is a Christian—sometimes wonders deep in his soul whether God really exists or whether He is just a myth that the ancients created out of fear. Then he watches you and experiences you. He notices that you take God seriously. He may know that you pray to that God, that you seem to relate to that God, not only as if He exists, but as if He's a friend, a person, someone who can actually be known and related to. He perceives that you are not acting that way out of fear, but out of confidence and peace. You clearly believe in God, as if He's actually real. And he slowly notices that that affects pretty much everything about you—how you see your work, how you try to relate to others, how you talk about your wife, how you spend your time, what seems to matter to you, how you handle your failures and mistakes, on and on.

In short, iron begins to sharpen iron. You are making an impression, an impact, a difference on another man's soul. In short, you become what this book is all about: a man of influence. You may not even be aware of it. But by some mystery, God is drawing that man to Himself through you. That's the ultimate mystery of mentoring—

from a Christian point of view, anyway.

In the next chapter, I want to mention a few of the specific areas that commonly come up as men relate to men in regard to the deeper areas of the mentoring relationship.

CHAPTER 14

SOME COMMON THEMES OF MENTORING

For about the past twelve years, I've met with a handful of other men for breakfast every Wednesday morning. To an outside observer, I'm sure that gathering looks pretty informal. That's because it is, at least in the sense that we don't have a set agenda and we don't follow any sort of "plan." Nor do we have any "rules." Basically, it boils down to two commitments: (1) show up every week (unless you're sick, detained, or out of town), and (2) pray for the other guys in the group. That's it!

Upon hearing that, some may react, "That's all?! What good will come of that? That's just a men's fellowship group—maybe not even that."

Well, that would be a mistake, because every man involved regards that group as one of his lifelines to staying grounded. By now, pretty much every single area of each man's life has come on the table countless times: his marriage and family, his work, his relationship to God, his deepest hurts, his hopes and dreams, his shame and regrets, his doubts and fears, his history, his thoughts about the later years of his life, his feelings about death, and so on.

That group is an example of peer mentoring, and it's about as clear a piece of evidence as I can offer to the truth that "iron sharpens iron," particularly over time. Certain themes surface in a group like that, and that's not by accident. Every man faces certain inescapable realities, as I began to describe in the last chapter.

You don't have to go into those deeper realities to have a positive influence on another man. You may not feel comfortable getting very far beneath the surface. That's fine. But I will tell you that the deep waters are where the real treasures exist, and that getting to them is not as difficult or as daunting as it may appear. But it's your call whether you go there.

Regardless, if you interact with other men in mentoring relationships, here are ten common themes that you're likely to encounter.

I. A MAN'S STORY

Throughout the book, I've stressed the importance of *The Story of Me*, the story of one's life from birth to the present—the "writing" of one's story goes on for as long as one is alive. Each of us as men is living out our story, day by day. But, sadly, few men are telling their story to other men. Which begs the question: If a story remains untold, was it worth being written in the first place?

One of the best things you can do for another man is to invite him to tell you his story—*but only if you're genuinely interested in hearing it*. Otherwise, leave it alone. If you are interested, I suggest extending that invitation as early in the relationship as seems appropriate.

What good will it do? you may wonder. More than you can imagine! In the first place, just telling his story to someone else causes the storyteller to feel more alive and, if I can put it this way, more "weighty"—like he matters, like he has significance. I can't explain exactly why that is so. It's a bit of mystery. But it's true.

In addition, by telling his story, a man tells you what has happened to him, and that provides insight into how he has come to be what he is now that you've met him. I have often thought that if I could crawl inside someone else's skin and experience everything he has ever experienced—every relationship, every interaction and conversation with others, every thought, every feeling, every conflict, every joy, every danger, every failure, every tragedy, every gift—if I could somehow retrace every step in the twists and turns of his life and experience them the way he has, I would instantly say, "No wonder you are who you are by now! No wonder you see the world as you do! It makes perfect sense!" Hearing a man's story is a scaled-down version of doing that.

By hearing a man's story, you will not only have greater insight into him, but hopefully greater compassion for him. You will be less prone to judging him. You will also have a lot of clues as to where he may need help, particularly at a soul level. You may or may not be the one to supply that help, but at least you know what he needs and can roll that into whatever else you're going to help him with.

Helping Him Tell His Story

There are several ways to help a man tell you his story. The obvious strategy is the direct approach: "So, let's go back. I want to hear your story—all the way back to the beginning." I've occasionally done that with a few men. It's usually happened when we've set aside time for that very purpose. For example, a couple of years after my buddies and I started our breakfast group, we all went on an overnight retreat together. While feasting on grilled steaks, sitting up late around a campfire, and enjoying coffee after breakfast the next morning, we listened as each man stepped up and told the narrative of his life, from birth to the present. Probably nothing has bonded us more than that weekend.

But hearing a man's *Story of Me* doesn't usually happen that way. More often, he tells it to you in bits and pieces over time. You may try to speed things along by saying, "So, tell me about yourself. Tell me about your background. Where was growing up for you?" Most men will willingly talk about their early years. But in the early going, a man is likely to tell a somewhat surface, factual account of it all: where he was born, where he grew up, what his dad and mom did for work, how many siblings he had, what activities he did in high school, and so on. He's not yet going to trust you with the deeper details of what happened—particularly the sad or hurtful events that took place back there.

However, if you keep the relationship going over time, other pieces of his story will gradually begin to come out. You'll learn more about his relationship to his dad. You may learn the details of a tragedy that occurred when he was young, an incident he only alluded to earlier. A revelation like that indicates that you've started to gain significant trust with that man. That trust tends to invite even greater vulnerability.

So Where Does It Go?

Now let me point something out. So far, all you've done is provide a listening ear and a safe space for a man to tell his story. That's really not that difficult. But notice that you don't have to be a trained counselor or psychologist to do that. You don't have to get into his potty-training and try to analyze him. All you have to do is actively listen and *attend* to another man.

As you listen to his story, you'll start to see the story as a whole. You'll see what I call the overall "trajectory" of the man's life. It may be a case of the tortoise and the hare, the underdog who has come from behind to achieve great things. It may be the narrative of a fallen hero, the man who seemingly had it all, then everything came apart, and now he's trying to pick up the pieces. Some men's lives have been sheer chaos: up and down, up and down, up and down, one misstep and misfortune and miserable event after another. Or it may be a story of redemption—like that of my dad, who was growing up on the streets of Philadelphia, lost as a lamb and was probably destined for a life to Nowhere, when God just plucked him off the sidewalk one day through an uneducated tool and die worker who happened to love Jesus.

Don't assume your man has ever seen any of that! I'd say that the vast majority of men I've encountered have spent most of their lives running around in the trees, and no one has ever taken them up in a helicopter to survey the forest at ten thousand feet. You could be the one to show a man that vista—and with it, countless insights into how the different parts of his story connect to each other, as well as relate to the whole. Men's lives are not random: things that happened earlier tend to be linked to things that happen later—both the good and the bad. There's a reason for that.

I could write a whole book talking about the benefits a man can receive by telling his story to another man. But let me just point out that the more you hear his story, the better you know him. That means the better you know what you're working with.

I don't mean to objectify or depersonalize the man by stating things that way. What I mean is every man comes to you in whatever condition he comes to you. You usually can't read that condition on the surface[1]—and neither can he. His story begins to take you beneath the surface, allowing you to see what condition he's in—a reality that ought to inform everything you do with him. For example, he's come to you for guidance on how to get along with his wife. He doesn't realize that in growing up, he never learned to have healthy conflict and find resolution to it. You could give him a dozen principles of conflict management and scores of verses on seeking peace and harmony in relationships, but if that earlier part of his story remains untold and therefore unexamined, what do you really expect to accomplish? Your efforts, well-intentioned as they may be, have not touched his soul, where the real transformation takes place.

One Caveat

Before leaving the issue of telling stories, I would be remiss if I didn't give you one major caution: *Whatever you do as you listen to a man's story, you have to suspend all judgment.* Not discernment, but judgment. Judgment means making a moral appraisal of the man's behaviors, attitudes, character, opinions, reactions, perceptions, conclusions, language, or humor. Okay, maybe you can *think* poorly of something he's told you. But just don't *say* it—at least, not then. If you do, you'll shut him down. You may also seriously compromise, if not end, the relationship.

When you invite/allow a man to tell you his story, you're not staging a debate. It's not about right and wrong. You're not there to correct him. He's not on trial. *Whatever else, the invitation to tell you his story is an invitation to trust you.* For once in his life, likely, he's being asked to just tell what has happened in his life, and to tell that as he sees it from his perspective. You may question some of his facts. Why, you may know for certain that some of his facts are wrong. It doesn't matter! Not at that moment. At that moment, all that matters is that he feels safe enough to go back and retrieve and recount his lived experience as he remembers it.

Remember what I said earlier about crawling inside his skin to experience the world as he experiences it. That's what you're trying to do in listening to his story. If you start judging him for what he's told you, you'll never get to the real truth about that man. In essence, his story will remain untold. And what good is an untold story?

2. A MAN'S STRENGTHS

God has given every man a unique set of core strengths and natural motivation to do things that he finds satisfying and productive. We refer to those strengths as the man's *giftedness*. His giftedness is what he is born to do.

Every man is born to do something. One man loves to solve problems: he's never met a problem he didn't want to tackle. Another man wants to build something and produce a finished product. Another wants to inspire other people and motivate them to action. Another wants to wrap his mind around a subject and gain an in-depth understanding of every last thing about it. Yet another has imaginative ideas that he brings into reality through a creative expression—a song, a novel, a sculpture, a painting. Someone else is fascinated by the concepts of math and physics and seeks to explain the mysteries of string theory and the eleven dimensions of space and time. Another man just wants to reach a goal and "git 'r done."

Every man has his own unique giftedness, but most men don't know what their giftedness is. That's because they live inside their skin. They can't see their giftedness any more than they can see their own face. They can see other people's faces and, likewise, other people's giftedness. But when they're using their own giftedness, they don't notice it. It doesn't seem remarkable to them. They wouldn't think of doing life any other way. As a result, most men remain unacquainted with their real strengths, except perhaps at a very rudimentary level.

You could change the course of a man's life simply by helping him discover his strengths. Many younger men in particular wonder whether they even have any strengths. Imagine what could happen if they discovered they do! They would gain real confidence. They could make better choices about what jobs and careers to pursue. They could make decisions and take action with a degree of authority, being sure of what tasks fit them and which ones they should let go of.

If you'd like to know more about helping a man discover his giftedness, see my book *The Person Called You: Why You're Here, Why You Matter & What You Should Do With Your Life.* That book will give you the details on giftedness, and in the back is a simple story-based exercise you can go through with another man to help him gain key insights into how God has designed him.

Hand-in-glove with the topic of giftedness are the topics of . . .

3. WORK, CAREER, AND CALLING

Elsewhere, I have pointed out that our culture does not know how to get people from high school graduation into the adult world of work. As a result, you may be approached by a college student trying to pick a major. Or a recent college graduate who went into the field of his college major—only now he wants to pursue something completely different, though he has no idea what that might be. Or a young professional who is three years out of law school and now perceives he made a terrible mistake going into law. Or a man in his late thirties or early forties who has realized he doesn't want to retire doing what he's been doing—but he doesn't know what his options are and has no framework for how to even think about any of this.

How can you help men with issues like these? Well, whatever you do, don't ask, "What would you like to do?" The answer is they don't know! If they knew that, they wouldn't be talking to you. They'd be pursuing what they'd "like" to do.

That's why I always start with the discovery of giftedness—as described in the previous section. A man's giftedness is given to him by God, among other reasons, as a means of adding value to the world—which is to say a means of earning a living in a productive, gainful way. Men need to pursue work that fits them. But in our culture, which confronts men with so many options, a man needs help thinking through, and brainstorming, how his gifts match some of those options. And then he needs someone to walk with him as he pursues those options to find the right match. Again, you can find out more about that and your part in it in *The Person Called You.*

Another key way you can help men think about their work is to see it as something God cares about. Too many men have the mistaken idea that work is a part of the curse. Wrong! The truth is that work was given to humans by God from the beginning. Our work is the means whereby we cause the world and its people to flourish. Yes, sin and the fall have drastically affected work and made it seem much more difficult than it was ever supposed to be. But every form of legitimate work has dignity and value before God, and He tells us to do it as if He were our boss—because, in fact, He is.

If all this comes as new news to you, I heartily encourage you to check out books like *Every Good Endeavor* by Tim Keller and Kathryn Alsdorf, or *Where's God on Monday?* by Alistair Mackenzie and Wayne Kirkland. You might also look at a website called The Theology of Work Project,[2] which examines every book in the Bible to explain what each one says about work from God's perspective. Consider working through these resources together with the man you're working with.

4. A MAN'S CHARACTER

Even a casual glance through the book of Proverbs shows that most of them are aimed at the issue of character. And that's as one would expect, because "iron sharpening iron" implies a shaping and influencing of a man's central core, the very stuff that he is made of. If you want to know what a man is made of—if you want to know what *you* are made of—watch what happens when he is tested to his core.

Sooner or later, the man you're working with will be tested. The three venues where it most often happens are at work, in his marriage, and at church. He'll find himself faced with a matter of integrity—a lie that his boss has asked him to tell, some numbers he is tempted to manipulate, a piece of juicy news he overheard at the dinner table, a situation where a pastor has told him not to remember something he actually witnessed.

The man doesn't quite know what to do, so he turns to you for guidance. How do you respond?

Your impulse may be to just give him "the answer." You lay out what's right and what's wrong, and you remind him he needs to do what's right. Case closed.

Sometimes it's that simple. Sometimes the situation is fairly black and white, and the man just needs some fortitude to do the right thing.

But think about the larger objective you're trying to achieve with him. Is it to arm him with "the right answers," or to help him develop a godly conscience and the ability to think things through with godly wisdom?

Remember what I said above about the "condition" a man comes to you in. When it comes to character, many men have grown up in a background where moral and ethical choices were made on the basis of expediency, pragmatism, and personal preference. Any thought of God or what He might have to say about matters was completely missing. So just saying, "The Bible says . . ." may not register for such a man. He's liable to respond, "Okay, but I think . . ."

Don't take that as an automatic rejection of God's ways. Instead, realize that you're dealing with a man who is still on a journey of learning that God is the Lord and His ways are given to us, not so much as a bunch of rules to be followed, but as pathways into life and health.[3] What, then, are ways you can help this man begin to place God's ways above his own thoughts about what's "right" or what "works"?

One other way you can help a man come to grips with his character is to acquaint him with his "dark side." The dark side has to do with using his core strengths—his giftedness—in sinful, selfish, or evil purposes. The worst sins that people commit are not out of their so-called "weaknesses," but out of their core strengths aimed in exactly the wrong directions. King David's strength as a warrior was exactly what Israel needed to vanquish its remaining enemies (the Canaanites who remained in the land) in order to secure Jerusalem for the building of the temple. But that same gift was turned against Uriah, with tragic consequences.

As you help a man discover, celebrate, and begin to use his giftedness, let him know that every gift has a potential dark side. Ask him how his gifts might be used for purposes other than what God intended for them.[4]

5. THE FATHER WOUND

Several years ago, I was just waking up one morning and I was in that netherworld between being fully asleep and fully awake. For whatever reason, my mind drifted toward thoughts of God, and the wonderful sense of God as my heavenly Father began washing over me. It was an incredibly peaceful, comforting sensation! Then my mind shifted to my three daughters, and I couldn't help but contemplate my own relation to them as their father. Suddenly the thought seized my mind: "You know, Bill, before your daughters were ever old enough to know God as their heavenly Father, you were their first experience of what 'father' is all about."

With that, I sat right up in bed, terrified! My immediate thought was, "O God! Then what hope do they have?"

In His kindness, the Lord eased me away from the ledge that morning, reminding me that His grace is sufficient to override the failures of men. He also showed me that despite the many mistakes I had made as a dad, there were still ways in which I was (and am) a "good enough" father.

But the chilling reality remains: for each of us, our first experience of "father" is with a fallen, sinful man who falls far short of what we have in our heavenly Father. One of the lingering effects of that shortfall is The Father Wound. In the ideal, a boy and his father develop a strong relationship in which the boy feels loved and supported by his dad. To the extent that doesn't happen—for whatever reason—the son can feel hurt, a hurt that inflicts a lingering wound.

Because of our fallen condition as humans, I suppose every man has a Father Wound to some degree. We all need a relationship with our heavenly Father to find healing, restoration, and an experience of true fatherhood. But some men are more wounded than others because as boys they were perhaps abandoned, or neglected, told they were no good and/or would never amount to anything, physically and/or emotionally abused, sexually molested, manipulated, cheated, lied to, betrayed, or mistreated in other ways.

Men with Father Wounds can end up feeling shame, guilt, low self-esteem, depression, anxiety, helplessness, hopelessness, inadequacy, anger, rage, or a sense of abandonment. They can have significant difficulty feeling worthy, feeling lovable, making and keeping commitments, or holding a job. Not surprisingly, they may seek relief through drugs, alcohol, sexual promiscuity, gambling, or countless other addictions and high-risk behaviors.

That's grim stuff. But we're foolish if we act as if it's not true. There's no way to know exactly how many men in our culture, let alone throughout the world, are walking around with a Father Wound. But chances are high you will run into one as you engage in mentoring—you may have a Father Wound yourself.

I do not believe that a mentoring relationship is the place to "work on" a Father Wound. That's the job of a trained counselor. But that doesn't mean a mentor can't be invaluable to a man whose father has left him a legacy of pain. For one, a mentor may be the first man who has ever had enough compassion to let a man know that his father failed him in some serious ways.

When a man grows up in an abusive home, abuse may well become the "norm" for him. He may assume all dads are abusive. His father may have even told him so. Until someone comes along and explains to him that abuse is not only not "normal" but also harmful, he'll never realize what's been done to him. Imagine, then what a profound breakthrough it could be when a man he's come to trust gently tells him that fathers are supposed to love their sons, and that he's sorry and saddened to know that didn't happen for him. And then he helps that man find some professional help to begin the long road of healing from that injury.

Another way a mentor proves helpful to a man with a Father Wound is by remaining faithful, reliable, trustworthy, and safe. A man with a Father Wound is liable to say and do some pretty foolish things. He may get himself into all kinds of trouble. Whenever that happens, he's come to expect rejection, condemnation, abuse, and/

or punishment. Imagine the impact a man makes on him when he doesn't go away, doesn't fly into a rage, doesn't tell him what a loser he is, and doesn't punish him for telling the truth. Obviously, a mentor has to set and keep healthy boundaries and not allow himself to be abused, nor to enable dysfunctional behavior. But often the only way a man can believe that there's an alternative to the way his father modeled manhood is to experience such a model personally.

This brings us to . . .

6. GENERATIONAL SIN AND GENERATIONAL GRACE

The older I get, the more I realize that people I've never even met and whose names I don't even know made choices, did things, and had things done to them decades and hundreds of years ago, and the effects of those things got passed down to my great-grandparents, then to my grandparents, then to my parents, then to me, and now to my own children. We call this sad legacy "generational sin."

Every family inherits a legacy of sin. The Bible even refers to this phenomenon. In the Ten Commandments, the Lord specifically warns against the sin of idolatry. Part of the warning says, "For I, the Lord your God, am a jealous God, visiting the iniquity of the fathers on the children, on the third and the fourth generations of those who hate Me" (Ex. 20:5). The idea is that one generation passes idolatry on to the next, and that generation to the next, and so on, with the result that multiple generations worship other gods. God makes it clear He will not overlook that.

In a similar way, I've seen families with several generations of alcoholism, several generations of sexual immorality, several generations of crime, several generations of drug abuse, several generations of abandonment, or several generations of violence.

As with the Father Wound, dealing with generational sin may be something you encourage a man to work on with a pastor or spiritual counselor. But his first step in seeking that help may come when you help him to simply notice that he has inherited deeply ingrained patterns of sin from his forebears. That alone could be invaluable.

Of course, God never leaves us in our sin. Just as there is generational sin, so there can be generational grace. To return to the Ten Commandments, God adds this encouraging word about the sin of idolatry: "but showing lovingkindness to thousands, to those who love Me and keep My commandments" (Ex. 20:6).

God never turns His back on those who trust and obey Him. Anyone in any generation can repent (turn around) from the old ways of living and begin to live according to God's ways. When they do, they introduce generational grace into their line. And that grace can also have far-reaching effects—for good—to children, grandchildren, great-grandchildren, and beyond.

That is the strong hope that a mentor can offer to any man.

7. SIN AND BROKENNESS

You can see that I've listed generational sin before getting to the man's own sin and brokenness. That's by design. I in no way mean to imply that inherited sin patterns relieve a man of his personal responsibility for whatever sin has him in its grip. But I do think it helps a man see just how far-reaching and pernicious sin is—that it ruins entire families for generations. That's one of the reasons he needs to take his own sins so seriously. He's now experiencing the terrible effects of his fathers' sins upon himself. Why would he want to pass that and his own sins along to future generations?

When you get to know a man through his story, you start to see patterns, some of which are sin patterns. For example: a childhood incident of sexual shame with his brother, a first exposure to porn in eighth grade, a girl in high school with whom he went "way too far," more challenges with porn and sexual immorality in his college fraternity, marriage, first child born, wife experiences post-partum depression, sexual frustration and recourse to porn, shame, guilt, more acting out.

I could draw out similar patterns for other besetting sins, like lying, cheating, pride, lack of self-control, bitterness, rage, jealousy, covetousness, gossip, and more.

How do you help a man whose sin becomes apparent in your interactions with him? The first thing you must do, of course, is the hard act of confronting him, to make sure he's aware that his sin is indeed sin. You can't just assume that he sees his sin for what it is. Remember, sin has a way of blinding a person to its presence. Over time, it can become the "new normal." So, you help him by speaking up. You certainly don't do him any favors by "looking the other way."

In speaking up, you don't need to condemn him. You might say something like, "Hey, man, do you notice this pattern? Do you know that God wants to free you from that?" You can then talk about the freedom that comes from owning our sin before God and experiencing His forgiveness at the cross. And then you can strategize with him on steps he needs to take to address whatever the deep roots of that sin happen to be. Those might well include some in-depth counseling, some pastoral work with a spiritual counselor, some new habits and spiritual disciplines—and, of course, your own willingness to walk alongside him, pray with and for him, and to believe in God's goodness on his behalf, to bring restoration to wholeness and greater holiness.

8. CRISES

If you work with men, sooner or later one of those men will show up with a crisis. You should count that cost before you agree to work with him. Because it *will* happen. And when it does, your commitment to that man will be put to the test. It's in that moment that he will see whether you really care, whether your *words* of support are backed up by *efforts* of support.

What do I mean by a crisis? Well, to name a few that men have brought my way over the years:

- loss of a job
- a wife who's run off with another man
- a serious medical diagnosis
- a car crash
- a lawsuit and/or criminal charges
- a financial loss
- the suicide of a family member
- a psychotic break
- a trip to the ER
- getting jumped, beaten unconscious, and left on the street
- the death of a spouse

When news of such an event reaches me, I quickly assess what my immediate response needs to be (if any). Then I begin thinking through what the larger and longer-term ways I could be helpful might be. One thing I *don't* do is to just turn away with the attitude, "Not my problem." Because once I begin investing in a man, I regard any problem he faces as both a potential problem and a potential opportunity for his growth. Remember what I said in the previous chapter: God is already at work in any man you choose to work with. So, when a crisis comes into his life, I assume that God is there in the midst of that crisis. Insofar as it depends on me, I want to ensure that my guy recognizes that and indeed finds God with him in his trial.

Most often that happens through the power of presence. Just by showing up—or being there when my man eventually shows up to get with me and talk about what has happened—I convey that I'm still there, I'm still walking alongside him, I'm still praying and believing God on his behalf. Sometimes, I can offer words of wisdom or practical help. Other times, it's just the reassurance that someone cares.

Whatever the impact, crises have a way of bonding the mentor and mentored. The relationship goes to a whole new level. Some of the greatest growth I've ever seen in a man has taken place in the aftermath of a crisis—when his back was to the wall, when he had no recourse but to trust God, and when he discovered new depths to his own faith, his own faculties, and his ability to take a punch. Sometimes I'm actually witnessing the severe mercy of the man experiencing brokenness (see chapter 5).

I never wish a crisis on anybody. But on the other hand, I try to never waste a good crisis.

9. MONEY

In chapter 8, I mentioned money as a key area for men to explore with a mentor. So, I'll address it only briefly here.

For years, I worked with men to envision great possibilities toward making their lives count and living into and up to their full potential. I would send them off with a cheer, and they would leave with excitement and a spring in their step to take the world by storm. Then I'd run into them a few years later, and the light had gone out of their eyes. It was as if someone had pulled the plug on their enthusiasm. They were earning a living and being responsible, but they seemed like men who had settled for far less than what they were capable of. I couldn't help but wonder: What gives?

It took me a while, but I eventually discovered that most of those men had crippling debt. It didn't matter what their gifts were or their prospects might be. When push came to shove, they just had to find a job that paid and start paying down their debt. Whether they'd racked up that debt through college loans, credit cards, medical bills, or financial mismanagement (or a combination), their financial condition had already hamstrung them before they even got started in life.

Many men reading this section are exceptionally gifted in the area of finance and financial management. If I could make one appeal to you, it would be that you grab younger men and help them learn what money and stewardship are all about. The other stuff on *The Story of Me* and The Father Wound and generational sin and the like may be way outside your comfort zone. But if you "get" money, I implore you to help the rising generations get on top of their finances. Help them learn what money is all about: how wealth is created, how it can be used for good (or ill), how it must be managed and preserved, and how one must guard one's heart against its dangers.

10. THE ULTIMATE QUESTION

My friend Grant Skeldon is a millennial and he has a gift for helping people my age understand millennials. In his great book, *The Passion Generation*, he answers a question I hear boomers asking all the time: "So what is it that millennials want? Here it is in a nutshell: millennials want to change the world. They want a cause to fight for and a community to belong to."[5]

And that's what I love about millennials! They want to change the world. No, actually, it's more than that. They believe they *can* change the world. And I believe they can, too.

But now, dial back the clock to 1968—a tumultuous year, if ever there was one (I was thirteen at the time). *Time* magazine named it "the year of student power" in its June 7 issue, with a cover photo featuring a graduating baby boomer. Inside, the magazine declared, "This generation of students has an instinct for humanity that may help redress what many of their elders concede is an imbalance in American life."[6] It was a generation that "combines an idealism with a cynicism about society's willingness to embrace their ideals."

I can validate that. I vividly recall that we boomers were "idealistic" enough to believe that *we* could change the world, too—just like our children now do. And that's how Brian Weiss, the now seventy-one-year-old student on that cover of *Time*, also remembers it: "We were optimistic, at that point, that we could affect very substantial changes. . . . At that point, with the optimism of youth . . . we thought we would stop a war and perhaps stop all wars."[7]

In light of these parallel experiences of the two generations, I have to ask: What if it's not about when you were born or which generation you're a part of? What if it's just natural for young adults to desire changes in the world they've grown up in, and to believe it's up to them to bring about those changes?

If so, then one of our main jobs as mentors is to stoke the fires of "youthful optimism," energy, and passion that young adults bring to the world (their so-called "idealism"), while schooling them in the realities they will face as the work to reshape the world they are inheriting.

RESTORATION VS. REDEMPTION

I couldn't be more thrilled that millennials want to change the world. But some, like some of their parents, speak as if their mission is not merely to change the world, but to save it. They seem unaware that there's a world of difference between the two.

Changing the world means finding a solution to one particular problem in the world, while accepting the reality that you can't solve all the world's problems. By contrast, saving the world means operating with the belief—really the delusion—that you can come up with the magic cure for all the world's ills. Or, increasingly in our time, saving the world can also mean that you must stand between the world and certain disaster.

Those who change the world make a tangible difference on something somewhere, not everything everywhere. William Wilberforce helped to bring an end to the British slave trade. Martin Luther King Jr. helped to reverse an ingrained system of racial discrimination in the United States.

Today, in my own part of the world, my friend Reid helps to create safer neighborhoods for impoverished families in Dallas by eliminating drug houses. My friend Brittany helps women in Africa provide for their families by making jewelry. My friend Parker helps disadvantaged people in Dallas, Detroit, and India get treatment for their type 2 diabetes. My friend Jenny helps women in China leave the sex trade by developing an alternative means of income.

I could give countless examples of people changing the world. Not just in the social sector, but in the business world, education, health care, the arts, government, and every other sector. Everywhere you look, change is desperately needed. And not surprisingly, God raises up change agents to lead in the direction of restoring the world to the way it was intended to be.

Saviors, by contrast, seek to remake the world into what they think it should be. The flaw in that plan, however, is that God has reserved the salvation of the world for Himself—because only He is capable of saving it. If humans were able to save the world—which is to say, ourselves—then no salvation would be needed. If a lost dog can find its own way home, then it is not lost. But if the world and its humans are indeed lost and broken, such that we need saving, then something beyond us must do it. As the poet W. H. Auden put it, "Nothing can save us that is possible."[8]

God has reserved to Himself not only the ability to deliver that miracle, but also the responsibility for it. After all, He owns the world, having made it. That's the other thing saviors forget. The world is not ours to save, but God's. His vision of the world is the world as it was intended to be. Any visions humans come up with for bettering the world need to dovetail with God's overall vision, not set it aside as if it doesn't matter—or doesn't even exist. God cares about the world and its people infinitely more than any of us can or do, and He has pledged Himself to reconcile all that He has made to Himself (see, for example, 2 Cor. 5:17–19 and Col. 1:13–20).

THE STORY OF GOD

Two implications for mentoring flow from the distinction between restoration and redemption, it seems to me. The first has to do with a man's *Story of Me*. I've been emphasizing the importance of a man telling that story frequently during his journey through this life. But in light of God's vision for the world described above, every man's *Story of Me* needs to be placed in its proper context, which is the much larger *Story of God*. I believe that rarely happens, unless someone intentionally helps to make it happen, which is where you as a mentor come in.

Here's why it rarely happens. The vast majority of people in our culture, including many Christians, are what could be called "secularists." That is, they live their daily lives with little if any practical thought given to where and how God might relate to their experience. They may "believe" in God, which can mean different things, but God has no real relevance to their life, except perhaps as a kind of spiritual comfort—or, under extreme circumstances, a divine 911 service. In short, secularists are those for whom *The Story of God* either is unknown or doesn't matter.

So what about those who have responded to Christ's call to salvation? They obviously are much more aware of *The Story of God*. Except that in many cases, their version of that story keeps them as the main character: God is to be praised and followed because *He has saved them from their sins.*

There's nothing wrong with that view. It's a biblically true statement. But it's a mere subplot in the larger *Story of God.*

When humans tell the story of God, they usually tell it as a story about humans: God is turning sinful people into redeemed people. While that's absolutely true, the story is also about God's glory and honor.

A cosmically massive lie was told about God back in the beginning of the universe: God is not good; He can't be trusted. But He is indeed a good God. Unfortunately, humans buy into the lie and rebel against God, and one result is that the whole universe is bound under the curse of death. So, at first it looks like sin, death, and the lie win, because God's creation is in a terrible state.

But just as it looks as if all is lost, God acts to set things right and vindicate Himself. He does the unthinkable—and really the impossible—and becomes one of His human creatures in the person of Jesus Christ, subjecting Himself to all of the terrible brokenness and evil of our world. That includes death—and a horrible death at that.

As Jesus' death approaches, God makes it crystal clear that

Christ's death is an act of selfless love, of undeserved goodness shown to humanity.

Jesus does indeed die. But then God does something even more extraordinary and outrageous and unthinkable than what He did in becoming a human: Christ comes back from the dead! And in raising Christ from the dead, God validates the truth about His Son, proves that He is good, and overcomes sin and death.

Upon Christ's resurrection from the dead, God goes to work right away to reverse the curse and restore His human creatures to what He intended for them all along. By His Spirit, God turns sinful people into redeemed people who share His goodness. That project continues to this day!

But the story doesn't end with Christ coming back to life. Despite what is now obvious—that God is not only all-good but also all-powerful—lies about God and rebellion against Him continue to persist. And now new lies are being promoted, that Christ never rose from the dead. Indeed, that Christ never even existed. Or if He did exist, he wasn't really God. More recently, the lie has morphed into the notion that there is no God, that He never existed in the first place, that we humans are more or less on our own to figure out how to live in a hostile universe.

However, God saw that one coming, too. Just as Christ said He would rise from the dead, He also said He would be coming back again—this time to do away with the liar and to set all things right once and for all. He didn't tell us what day on the calendar He would be back, only that such a day exists.

Therefore, He said, we should watch and wait and be prepared, because that day will come as surely as a person who has bought a priceless treasure will return to take possession of it. God came once and showed He is good. He's coming back to establish His goodness forever.

Now, it's important to know that there is more to God's story. A great deal of it has not been told to humans. But enough has been told for us to know where we fit into the story. And also to make it clear that God is indeed good, and He has our best interests at heart, and He can be trusted.

I suggest that you and the man you're working with discuss *The Story of God* and its implications. Among the questions you might ask each other are:

- What is your overall reaction to reading *The Story of God*? Have you ever heard this story before?

- How does this story affect how you see God? Does it suggest any new ideas about Him? Does it challenge any of your existing perceptions of or feelings about God?

- What part(s) of the story makes the biggest impression on you? Why do you think that's the case?

- Where does your *Story of Me* fit into *The Story of God*? In other words, where do you see yourself in God's story? Or do you even see yourself in His story?

- Does *The Story of God* speak to any particular moments or details of your *Story of Me*? Describe those connections. What difference does His story make?

- As you think about your *Story of Me*, are there any parts where it shows that the lie that God is not good has been told to you, and you have bought into that lie? Where (or how) do you most need to experience God's goodness?

- *The Story of God* says He is restoring His human creatures to what He intended for them all along (turning trash into treasure). In what ways do you think God is turning you into the treasure He intended all along?

- *The Story of God* says He is coming back. How does that affect your *Story of Me*? How does it affect how you are living your life right now?

- After reading *The Story of God*, are there ways in which you might want to change how you tell your *Story of Me*?

WHO'S IN CHARGE?

I've mentioned the secularist mindset by which most people in Western culture live their lives. By now that mindset tends to follow a widespread narrative that says the world is solely in the possession of humans. Whatever preceded us and whatever comes later, we're in charge now. It's up to us to make of the world what we will. If we act wisely, we can maximize its potential. If we act foolishly, we will precipitate disaster.

Can you see the half-truth in that narrative? It's that humans actually are in charge of the world—to a degree. Remember the Scripture I quoted back in chapter 2? "Prosper! Reproduce! Fill Earth! Take charge! Be responsible . . . for every living thing" (Gen. 1:28 MSG). In God's narrative, He has put us humans in charge of the world to cause it and its people to flourish.

But in what sense are we "in charge"? God's narrative says we have a *delegated* responsibility. We have been *given* authority by a higher authority—God, the God who made the world and its people, and therefore owns it all. The God, moreover, who is taking responsibility for rescuing the world and its people from their fallen, broken condition.

So again, what does that mean for mentoring? Well, the issue of *Who is in charge?* looms large for every man, including every man who comes your way. He may well have been significantly shaped by the secularist narrative that says we humans are solely in charge. And even if he's come to faith, the residue of that mindset will tend to linger in his thinking. His posture toward God will be that God is there to help *him* with *his* plans and *his* aspirations. God is there to meet *his* needs and help him with *his* problems and bring blessing to *his* life and loved ones. God is seen as great because He's got great things in store for *his* life.

As that man's mentor, you have an opportunity to help him grapple with the practical implications of a "new" narrative, of God's narrative. That means living his life as a subordinate of God—a steward, a manager, a trusted representative or agent with delegated responsibility—as opposed to simply doing whatever seems to best serve his own interests, or treating God as a supernatural concierge who's there to handle the more unpredictable parts of his personal life plan.

From a practical point of view, the issue of *Who is in Charge?* is perhaps the ultimate question. Because as a man lives his life and makes his choices and writes his *Story of Me*, sooner or later he has to come to grips with a determinative decision: Is it going to be "my will be done" or "Thy will be done"? In deciding that question, he will decide the course of his life.

CHAPTER 15

WHAT SHOULD YOU WATCH OUT FOR?

In chapter 9, I described a number of potholes and hazards that men seeking mentors should watch out for along the road of mentoring relationships. So, what are some dangers that mentors should anticipate on their side of the equation?

PROBLEMS OF TIME

One of the most common areas of frustration has to do with time. For example, the relationship may seem to require too much time for you as a mentor. Indeed, lack of time is the reason many men give for not engaging in mentoring at all.

Only you know your schedule and your priorities, so only you can determine whether you actually have time to give to another man. But I would point out that as you get older, you tend to have more control over your time. So, should you choose to serve as a mentor, you likely can find at least some discretionary time somewhere in your schedule to give to the relationship.

I would also say that mentoring can actually take far less time than most men realize. Obviously, you can pour as much time into the relationship as you want, which would be true for any relationship. But mentoring is a situation where great gains can be realized for a relatively small investment. Why? Because in mentoring, there's a purpose for getting together. It's not just a social time; it's a growth time. And it's the growth of the man you're working with that's on the line. So, the monkey is on his back, so to speak, to devote himself to the process. If anyone should be complaining about a lack of time, by rights it should be him, not you.

WHEN YOU SEEM TO HAVE LITTLE TIME

So, if you're doing all the work, you need to pause and revisit your understanding with the other man. You are mentoring him, not the other way around. Therefore, he needs to be doing the lion's share of the work.

That brings up a fundamental law of mentoring: don't do anything for the other man that he could do and should do for himself. Otherwise you make him dependent on you, which is the exact opposite of what mentoring is designed to accomplish—namely, helping him grow and develop the ability to stand on his own two feet.

Another possibility is that you and/or the man you are working with are operating with unrealistic expectations about what is involved in getting together. In that case, reevaluate what you've agreed to work on together and what that should entail. Consider whether that agenda is reasonable or too ambitious. If either one of you is asking too much, you need to rethink and scale back the expectations.

There's nothing wrong with having an ambitious set of learning objectives. If you've got a hard charger who wants to go for the gold, that's great! More power to him—if he can pull it off. Some can. But if he's got a highly ambitious plan mapped out, you may need to consider whether you alone can service all of his expectations. It may be that you need to agree to help him with just a part of his agenda, and then help him find other people to help him with the rest. Nobody says you have to do everything.

One other thought: If you're feeling that mentoring is taking up too much of your time, it may be because, in fact, you actually don't have enough time. An indication of that is that the relationship feels rushed. You and the other man are always scrambling to get things done. In that case, you may not have budgeted enough time for your interactions with him. You and he will need to adjust the timeframe accordingly.

Of course, sometimes feeling like the clock runs out too quickly suggests a blessing, not a problem. It's a sign that the relationship is extremely satisfying and productive. You just can't get enough of it. That's a good problem to have.

My dad used to tell budding preachers at Dallas Seminary to leave their listeners "longing, not loathing." That is, stop speaking just at the point where people are supremely satisfied. Don't go any farther than that. You want people to say, "No, no! Keep going!" You want them longing to hear more, which means they'll come back for more. A similar principle applies to your interactions with another man. Better to leave him longing, not loathing. Bring your sessions to a halt just at the peak of his motivation, just at the point of saturation. Never stretch things out to "cover" all that you think needs to be "covered." You'll only end up overwhelming him, or worse, boring him. That's the kiss of death! You never want someone to get to the point where he leaves his time with you thinking, "Man, I'm glad that's over with. I thought we'd never finish!"

WHEN THE OTHER MAN HAS LITTLE TIME

The flip side of the time-related coin, of course, is when the man you are working with can't seem to find time for the relationship. For example, he no-shows for your sessions. When he does show up, he's late. He doesn't put much effort into his work. And overall, you get the sense that his mind is elsewhere.

When you're seeing symptoms like that, having his mind else-where is actually a real possibility. He may, in fact, be distracted by a problem he is struggling with. Rather than be put off by that, see it as a potential moment of opportunity. Seize the day by opening the door to exploring what might be going on: "Hey, man, can I shoot straight? You seem kind of distracted these days. Like your mind is kind of wrapped around the axle with other things. Is there anything going on that you'd like to tell me about? If so, I'd be glad to listen and, if I can, help you with it." You never know what may come crawl-ing out from under that rock when you turn it over. But whatever it is—if there's indeed something there—there's a good chance it will lead to positive growth.

Of course, if your man genuinely can't find enough time for the relationship—for whatever reason (and there can be many)—he probably needs to reevaluate whether right now is the best time to be involved in any sort of regular interaction. There's no shame if he comes to the conclusion, "Yeah, I need to pull back. I've got some other business I need to take care of in my life right now." In fact, you may need to give him permission to withdraw so that he can take care of his priorities.

JEALOUSY

Jesus told His followers that eventually they would do bigger and better things than He had done (John 14:12). He wasn't just flat-tering them; He delivered a statement of fact. The whole point of developing others is to help them do what you can do at least as well as you can, if not better (see Luke 6:40). So, that begs the question: Are you willing to see the man you are working with eventually outdo you? Is it okay if he someday becomes more successful than you are?

Not every man can accept that. History is filled with examples of mentors who simply could not deal with the mounting success of their followers. For example, the film *Amadeus* brilliantly portrays an eighteenth-century court musician named Antonio Salieri, who was so driven by jealousy of his star pupil, Wolfgang Amadeus Mozart, that he plots his death. Likewise, the pioneer of psychoanalysis, Sigmund Freud, became so embittered at the growing acclaim of two of his followers, Carl Jung and Alfred Adler, that he reworded some of the footnotes in his writings to avoid crediting them.

Those may seem like extreme cases, but my dad and I have both known men who have cynically disparaged the accomplishments of men they helped to mentor. Some have even resorted to dirty politics to block their success. Yet if challenged, those embittered men would deny it—though they could hardly disguise their envy. "Look at him eat up all that praise," they'll say with contempt. "It's sickening! He's way overrated. Why, he wouldn't have gotten anywhere if it hadn't have been for me!"

Do you think you're immune to that attitude? If so, you might want to consider 1 Samuel 18. When King Saul returned from defeating his enemies, the Philistines, women greeted him with tambourines and dancing. That was the usual way of celebrating victory, and Saul's triumphant return was a grand and joyous occasion. "Saul has slain his thousands," the women chanted wildly. But then they added, "and David his ten thousands" (v. 7). Scripture tells us that upon hearing that, "Saul became very angry, for this saying displeased him; and he said, 'They have ascribed to David ten thousands, but to me they have ascribed thousands. Now what more can he have but the kingdom?' Saul looked at David with suspicion from that day on" (vv. 8–9).

Do you fear that a man you are working with may someday capture your kingdom? Well, guess what? He very well may! In fact, if you've done your job right as a mentor, he shouldn't have to capture it. Maybe he should inherit it and build on your legacy, far beyond anything you ever imagined. That's the ideal you should be shooting for. Are you prepared for that?

Envy is like poison to a mentoring relationship. And sad to say, too many leaders today are sipping that poison, which kills any motivation to cultivate new leaders. Too many men are building their kingdoms, when they ought to be building Christ's kingdom. As a result, they have no interest in a ministry of multiplication. They can't be bothered with reproducing themselves in the lives of up-and-coming men. "Why train my competition?" is their attitude.

You know what the Bible says about that? It's an attitude directly from the pit: "This wisdom is not that which comes down from above, but is earthly, natural, demonic" (James 3:15). James is warning us about harboring bitter envy and selfish ambition in our hearts. If that describes you, then you need to repent of (turn away from) that before it ruins your life. You need to pray that God replaces the hellish poison of envy with the pure water of His wisdom (see James 5:16).

It can be hard to see someone surpass us, no question about it. It can resurrect every fear we've ever had about our self-worth, our competence, and our significance. As the crowds start chanting someone else's name, it dawns on us that they've forgotten ours. That hurts!

So what do we do with that hurt? The devil holds out the toxic salve of envy. The Lord holds out the salvation of grace. Which one we choose determines whether we end our days in jealousy or joy.

A LACK OF MOTIVATION

Have you ever swallowed a soft drink after all the fizz has gone out of it? Blah! It's pretty disgusting! All sweet and syrupy, and altogether unsatisfying. Sometimes mentoring relationships end up like that. Either the mentor or the man being mentored (or sometimes both) loses interest, and the thing goes flat. The motivation seems to evaporate. For example:

- One or the other can't find time for the relationship
- The sessions are boring and unproductive
- Assignments are not carried out
- More time is spent analyzing the relationship than doing productive work

- The discussions drift away from the agenda onto rabbit trails and superficial matters

There are many possible reasons to explain why the energy might be draining away. To look at them all would require a comprehensive examination of human motivation. For our purposes, it is enough to consider the advice of the tall Texan my dad ran into shortly after moving to Texas in the late 1940s. One day, Dad used the old adage that "you can lead a horse to water, but you can't make him drink." Without a moment's hesitation the old boy said in his thick Texas drawl, "Well, yer sure wrong about that, son. You can always feed him salt!"

What a great insight into human nature! You can never force anyone to change. You can only provide a climate in which change becomes increasingly desirable. So, if either you or the man you've been working with (or both) has lost motivation, don't ask, "What's wrong with this guy?" or even, "What's wrong with me?" Rather, ask, "What can I do to rekindle his passion, so that he wants to make strides in his life?"

You see, you can temporarily—and I stress *temporarily*—motivate most anyone through rewards, guilt, or even manipulation. But that's not compelling him; that's coercing him. You're merely imposing outside factors that make your agenda temporarily attractive to him. But you're not cultivating any internal commitment in him to pursue the process.

The better way is to seek out his intrinsic motivation, the internal factors that trigger his interest and effort. Then put him in situations that stimulate those factors. I'm referring, of course, to the man's giftedness—which we discussed in the previous chapter. Intrinsic motivation is a function of a man's God-given bent. If you can help him discover his giftedness and then give him exercises and assignments that fit that wiring, he'll have no problem staying motivated, because a man always prefers to function according to the way God has designed him. It's as natural as breathing.

THE MENTORING LIFE CYCLE

There is one other factor to consider as you troubleshoot a lack of motivation. It may be that the relationship has run its course. This brings us to the issue of life cycles in mentoring relationships.

In a few cases, you and the men you're working with will end up as lifelong friends. You may or may not interact frequently, but whenever you do, it's as if the conversation picks up right where it left off. By now, he knows precisely when to get ahold of you for your input. And even when he doesn't have any particular "issue" to discuss, you still enjoy each other's company and the wealth of wisdom and memories you share together.

But most mentoring relationships don't end up that way. Instead, they go through a fairly predictable series of stages. Experts differ on how many stages there are, but we can identify at least three. By recognizing this life cycle, you can anticipate certain dynamics in your relationship with other men.

The first stage is *definition*. This is the initial period during which the relationship is getting established and defined, and everything is somewhat tentative. Someone is checking you out as a potential mentor, and you're sizing him up to see what and who you have to work with. You're each deciding whether to commit yourself to the other person, and under what terms. (Note: this evaluation may take place totally in the background, nonverbally, even as you and the other man interact about "top level" matters.) If you both decide to proceed, this stage ends with some sort of understanding that you're going to work together.

The second stage is *development*. This tends to be the longest and most intense period of the relationship. You and the other man interact in ways that help him grow and develop. You tend to meet regularly, or at least at key points along the way. This period is like a house or building under construction, with dirt flying, hammers banging, and power saws whining. The other man is hard at work, working on his agenda under your guiding hand.

But after a while, the structure is essentially complete: the man you are working with has more or less finished what he came to you for help with. It's not that he has reached full maturity—remember "top level" versus deeper matters—but he has made substantial progress on whatever he came to you for in the first place.

That brings the relationship to its third and final stage, the point of *departure*. Departure may be sudden or it may take a while. But sooner or later the man perceives that his need for your input has come to an end.

There are several common ways that that can happen. The most difficult, unfortunately, is through a painful break. One day, seemingly out of nowhere, there is a conflict—I say "seemingly" because a closer examination usually reveals a history of growing tension in the relationship, which has finally spilled over into open conflict. You and the other man go back and forth, as in previous disagreements. Only this time, the conflict escalates until one of you decides, "That's it! I'm out of here!" Paul and Barnabas may have parted ways through that kind of argument (see Acts 15:36–41).

The impetus for a break like that can go either way. A mentor will say, "Well, if that's the way you feel, why don't you just go do your thing," and his follower says, "Okay, I will!" And he does, and they never really get back together. On the other hand, the man being mentored might say, "Look, I think it's time I did things my way," and the mentor says, "Okay, dude, go ahead." And so the man goes off on his own. There may be a reconciliation later on, or there may not. But the break is clear, even if it is not clean.

Another possibility quite common is that the man being mentored sort of drifts away over time. His need for the mentor is no longer critical, so he contacts him less and less. You'll see this a lot in colleges and universities. While still in school, a student will latch onto a professor, and the relationship will prove transformative in the student's confidence, maturity, and development. Graduation comes, and both student and professor promise to stay in touch.

But life moves on. The student gets involved in his career. The professor meets new students. And before long, the two have moved on. Practically speaking, all that remains of the relationship are a lot of positive memories.

A third possibility—and this can occur whether the break is sudden or gradual, heated or "cool"—is a redefinition of the relationship, in which the two men become associates or colleagues rather than mentor and follower. The ground between them levels out and to a large extent they become equals. In a way, this is the ideal outcome. It indicates that the mentor has done his job. He has helped the other man step up to his own level. He's helped him become his own man. In fact, it's possible that the two men will develop a peer mentoring relationship, especially if they are roughly the same age.

Such is the mentoring life cycle. There's no standard timetable for how long this cycle lasts or its stages take to complete. Some experts estimate that the average mentoring relationship lasts between two and six years. But who really knows, especially in light of all the informal mentoring that takes place? What is certain is that most mentoring relationships come to an end at some point.

How do you know when you've reached that point? Probably when you or the man you're working with just sense it. For his part, he'll have a sense that he's completed his agenda and has gotten whatever he hoped to get out of the relationship. Or on your part, you sense that you've helped him as much as you can. In either case, the relationship itself may actually continue, but not in terms of mentoring. You've helped the man get "launched" into the world, and he's ready to move forward on his own.

SAYING GOOD-BYE

Sometimes both you and the man you're working with know that the relationship is coming to an end, at least in terms of the way you've been interacting. For example, a milestone is looming that spells a change in your circumstances: a graduation, a transfer, a wedding, a retirement.

Unfortunately, many mentors drop the ball at that point. Having done a superb job of bringing someone along and building into his life, they fail to put proper closure on the relationship. And you can see why: no one likes to say goodbye. But if the mentor misses that moment, he loses a great opportunity to seal his work with a permanent, positive impression.

If you've poured countless hours into a man and invested emotional energy in him, your relationship with him deserves a proper send-off. So, if possible, honor what you have had together by setting a time to get together and wrap things up. In reviewing the relationship, talk about some of the highlights of your work together—as well as some of the lowlights. Solicit his impressions of what he has learned and how he has grown, and share your own observations along the same lines. Also talk about his future, both how he sees it and how you see it. Then pray together that God's hand will rest on his life.

Whatever you do, be sure to tell your departing friend what the relationship has meant to you, and what *you* have gained from *his* life. He likely will not see that one coming, but he deserves it. The relationship may not have been perfect, and from your perspective it may not have seemed particularly close. But the fact that it even happened is significant. Whether it's been the best possible relationship or not, you and the other man have shared something for which millions of men today hunger, but few ever experience. That alone is worth celebrating.

So, give him a hug, shake his hand, and then send him on his way, knowing that a part of you is going out into the world wherever God chooses to take him.

WHAT WILL BE YOUR LEGACY?

With ten thousand baby boomers turning sixty-five every day, there is now no end of books, blogs, podcasts, and other resources being produced on the themes of "finishing well," "leaving a legacy," "what really matters," and "what will you be remembered for?"

All of that is driven, of course, by the inescapable reality that our days in this world are limited. As John Ortberg so poignantly reminds us, "When the game is over, it all goes back in the box."[1]

Well said. And as men get closer to the end of the "game," they tend to feel a natural impulse to pass down to younger men some of the lessons they've learned and wisdom they've gained during their turns on the gameboard. I mentioned this in chapter 2. It's called the phenomenon of *generativity*, a sense that: *Time is growing short. I have something inside me that I need to impart to someone else. Someone needs to benefit from what I've seen and learned.*

Mentoring is a perfect way of passing on that legacy.

IT'S NOT ABOUT YOU

But in thinking about legacy, let's go back to an earlier time in life, the time when you were thinking through what your purpose was all about in the first place. For many boomers, the guidebook for figuring that out was Richard Bolles's *What Color Is Your Parachute?*, first published in 1970 (and still being updated today).

More recently, Rick Warren has written *The Purpose Driven Life: What on Earth Am I Here For?* In helping people today think about their purpose, Rick opens with what may be the best first sentence of any book since the book of Genesis: "It's not about you."

I couldn't have said it any better! It's not about you, or me. And that becomes apparent when we consider *The Story of God* that I told in chapter 14. *The Story of God* shows that while *The Story of Me* is important, it derives its importance from being a subplot in a much larger story, which is the main story—God's story. I pointed out that the men you mentor must come to see themselves in light of who God is and what He's up to, not the other way around.

But the same thing applies to you and me—including our legacy. As I look through all those resources on what we will be remembered for, I'm struck with how *me-centered* most of them are. And why not, since it's aimed at baby boomers, right? The Me Generation. It's about *my* legacy, *my* memory, what *I'm* leaving behind, what *I* will be remembered for.

Can I be honest? I mean, brutally honest? The day is coming—and relatively soon—when you and I will die, and whatever our life has amounted to will all go back in the box. Before the sun has even set on the day of our departure, the world will move on. Our family and friends will gather to mark our passing and mourn our loss, but they too will go on with their lives. In time, they too will pass. Rather quickly after we're gone, our earthly possessions will be scattered to the four winds. A hundred years after we're gone there will not be a single person alive who knew us personally. And with the extraordinarily rare exception of a Caesar or a Lincoln or a

Queen Victoria or a Mother Teresa, any memory of us will be gone, practically speaking.

SOMETHING IS COMING

In light of that fleeting, transitory nature of a human life, what is the "something" that we're supposed to "pass on" to those we leave behind? Is there anything that will actually "last"?

I began to answer this question in chapter 2 when I said that this world is actually just the practice field for the real game that is coming. Obviously, I'm distinguishing between this life and the life to come. We all are familiar with this life. But God has told us very little about the life to come. I'm not sure why that is. Perhaps because we couldn't handle it? Whatever the reason, humans have reacted to that dearth of information in two unfortunate ways. One has been to dream up a caricature of "heaven," with angel's wings, clouds, harps, and so on. The other has been to write the whole thing off as myth.

What strikes me, however, is not that we know very little about the life to come, but that we know anything about it at all. Why should we?

Well, there's no mystery there. In almost every case where the Bible reminds us that "a day" is coming or that there's another realm awaiting us or that Jesus is coming back, it accompanies that news with a strong message—sometimes a message of excitement, sometimes a warning—to *be prepared*: "Be on the alert." "Be ready." "Be dressed in readiness." "Be like men who are waiting." "Wait eagerly." "We are waiting." "Let us be on the alert and sober." "Look for new heavens and a new earth." "Wait anxiously."[2]

Could God be any clearer? Over and again, He's told us that something is coming and He doesn't want us to be caught off guard—or worse, to act as if we have no clue about it. Quite the contrary! He wants us to be ready. But also to be excited about it! Apparently what's coming is a whole lot better than anything we've been experiencing so far in this world.

GETTING READY

Now this idea of getting ready for something exciting that awaits us in the future is about as common and as down-to-earth an activity as I can think of. For instance, if you're married, just think back to your wedding. Remember all the preparations that (maybe) you and (definitely) your fiancée (and her mom) made to get ready for that big day? Something that wasn't even going to happen until six months, a year, or even further in the future somehow became the governing factor in all the days leading up to it.

Or what about whatever education you've had, whether vocational school, college, or graduate school? You set a goal to become an aircraft mechanic, a computer programmer, an engineer, an accountant, a lawyer, a doctor, or whatever. With that vision in mind, you put countless hours into studying, taking tests, memorizing information, getting certifications, gaining knowledge, developing skills, and earning degrees. You did all of that, *why?* So that once you found yourself working with planes or computers or bridges or numbers or legal matters or patients or whatever, *you were prepared.* You were ready. You had your game together.

The time to get your game together is on the practice field. And this world is the practice field for the actual game that is coming.

In pointing that out, I don't mean to diminish any of the efforts or accomplishments that any of us achieve in our lifetime. God has put it in our hearts to strive after greatness. So, we should certainly do our best and aim high. But we must never mistake the applause and honors of this present world for the far greater glory that is yet to be revealed to, and conferred on, us (see Rom. 8:18–21). Of course, we want to do well *now*. And we should give it our very best, right now. That's what champions do in practice. But let's not lose perspective: no one is ever remembered for the outstanding play he made on the practice field. That's exactly what he's *supposed* to do in order to get ready for the game. But the glory is reserved for the outstanding plays he makes in the game, where it counts.

It Starts Now

That sets up a fascinating relationship between the practice field and the game. The things we will face in the game determine what we need to practice; and the things we do on the practice field prepare us to play the game well.

So what things will we face in the life to come? As I say, God hasn't told us just a whole lot about that. But if we examine what He *has* told us, we'll notice that the life to come bears striking resemblances to life now—only without sin, evil, or death. For example, we're told that in the life to come there will still be people (humans, without sin). There will still be work (without the curse). There will still be authority structures (that follow justice). There will still be cultures and people-groups (living in peace). There will still be commerce (conducted honestly and fairly). There will still be houses (that are safe). There will still be feasting (with plenty of provisions).[3]

I can't help but think we're mistaken to assume that this world and the world to come are somehow incomprehensibly different. All the evidence suggests that they have a great deal in common—the one key exception being that in this world, as it stands, many people remain estranged from God and in rebellion against Him, whereas in the world to come, all the people *there* are in right relationship to Him.

So, how do we get ready for that world, and how do we prepare other men to get ready for it? The answer given in the New Testament is, first of all, to get into right relationship with God, by His grace.[4] Then, on the basis of that, we *start practicing*—in the ways we live right now—the ways we'll live then. For example: we can start pursuing values like love, joy, peace, patience, kindness, goodness, faithfulness, gentleness, and self-control (the fruit of the Spirit; Gal. 5:22–23). The day is coming when those values—along with others like them—will govern the world. That's why we pray, "Your kingdom come. Your will be done, on earth as it is in heaven" (Matt. 6:10).

So, applied to our work: How would those values express themselves in our current jobs? How would they affect how we do the work itself? How might they affect how we think about and treat our co-workers? Our boss? Our customers? Our vendors? Our community? How would they affect what we do with the money we earn from our job? We're already working for Jesus—right now, in this life: "It is the Lord Christ whom you serve" (Col. 3:24). Are we training ourselves to be conscious of that and what it means as we clock in every day?

Another reality of the life to come is that apparently we will be given authority.[5] Well, we've also been given authority in this life. And guess what? How we exercise authority now should look identical to how we will exercise it in the world to come: "Whoever wishes to become great among you shall be your servant, and whoever wishes to be first among you shall be your slave" (Matt. 20:26–27). So, how does Jesus' model of "servant-leadership" show up in your position of influence and authority? If you have anyone reporting to you, you are their "shepherd." In what ways are you "laying down your life for your sheep" (see John 10:1–5, especially v. 11)?[6]

A WAY OF LIVING

What I'm suggesting is that the legacy we most need to pass on to other men is a way of living. That may happen through what we tell them, but it's mostly through what we show them—how we actually live. We may give them the relevant Bible verses and use religious language to try to explain why we live the way we do, but that's not mainly what they'll remember. How we lived is what they'll remember. What sort of person we were is what they'll remember. That's because men can never forget what God looks like in human form.

"Shine through me," someone has prayed, "shine through me and be so in me that every soul I know will feel Your presence in my soul. Let them look up and see no longer me, but only You."[7] That's certainly my prayer—that through me others would experience some dimension of God that they otherwise would never get to experience.

I pray the same for you—that in knowing you, men will experience something of God Himself in you. Maybe it will be a reputation for patience or a spirit of compassion and mercy or a profound sense of gratitude that welled up time and again. Maybe you'll be remembered for your generosity—especially through the quiet, unseen ways in which you helped an individual here and there. Or maybe someone will take note of the way your life was consistently marked by prayer and a childlike trust in God. Or perhaps it will be your courage in pursuing justice for the marginalized and forgotten. Maybe the fact that you just kept showing up faithfully, day after day and time after time, despite great burdens and adversities. How you treated children and the delight they found in your presence might be your legacy. Or your steadfast care for an invalid wife may leave an indelible impression of devotion and sacrifice. And then, too, the simple fact that somehow you always seemed to make time for a man who really needed your help may be the thing someone most recalls.

One way or the other, we *will* leave an impression—as iron sharpens iron. To the extent that our heart is sold out to God and we're intentionally allowing Him to reveal His life through ours, we can trust that the impact we make, all in all, will be quite good.

But here's the crazy part: we'll probably never even know or be aware of exactly how we've made an impression on other men—at least, not in this life. That's the mystery of mentoring that I've stressed over and again. For reasons of His own, God uses a man to make a deep, lasting impression on another man's soul—usually without the man making the impression even being aware of it. The transformation takes place at a level he cannot see and in ways he cannot imagine. But it's real. God has used him. We know that when the other man, looking back, is quite certain that "I never would have become who I am were it not for that man's influence."

FORMAL MENTORING PROGRAMS

In chapter 7, I made a distinction between formal and informal mentoring relationships, and I focused mostly on informal interactions throughout the book. But I would be remiss not to offer a few thoughts about formal mentoring relationships (and now I'm talking about mentoring for both men and women).

I think it's fair to say that what we would call "formal" mentoring mostly takes place at or through organizations, whether for-profit businesses, social sector ventures, or government agencies. Someone in the organization decides that mentoring would serve the purposes of the entity, and an intentional, usually structured, "program" of some sort is then devised to facilitate mentoring relationships.

WHAT ARE YOU TRYING TO ACCOMPLISH?

Whether you're exploring the idea of establishing a formal mentoring program or you already have one in place and are trying to improve it, the core question you have to come to grips with is: What are we trying to accomplish through mentoring?

I'm sure every group answers that question in its own unique way. But I can think of only one basic answer, and that answer underlies whatever other answers might be given, because it goes to the heart of mentoring: *The reason for mentoring is to develop people.* Mentoring is all about people-development.

For some organizations, people-development *is* their core mission (or a large part of it). Local churches are the most obvious example (for more, see Appendix B: Formal Mentoring in Churches).

Other enterprises aimed at people-development—and for that reason need to be involved in mentoring—include schools, colleges, and universities; leadership development programs in the military; nonprofits aimed at building character and healthy habits in children and youth; programs in prisons and juvenile facilities focused on reorienting and rebuilding lives; fellowships and gap-year programs for young adults; and residency and post-graduate training programs at hospitals, psychiatric facilities, schools, churches, and more.

For most organizations, however, the core mission is *not* about people-development. For instance, construction firms build buildings. Law firms handle legal matters. Hospitals cure the sick. Farms grow food. Police look out for public safety.

And yet, while such enterprises are not "about" people, they can accomplish their core mission only *through* people. As a result, developing people becomes mission-critical. Even if not explicit in the mission statement, people-development must be a core value of the enterprise.

WHAT DO WE MEAN BY "PEOPLE-DEVELOPMENT"?

But what does that really mean, to develop people? Again, your group may have its own special definition of "people-development," along with a list of competencies and/or qualities that a person will display once they are at last "developed."

But I come back to the difference between top-level skills and knowledge, and the deeper issues of a person (see chapter 13). Organizations whose core mission involves people-development invariably seek to get to those deeper issues. But that's not always the case for organizations that are not about people. Their work tends to be more "transactional." Yes, they may see the need to develop people, but mostly in the interest of benefitting the work of the enterprise. If the developmental process ends up helping someone as a person, that's great. But that's not what's driving the process.

And yet, as our world gains more experience with knowledge work and workers, we're discovering that it's virtually impossible to ignore the workers as *persons*. Frankly, it can even be perilous! I remember in the early 2000s trying to explain to someone the importance of a worker's personhood to an enterprise. This individual was in finance, where they read spreadsheets and worked with hard data to evaluate companies. The more I talked, the less convinced they were. To them, everything I was saying felt "soft." As they saw it, the "people stuff" was something of a luxury that contributed little to the bottom line. Finally in exasperation I said, "Well, let me ask you: What took down Enron? Was it the hard stuff or the soft stuff?"[1]

Henry Ford said that when you "hire a hand," you get the rest of the body thrown in. How true! People bring all of who they are to their work—the good, the bad, and the ugly. You employ someone to "do a job," but in the doing of it their *being* is revealed. That being affects both their doing of the work, as well as all the other doers/ beings around them. An employer can look at that as a big hassle. I prefer to see it as a huge opportunity. Quite simply, if you employ someone (or oversee them) *you have an opportunity to affect their soul.*

I'm pleased to say that as I interact with organizational leaders these days, I'm finding more and more of them who sincerely desire to positively influence that deeper stuff, particularly as they develop future leaders. They know full well that competence alone is not enough.

A CULTURE OF PEOPLE-DEVELOPMENT

The most effective efforts at formal mentoring occur in organizations where people-development is not so much a program as part of the culture. Culture doesn't mean a set of platitudes on the wall. Culture means The Way We Do Things Around Here.

In organizations that have a people-development culture, you'll see a high priority on training—perhaps using formal classes or on-line modules, but also through on-the-job, real-time interactions between workers, with both managers and experienced people explaining, showing, and helping newer recruits learn the ropes and improve their game.

But hand-in-glove with that tactical training you'll hear explanations for how the tasks tie back to the core values of the enterprise. In effect, "We do it this way, and here's why." That constant repetition of core values, especially when tied to actual behaviors, has a way of embedding those values deep inside a person's psyche. At some level, even if it's unconscious, it compels the person to ask: "Do I really believe that? Am I committed to that? That makes sense, so how can I begin to naturally behave that way?" Over time, the person lives out the core value without even thinking about it. It's become part of who they are—they've developed as a *person*.

But let's go a step further. In addition to formal learning and training, people-development cultures are characterized by people who tend to engage in lots of informal, one-on-one conversations—both on the job and outside of work. They work side by side on projects and talk about what they're doing. Workers in people-development cultures drink a lot of coffee. They also tend to value hospitality—food, meals, birthday cakes, home-baked goods, happy hours, and so on. Perhaps most notably, their leaders spend a lot of time out among the troops, meeting with small groups and individuals in order to favor the odds of influence taking place.

That kind of stuff happens, not because people are told to do it, but because "that's just the way we do it here." Everyone kind of instinctively knows (or senses) that high-touch, highly relational interactions humanize the workplace. The people doing the work are treated like *persons*, not just employees.

THE KEY TO MENTORING: MENTORS

If you asked me how to start a formal mentoring program in your organization, I would immediately respond, "It all depends." So many factors affect how you should get started: The mission of your venture and the nature of your work. What your core values are. The size of your team and who you want to influence. Your geography. How much time your people have. What you hope to accomplish through mentoring. Where your enterprise is in its life cycle. The health of your organization and its level of employee engagement. Who your leaders are. What their experience with mentoring has been like and what their commitment to it is. Who will lead the program and what experience they have. What your budget for the program is. How you intend to measure the program's effectiveness. Needless to say, there is much to be considered!

But you have to start somewhere. And for my money, the key is to first identify the people you want to clone. Those are the people you want as mentors. As Gordon MacDonald pointed out years ago, "Organizational programs rarely create leaders. Leaders create leaders. Leaders are mentored."[2] So, notwithstanding the characteristics of an ideal mentor that I mentioned in chapters 5 and 11, you want your "best" people reproducing themselves in others. Which is to say you want the people you're trying to develop to be influenced by the "best" of the people you already have. Find those modeling individuals and then figure out how to build the program around them.

LEADERS CREATE LEADERS

I'll give two real-life illustrations of how leaders create leaders, one in a company and one in a church. The company is Southwest Airlines. Its founder, Herb Kelleher (1931–2019), was a larger-than-life personality and a born entrepreneur. But he also was a genius at people-development. His business philosophy was quite simple: *The business of business is people.*

My friend Dave Ridley tells this story in its entirety at his website.[3] But the gist of it is that when he was in his mid-thirties, he went to work for Mr. Kelleher as Director of Marketing on June 10, 1988. On that first day, Dave's vice-president of marketing informed him that they were scheduled for a "Herb Meeting" at 4:00 p.m. A Herb Meeting was a monthly gathering between Herb Kelleher, Southwest's marketing executives, and the company's ad agency, to review advertising and marketing strategy. Dave asked how long the meeting would last. He was told that dinner would be brought in, so he should expect to stay until 7:30 or 8:00, possibly later.

On that particular evening, the meeting didn't break up until 10:45! But no one seemed to notice, because one of Dave's most lasting memories is that by the end of it his jaws were hurting from having laughed so hard during the course of those six hours. Herb loved to tell a funny story, and it usually ended with his signature bellowing laugh. He had a lightning wit, to boot, which always sparked even more laughter. But through it all, he kept everyone engaged in some serious strategic thinking. Then out of the blue, he would turn and ask someone, "Hey, I know your daughter was recently in the hospital for knee surgery. How'd that go?"

Dave was stunned. Not only had he gotten to spend six hours with the CEO on his first day on the job, he watched his leader reach into the hearts of every person in that room and create a bond with his team. He saw firsthand the veracity of another of Herb Kelleher's mantras: *An organization that is bound by love is more powerful than one bound by fear.*

The tradition of the monthly Herb Meetings went on for years. Did that help Southwest's bottom line? Sure, but the benefit to the leaders who got to have dinners with Herb was incalculable. Just by being around him, they absorbed the vision and values he wanted his company to express. Dave later told an interviewer, "Within weeks, he knew my wife and children's names, what my outside interests were, and a lot about my background. I knew within three months of going to work at Southwest that Herb would fall on a grenade for me or any member of my family. His love for people was palpable."[4]

Who wouldn't want to work for a leader like that? More importantly, after spending time with such a leader, who wouldn't be inspired to lead like he did? Dave certainly was, because leaders create leaders.

The second story is about Randy Pope, founding pastor of Perimeter Church in Atlanta, Georgia. Perimeter began in 1977 with a vision for reaching people "all around the perimeter of Atlanta and the world." By the 1980s, it had already planted several churches. As Perimeter likes to say, it was multisite before multisite was cool!

In the late 1980s, Leadership Network (LN) gathered a number of pastors and church leaders to Glen Eyrie in Colorado Springs to discuss the topic of church multiplication. Most of the well-known megachurches of the time were represented, including Randy and Perimeter. Because I had worked on a related project for Bob Buford and LN, I was invited to attend as an observer.

Throughout the first day, leader after leader presented his church's strategy for reproducing itself. It was a yeasty time, to say the least! I mean, we heard about cutting-edge best practices from the best of the best: surveys and questionnaires, demographic studies, census data, marketing segmentation, insights from Scripture, protracted prayer vigils that had resulted in timely promptings, providential opportunities, real estate miracles, you name it. Clearly, when it came to replicating churches, these people had thought it through, prayed it through, and seen it through. They all had thriving, growing, reproducing churches.

Interestingly, Randy Pope had been mostly a spectator all day until someone finally said, "Randy, you haven't said much, but your church has planted a number of churches. What's your take on all this?"

In reply, Randy was amazingly self-effacing. "Boy, my reaction is, I'm just sitting here amazed at all I've heard! I mean, I've been taking notes all day long. You guys are way beyond anything we've been doing."

Then he got around to answering the question. "I'll tell you how we've done things at Perimeter, but it's nothing like what you guys have done. I just start by recruiting seven or eight men that I've picked out. I approach them and ask them to make a three-year commitment. I ask them to meet with me once a week for two hours during those three years. The first year we cover the Bible and the basic doctrines of the faith. The second year we get into their personal and spiritual life: their spiritual disciplines, their marriage and family, their sin patterns, their walk with Christ. In the third year we talk about ecclesiology and what the church is all about. That includes pastoral issues and church governance, and what it takes to lead a church.

"Throughout that three-year period, they each have to recruit and lead a group of men themselves. During that third year, we identify a group of people in the church who are going to plant a new church. And at the end of that year, we hive off that group with those trained leaders, and they go plant a new church. Then I go recruit a new group of seven or eight men, and we start the process over again. That's how we've planted most all of our churches."

Today the Perimeter website lists twenty-seven daughter and granddaughter churches around metro Atlanta,[5] all from a strategy that is time-consuming (and therefore expensive), unrelated to the immediate concerns of the lead church, and not particularly "sexy" in terms of analytics or cutting-edge best practice. Indeed, it's actually a pretty archaic approach, dating all the way back to the first century. Yet somehow this dinosaur (or is it a unicorn?) of life-on-life leadership development seems to have served the region of northern Georgia extraordinarily well.

COMMITTING TO THE LONG HAUL

The CEO of a mid-size company once told me that his horizon for performance was five quarters. "If I don't have the stock price up within five quarters, my board will go find a new CEO," he said. I guess if a company exists only to maximize shareholder wealth, then that makes sense. But I side with Forrest Mars, Sr., founder of the Mars Company (candy bars), who in 1947 wrote out the purpose of his enterprise as follows:

> The Company's objective is the manufacture and distribution of food products in such a manner as to promote a mutuality of services and benefits among:
>
>
>
> CONSUMERS
>
> DISTRIBUTORS
>
> COMPETITORS
>
> OUR DIRECT SUPPLIERS OF GOODS AND SERVICES
>
> ALL EMPLOYEES OF THE COMPANY
>
> AND
>
> ITS SHAREHOLDERS
>
>
>
> This expresses the total purpose for which the Company exists—nothing less—and it is expected that the Board of Directors, all Management and employees of the Company, will be motivated by this basic objective, and will keep it constantly in mind as the guiding principle in all their work for the Company.[6]

That's what I call taking the long view. Obviously Mr. Mars was interested in making money for his shareholders. But notice that he placed them last on his list of stakeholders in the Mars Company.[7]

Organizational leaders have to take the long view when it comes to building into people. That's because people take time to develop and grow. There is no shortcut to the process.

Another way to say it is that people-development is inherently altruistic. I build into you because I believe in you. I want to see you prosper and thrive long after I'm gone. If I'm only out to build my own kingdom and make a name for myself, then I don't care what becomes of you. You matter to me only to the extent that you serve my self-interests.

Organizations led by self-centered superstars tend to have a very short lifespan, because when the star is gone, there's nothing left. By contrast, organizations that operate as star factories, constantly spawning new leaders and cultivating their unique gifts, can last pretty much indefinitely.

So, I return to my point about identifying the people you want to clone. Think most carefully about that. One's first impulse may be to name that superstar, the person on whom everything seemingly depends. Often, such peak performers have a dynamic personality and a charismatic style that makes them the "face" of the organization. Or perhaps they have some other over-sized asset—a towering intellect, an ability to out-think everyone else, a ruthless but remarkably potent talent for getting deals done, or a charm that cannot be resisted.

It's fun to imagine what you could do with an army of troops like that person. But the question I would be asking is: Does this individual have any humility? Humility means that one uses whatever gifts one has not in the service of making oneself great, but to make other people great, to make one's organization great, and to make one's society and the world great. Humility takes the long view by setting others up to become far more successful than oneself long after one is gone.

FORMAL MENTORING IN CHURCHES

The organization I know best is the local church. If any enterprise should be deeply involved in mentoring, it should be the local church. That's because people-development *is* the mission of the church. Jesus couldn't have been clearer about that: "Make disciples" (Matt. 28:19).[1] Literally, make learners, make apprentices, make followers (of Jesus). That is pure people-development. So, mentoring makes perfect sense for every local church.

MENTORING VS. DISCIPLESHIP

What's the difference between mentoring and discipleship? From one point of view, that's a pointless question because they are the same basic process of personal transformation and growth as a result of being influenced by someone else. Churches sometimes assume they "own" discipleship because that term has been used by churches for two thousand years. But there's nothing inherently "Christian" about discipleship. Nor, by the same token, is there anything "unchristian" about mentoring. Discipleship is a perfect example of mentoring, and mentoring is inherent to life-on-life discipleship.

That said, I will concede that if we understand "discipleship" to mean becoming an apprentice of Jesus, then there are additional means of doing that besides having a one-on-one relationship with a spiritual guide (or mentor).

But whatever one wants to call it, the fact is that neither discipleship nor mentoring are taking place to any significant degree in the vast majority of churches today. A 2015 Barna study[2] found that 52 percent of Christian adults say their church "definitely does a good job helping people grow spiritually," and another 40 percent say it "probably" does so. That's what all the sheep believe, anyway.

Meanwhile, their shepherds (who are supposed to know better) say the exact opposite: only 1 percent of church leaders say that "today's churches are doing very well at discipling new and young believers." Sixty percent rank the job churches are doing of discipling their people as "not too well."

A closer look at the data shows that only 20 percent of Christian adults are involved in some sort of "discipleship activity," which Barna classified as (1) attending Sunday school or a fellowship group, (2) studying the Bible with a group, (3) reading and discussing a Christian book with a group, or (4, and ranked last) meeting with a spiritual mentor. Among "practicing Christians," only 17 percent say they meet with a spiritual mentor.

Shockingly, among Christians who claim that spiritual growth is "very important" or "somewhat important" to them, 38 percent say that their preferred method of discipleship is "on my own"! (I'm still trying to wrap my mind around how one gets "discipled" on one's own.)

Barna's research echoes what Willow Creek discovered in its 2007 *Reveal* study: "Does increased attendance in ministry programs *automatically* equate to spiritual growth? To be brutally honest, it does not." Indeed, "Church activity alone made no direct impact on growing the heart. . . . It was a flat line—and a stunning discovery for us."[3]

Stunning indeed! I see churches doing lots and lots of activities. But if the hearts of the people are not growing in an increasing love for God and for other people (Willow's definition of spiritual growth), what's the point?

Buried in a sidebar of the *Reveal* report is a statistic on people who were found to be "dissatisfied" (or unhappy) with their experience at Willow. The Dissatisfied agreed with the statement, "My faith is central to my life and I'm trying to grow, but my church is letting me down." That segment represented 10 percent of those surveyed. One of two statements rated lowest by the Dissatisfied group was:

> "The church helps me find a spiritual mentor." Just 4 percent reported being satisfied versus 25 percent for the total (meaning the total number of people surveyed), a multiple difference of more than six times.
>
> Although the Dissatisfied segment appears totally aligned with the attitudes and behaviors related to a Christ-centered life, they still want the church to help "keep them on track," to hold them accountable and keep them challenged. A tool like a personal spiritual growth plan might address some of those needs. But they also seem to want a personal growth coach or spiritual mentor. That may be what would truly "keep them on track" and from walking out the back door.[4]

A DIFFERENT MODEL

Would a personal growth coach or mentor "keep people on track"? The only way churches could ever know is if they tried it. But most don't. According to Barna, only a third of Christian adults report that their church recommends meeting with a spiritual mentor. That may be why only 23 percent say they are currently being discipled by someone, and only 19 percent are discipling someone themselves.[5]

The discipleship strategies of most churches involve small groups, growth groups, fellowship groups, discussion groups, home groups, Sunday school classes, Bible studies, and other group-based programs. Sometimes, the leaders of those groups become mentors to group members, which is fantastic! We need more of that.

But in talking about spiritual growth and discipleship with a pastor-friend recently, I learned from him, "I think one of the challenges of our churches is that we are much more education-based than we are process-based. And people's primary experiences within churches are knowledge-based and information-based, and we don't have the life-on-life. You know, people helping people."

Education-based, knowledge-based, and information-based. I would add program-based, as well. Those descriptions certainly characterize how most churches do discipleship.[6] I'll leave it to you to decide how effective that model (which has been around for the past hundred years) has been in producing genuine transformation toward Christlikeness.

For my own part, I think it's time to try a different model—something more process-based, relationship-based, and experience-based. Something that's probably a combination of small-group interaction and one-on-one with a mentor. Something that fits with the way today's knowledge workers learn. Something that also fits with what millennials are desperate to find. Something that resembles the model of Jesus and the twelve. And something that also resembles what the apostles appear to have practiced as they took the gospel to their world.[7]

FIVE GUIDELINES FOR MAKING IT WORK

Would such a model work in our culture's churches?[8] We can know only if churches try it. If your church would like to accept that challenge, here are five recommendations for upping your odds of success:

1. *Mentors are the key.* It goes without saying that a model of discipleship built on mentoring depends on the mentors. Jesus said that a learner, "after he has been fully trained, will be *like his teacher*"

(see Luke 6:40, emphasis added). So I ask: What sort of person are you trying to produce? Your mentors should resemble that person.

In the New Testament, the primary models for mentoring are Jesus, Paul, and Barnabas.[9] That sets the bar pretty high! But I think if we look at things that way, we miss the point. Mentoring is *not* about pairing people with superstars. It's about iron sharpening iron. It's about people influencing other people. You don't have to be a superstar to do that.

You do, however, have to be an apprentice of Jesus yourself. Pastors and church leaders ought to be able to assess that in potential mentors.

But then, how do you get those modeling individuals into action as mentors? No one has completely cracked the code on that. Unlike a business, a church is predominantly a voluntary enterprise, so you can't just order someone to become a mentor as a condition of employment. Instead, you have to tap into the art and science of volunteer mobilization.[10]

But let me offer two suggestions. First, create an expectation (or value) at your church that the older you become in the faith, the more intentional you will be about mentoring someone else. That comes right out of Titus 2: "Older men are to be temperate, dignified, sensible, sound in faith, in love, in perseverance" (v. 2). Isn't that the kind of person you're trying to produce? Likewise, "older women" are expected to be "teaching what is good, so that they may encourage the young women."

Somehow in the age-and-stage model that most of today's churches have adopted, we've siloed people to the point that we've suffocated mentoring. By creating programs to meet the "needs" of children, youth, young adults, young marrieds, families, seniors, etc., we've overlooked Paul's insight that one of the most basic needs of any person at any age is life-on-life discipleship. We've got to recover that if we intend to develop fully devoted followers of Jesus.

But I know what you're going to run into when you try to coax a middle-aged person into becoming a mentor: "Oh, pastor, I'm not a very spiritual person!" "I'm just so busy." "I wouldn't know how to relate to these young people nowadays." "I've made too many mistakes in my life." I've heard dozens of excuses like that.

While you have to respect people's right to decide what they feel they can commit to, you also have to show them that many, if not most, of the usual objections are based on misperceptions about the process of mentoring. So, you may have to give them a reorientation as to what the process is all about.

But I also suggest an end-around strategy: appeal to a person's own life history. The next time you're in a conversation with someone and they tell you about a person who made a profound impact on their life—a coach in high school, a youth leader, a professor in college, a godly older woman at a previous church—seize upon that memory! Turn it into a sales pitch for mentoring: "Wow, Anne, it sounds like God really brought Ellen along at a key moment in your life. Hey, can I ask you something? Because of your experience with Ellen, I think you're in a position to do what Ellen did for you for someone else. You're older now and more experienced. We have so many younger women here at the church who are looking for an Ellen, someone they could talk to about the real issues. Someone, frankly, to just be a trusted friend, kind of like Ellen was for you. Would you be open to doing that for another woman?"

Notice you didn't even have to use the word "mentor." But that's of course what you're talking about—and what Anne was talking about. Anyone who has ever benefitted from a mentor knows the value of a mentor. I encourage you to appeal to that value. By doing so, you are essentially tapping into that mentor's authority, which is still quite present. It's as if, through your appeal, the person's mentor is telling them, "Look, what I did for you, you need to do for someone else."

And they do! Every year for decades, my dad held a 6:00 a.m., by-invitation-only discipleship seminar (non-credit) for a dozen students. He frequently told those groups, "I do this for you, so that you would do this for others." That was basically just an updated version of Paul telling Timothy, "Hey, I handed you the baton of faith. Now you need to pass it on!"

In short, if you're older in the faith, you have an obligation to help someone younger in the faith. If you've had a mentor, you have an obligation to mentor someone else.

2. It starts from the top. Life-on-life discipleship is as much a value as it is a practice and a process. It's a mindset. It's what my dad called a "ministry of multiplication." God created humans to multiply—not just numerically, but personally and spiritually. Likewise, Jesus left instructions to "make disciples." He wasn't talking about a one-and-done strategy. Inherent in the command is the idea of *making disciples who make disciples*.

That begs the question: If you're a senior leader in your church, who are *you* discipling? And how intentionally and how effectively?

My pastor-friend Chris lives in Fort Worth, which is just under an hour's drive (with traffic) from Dallas. Whenever he comes to Dallas, he brings a man from his church. That gives them an hour to talk on the way over, and an hour to talk on the way back. Genius!

My pastor-friend Tom spends many of his lunch hours visiting the people in his church at their workplaces. While there, they invariably talk about their work and the challenges they experience there. Often they ask Tom to pray with them and offer any insights he has. That may not sound like "discipleship," but I can assure you those people are far more likely to bring Jesus into their work after Tom's visit than they would have been if he had just stayed in his office back at the church.

My pastor-friend Gary believes he has an obligation to build into aspiring future church leaders. So, in addition to focusing on his elder board, he meets with a group of seminarians every week to talk about (1) their own lives and (2) what they are learning about people and the church as they participate in the life of Gary's church.[11]

The point is whatever the key leaders of a church emphasize and devote their time to, that's what everyone will think matters. So, if you want your church to be a disciple-making church, then show everyone what that looks like. It's a case of the old saw, "I'd rather see a sermon than hear one any day."[12]

3. *Use mentoring to strengthen programs, not add to them.* What I'm describing here is not really a program but a way of doing church and a way of doing discipleship. It's extraordinarily difficult to "program" life-on-life relationships. And the last thing most churches need is another program.

But what if you could strengthen existing programs by challenging the leaders—whether paid or volunteer—to become intentional about discipling people *on the way, as they are doing* their programs? In other words, have them learn to integrate mentoring principles into what is already taking place—and you might consider using the second half of this book as a guide to helping them do that.

For example, say Larry is your worship pastor. Every week he oversees an ensemble of musicians and vocalists who prepare for the worship services. *While doing that*, Larry should be on the lookout for what might be called "discipleship moments." Life-on-life discipleship (or mentoring) is heavily moment-driven. While you're just walking through life with another person, doors of opportunity open up along the way. It could be a need, a crisis, a comment, an incident, a question—really almost anything that life throws a person's way. But that moment may present a door of opportunity for discipleship.

So, let's say that one day Larry notices that Sidney the drummer is off. Not so much his performance, but his demeanor. He appears to be in a funk. Quite naturally, Larry asks him how he's doing. Sid volunteers that he's just received bad news about his dad's health. Bingo! There's a moment of opportunity. Obviously, Larry can stop right then and there to pray with Sidney about his dad. But if he chooses, he could also take it a step further and suggest that he and Sidney get together later to talk about it.

Will that get-together then lead to a mentoring relationship? Who knows? If that's the first time Larry and Sidney have ever sat down over coffee, it's too early in the relationship to tell. They might hit it off ("chemistry"), or they might not. But if it leads to another get-together later, or if it encourages Sidney to reach out to Larry again sometime, then maybe it turns into an impactful relationship. The point is Larry has created the conditions for life-on-life discipleship to take place. That's all one could ask for.

Some people would describe what Larry is doing as "pastoring," not necessarily discipling. Others would say he's just doing his job. Still others would say he's being a friend. I say, who cares what one calls it? Is Larry making himself available to help Sidney as he faces a tough situation? Will that have a positive influence on Sidney? Will Larry be, in effect, the hands and feet and heart of Jesus to Sidney in that moment? Whatever you call it, that's what we're looking for (and what Jesus is looking for: "If I . . . washed your feet, you also ought to wash one another's feet" [John 13:14]).

Larry's a paid staff member, so yes, I suppose we could expect it of him to follow-up on Sidney's need. And yes, by doing so he is modeling the value of life-on-life discipleship. Which is exactly what needs to happen because what a church should strive for is to see its members—everyday Christians—being inspired to spot those "discipleship moments" and seize those opportunities for life-on-life impact.

That's more likely to happen if life-on-life discipleship is a core value for the church that the senior leaders continuously model. And I should add, also explain, celebrate, repeat, reward, and measure. And, whenever that value gets ignored or violated, the infraction should be called out, and discipleship should be brought back to its place of priority. Leaders can reinforce a value in a thousand ways— through the worship services, the teaching, the illustrations, the staff meetings, the programs, the outreach activities, the meals and hospitality, and so on.

One of the most important ways to reinforce discipleship is

through the people who get honored. Is it an honor to mentor people at your church? Does a person get affirmed and praised and esteemed for doing that? Do they feel valued for doing that?

Likewise, are new believers and younger believers challenged, encouraged, and facilitated to seek out mentors?[13] Is anyone telling them, "Look, if you're serious about following Jesus, you need to find someone in this church who's been walking with Jesus for a while and start hanging out with them. Our classes and programs and the like are great, but nothing will beat having personal interaction with an experienced follower of Jesus."

4. Use top-level matters as a gateway. This follows from the previous point. Most church programs deal with top-level issues, meaning practical needs, problems, and desires. For example: parenting classes, recovery programs, money management seminars, pre-marital workshops, Bible study methods, and so on. There are also a variety of age-and-stage groups, as I mentioned earlier.

Quite often these groups pair individuals or a smaller group of learners with a leader or guide. To my mind, that offers a perfect opportunity or climate in which mentoring relationships can develop. The top-level activity provides a natural "agenda" for putting learners and leaders together. It eliminates a lot of the awkwardness that would exist if they got together just to get together.

Of course, the key, again, is to orient the guides to be on the lookout for those "discipleship moments" and the opportunities to go deeper. I'm not suggesting that the leaders try to force relationships to happen. Chemistry can happen only organically. But I am suggesting an openness for a relationship to form and, as I tried to illustrate with Larry, an availability to see what God might do.

What happens if a leader gets together with someone and the relationship goes nowhere? That actually happens a lot! Humans are just like that. But just because someone doesn't have chemistry with you doesn't mean they won't have it with someone else. As a leader, you likely know another leader whom the person might find it easier to relate to, for any number of reasons. You can easily suggest that the person seek out that other leader. Or better yet, arrange a get-together between the three of you so you can "hand off" the person to someone who may be in a better position to help them than you are.

5. *View this as a learning odyssey.* Church history celebrates a rich legacy of life-on-life discipleship (or mentoring) in times past. But the church in our culture has only recently started to reawaken to that model. Here and there are some exciting "new" initiatives that are showing promise and bearing fruit (not all are church-based). But if your church decides to go in this direction, just know that you will be embarking on a learning curve.

I myself love learning odysseys. You try some stuff. Some of it works, some of it doesn't. You debrief and reevaluate. You tweak and retool and try again. Over time you start to figure things out. You make lots of mistakes, but you get wiser. And if you've got the right people on the bus and you keep things in perspective, you have fun.

But I realize that not all churches or church leaders are that sanguine about experimentation. They want something proven, something they know will "work." If that describes your church, I'm not sure what to tell you. I know the old model never worked extremely well, even when the winds of culture were in the church's favor. Now that those winds have shifted around and are coming right at us with full force, the old model seems outdated and outmatched.[14]

But I do know that life-on-life mentoring works extraordinarily well, and always has. However, in adopting that model you have to commit to the long haul. You have to think in terms of years and decades, and even generations—for mentoring, like the church, is inherently generational.

Life-on-life is a slow (and messy) process because it moves at what I call "the speed of people." That means it takes as long as it takes—as long as it takes to grow a person spiritually and personally. Certainly, a lot can happen in three years, especially if one is teachable and has a good mentor. But we all know that sanctification is a lifelong process. Our approach to discipleship must take that into account.[15]

That's why there's so much value in setting an expectation at your church that when you're young you need a mentor, but as you get older you need to start mentoring others. Seen from that perspective, sanctification-as-a-lifelong process seems less daunting; it seems manageable. In fact, it seems quite natural and organic. It injects a sense of hope because it communicates, "This is how the Christian life works. You travel through a series of adventures in a lifelong pilgrimage toward Christ-likeness." To the young, it says, "See these older Christians? They started out where you are. You can learn from the journey they've walked." And to the old it says, "See these younger Christians? You were there once. You need to help them learn to walk with Jesus."

Discipleship (or mentoring) is all about learning, so what could be more interesting than a church learning about the learning process of discipleship? I believe churches that commit to that path will bear much fruit, and their fruit will remain (see John 15:16). Whatever they learn, they will be learning on behalf of the worldwide body of Christ. Their takeaways will prove invaluable to future generations of believers, because those believers will have the benefit of some solid, proven wisdom about the process of "making disciples who make disciples" of Jesus.

FORMAL MENTORING MODELS TO CONSIDER

There are countless resources now being produced on the theme of mentoring, so it would go beyond the scope of this book to try and list even "the best of the best" among them. But the entries below suggest a few models to consider. As you can see, mentoring appears in many forms. (*Note: by mentioning these resources, I am neither agreeing with nor endorsing everything about them or their sponsors.*)

BUSINESS, INDUSTRY, AND THE PROFESSIONS

Caterpillar Professional Development Programs[1]

Earthmoving equipment giant Caterpillar offers new recruits seven different programs designed to acquaint them with the company and cycle them through a rotation of the company's various divisions, facilitated by a professional mentor. The aim is to help them find their spot within Caterpillar and tee them up for long-term productivity and success with the company.

Deloitte Emerging Leaders Development Program[2]

Deloitte is a professional services firm offering auditing, consulting, tax, and other financial services. Its ELDP is a comprehensive, multidisciplinary professional development program designed for high-performing minority managers and senior managers to prepare them for the next stage in their careers. Each participant is assigned a partner, principal, or managing director mentor who commits to at least two years to help their protégés drive their own careers.

Feruni Ceramiche[3]

Dato' C. C. Ngei founded Feruni in 2010 with a vision of transforming the ceramic tile industry in Malaysia. He's done exactly that through a corporate culture that borrows heavily from the model of online shoe retailer Zappos. As an employer, Feruni has become a magnet for millennials in Kuala Lumpur by representing that "we don't just offer jobs, we help build careers." Company leaders develop a customized Career Transformation Plan for each team member that facilitates self-discovery, brings out their best potential, and guides them in achieving personal career goals.

Praxis Academy[4]

Praxis is "a creative engine for redemptive entrepreneurship, supporting founders, funders, and innovators motivated by their faith to renew culture and love their neighbors." Praxis Academy is a week-long immersive learning experience for young entrepreneurs to sharpen and accelerate their nonprofit and business ventures. The academy is led by a diverse group of twenty-five or more seasoned mentors from businesses, nonprofits, and social enterprises around the world, who speak out of their own career and life lessons. Those interactions foster ongoing mentoring and networking after the academy experience.

The Master's Program[5]

Founded by Bob Shank, a longtime friend of both my father and myself, The Master's Program "prepares Christian leaders to value and master a Christ-centered lifestyle." Most of the program's participants are leaders in business and the professions. Trained and experienced Leadership Mentors meet with groups in numerous cities across the country for twelve quarterly sessions over a three-year period.

EDUCATIONAL INSTITUTIONS

Edgerton Gear's Craftsman with Character Course[6]

This family-owned gear manufacturing company has partnered with local high schools to encourage students to explore careers in the skilled trades. The Craftsman with Character Course helps them find self-worth and purpose in the workplace by connecting students with potential employers who provide invaluable hands-on experience as they work alongside mentors.

Bottom Line[7]

Bottom Line helps first-generation students from low-income backgrounds get into and through college by pairing them with a counselor who meets with them in person, one on one, several times a semester. A study released in 2017 showed that Bottom Line students were fourteen percentage points more likely to still be enrolled in a four-year institution two years after high school than their peers who didn't receive such support. Other research shows that 81 percent of Bottom Line's six-year cohort graduated from college—versus the national rate of 59 percent.[8]

The William N. Garrison Faith-and-Work Fellowship, Dallas Theological Seminary[9]

As the Executive Director for Christian Leadership at The Hendricks Center at DTS, I oversee the Garrison Fellowship, which exposes future pastors and teachers to the realities that everyday Christians face in the work world, and also to a robust theology of work. The fellows spend a half-day each week visiting a workplace under the sponsorship of a Christian leader there. They also meet with a senior fellow, as well as myself and others, to interact on what they've seen and discuss the implications of it for helping Christians integrate their faith and their work.

GOVERNMENT AND THE MILITARY

MyVECTOR[10]

The United States Air Force uses its MyVECTOR Program to facilitate career development and mentoring relationships for enlisted personnel. More than 120,000 Airmen have enrolled in the initiative, and more than 15,000 have signed on as mentors. The program puts the responsibility on the mentee to manage the relationship by scheduling sessions, creating agendas, executing developmental activities suggested by the mentor, following up and briefing the mentor, and working with the mentor to develop a career roadmap.

SOCIAL SECTOR AND COMMUNITY SERVICE ORGANIZATIONS

Mercy Street Mentoring Program[11]

Mercy Street is a group of Christians with a vision for seeing the historically impoverished neighborhood of West Dallas transformed by the gospel of Jesus Christ. Their strategy is to raise up a new generation of leaders from the community to be the change agents of tomorrow. The heart of that strategy is mentoring, whereby Christian mentors are matched with public school children. Mentors are carefully vetted and trained, and they make a minimum two-year commitment—although the hope is for a mentor to walk with a child for a lifetime. There are probably thousands of ministries like Mercy Street across the United States, so their mentoring program is hardly unique. But it has proven highly effective over many years.

High Adventure Treks (HATS) for Dads and Daughters[12]

In 1996, Dallasite Kipp Murray decided that he and his daughter, Megan, should be able to experience the same kinds of challenging outdoor adventures together that he had had with his son, Reed, in Boy Scouts. So, he founded HATS in order to teach girls (and their fathers) advanced outdoor camping and survival skills in combination with building lasting father-daughter relationships. Through HATS, Kipp and his team have facilitated hundreds of father-daughter teams, producing women with greater self-reliance, responsibility, teamwork, confidence, compassion, and strength of conviction, as well as a strong sense of self-determination. And whether intended or not, the process has also mentored hundreds of dads in how to relate to their daughters (and by extension, to women in general).

CHURCHES AND PARACHURH MINISTRIES

The C.S. Lewis Institute[13]

CSLI exists to "develop wholehearted disciples of Jesus Christ who will articulate, defend, share, and live their faith in personal and public life." Their Fellows Program is a year-long discipleship program designed for believers who are already established in their faith. Fellows Programs exist in numerous cities in the United States, Canada, and Great Britain.

Radical Mentoring[14]

Radical Mentoring exists "to equip and encourage churches and mentors to build leaders and disciple-makers through intentional men's small group mentoring." Discipleship groups meet monthly with a mentor for a year.

Men's Fraternity[15]

Men's Fraternity aims "to provide men with an encouraging process that teaches them how to live lives of authentic manhood as modeled by Jesus Christ and directed by the Word of God." Groups meet weekly in churches to work through three, year-long studies: The Quest for Authentic Manhood, Authentic Manhood: Winning at Work and Home, and The Great Adventure.

Life-on-Life Ministries[16]

I've told the story about Randy Pope. He and Perimeter Church have founded Life on Life "to ignite movements of life-on-life missional discipleship in churches around the world." They train church leaders through a relational process that involves clinics, coaching, and a leadership community.

Man In the Mirror[17]

This organization grew out of a movement spawned by Patrick Morley's 1986 best-seller, The Man In the Mirror. It "helps leaders provide a discipleship pathway for every man in their church" through leadership training, a church-based program called Journey to Biblical Manhood, and consulting with church leaders.

The Navigators[18]

The Navigators are among the oldest and best known organizations devoted to life-on-life discipleship. Their motto is, "To know Christ, make Him known, and help others do the same." They emphasize personal mentoring/discipling relationships aimed at equipping Christ-followers to make an impact on the people around them for God's glory. Two of the Navs' best known resources are The Topical Memory System for Bible memory, and The 2:7 Series, a discipleship training curriculum for small discussion groups.

MentorLink[19]

MentorLink was founded in 2000 to develop leaders for the burgeoning global church by shifting the focus from content and skills to character and Spirit. The initiative partners with 250 ministries, agencies, and parachurch groups worldwide.

Made to Flourish Pastoral Residency Programs[20]

The MTF Pastoral Residency Programs originated out of Christ Community Church in Kansas City, founded in 1988 by Tom Nelson and his wife, Liz. Christ Community's Pastoral Residency is a two-year mentoring program designed to train and equip the church leaders of tomorrow. Based on the medical residency model of a teaching hospital, the program enrolls seminary graduates in guided, hands-on ministry activities. MTF is now scaling that model to other churches nationwide.

The Fellows Program at The Falls Church Anglican[21]

The Falls Church is an historic Anglican congregation near Washington, D.C. Its Fellows Program is a nine-month Christian leadership development process for recent college graduates that focuses on vocational growth, practical discipleship experiences, graduate studies, service opportunities, and family living in the context of a community of believers. The program has spawned numerous programs like it in churches throughout the United States.

The Forge at Pine Cove[22]

Pine Cove is a gospel-centered Christian camping ministry that strives to be "Christ-centered, others-focused, and seriously fun." The Forge is the leadership development ministry of Pine Cove, serving young adults in their twenties with the aim of developing leaders who embody a faith worth following. (In the interest of full disclosure, I have served several terms on the Pine Cove Board and often help The Forge in the area of giftedness and calling.)

ACKNOWLEDGMENTS

Often after I've completed a book, someone will ask, "Bill, how long did it take you to write that?" In the case of this book, the answer is: about sixty-four years. Yes, Dad and I wrote the initial edition, *As Iron Sharpens Iron*, in 1995, but many of the things I've added here have truly been a lifetime in the learning.

That being the case, I simply don't have space to name all the countless people who contributed to whatever understanding of mentoring I pretend to possess. I am an unbelievably blessed man, in that I have had so many people pour into me as mentors—some knowingly, probably most unwittingly. Some of them I've named or alluded to in the book. The vast majority, alas, must remain unnamed—but not for lack of gratitude. I thank God upon remembering every person who has "sharpened" me in some uniquely helpful way. As a result, I live with a haunting drumbeat in my brain: "To whom much is given, from him much will be required" (Luke 12:48 NKJV).

I must also thank the many people who have trusted me enough to invite me into their lives in what has amounted to the role of a mentor (as I've said, I never call myself a mentor; that's for the other person to determine). I think I can honestly say that I have learned something from every person I have ever worked with. So each of them also has a part in this book.

Of course, my primary source for what mentoring is all about is my dad, Howard Hendricks. Just as John Wooden's father was a mentor to him, so my dad was a mentor to me. But he was also a mentor to literally thousands of other men and women, not only at Dallas Theological Seminary, where he taught for sixty years, but worldwide. I have written testimony from hundreds of those folks who have said that what John Wooden was to basketball, Dad was to teaching and mentoring: best of class! So again: "To whom much is given, from him much will be required" (Luke 12:48 NKJV).

One group that I've mentioned in the book is my Wednesday morning breakfast group (Ben, Russ, Brad, and now Sam, and in times past Clanton and Robbie). Brennan Manning used to meet with a similar group of guys, and they called themselves The Notorious Sinners. I suppose our Wednesday morning group would fit the spirit, if not the name, of that motley crew. We are certainly sinners saved by grace. But by that same grace we are walking with each other through life, and I wouldn't trade the honor of that for anything.

Another group to whom I owe a tremendous debt of gratitude is the team I get to work with at The Hendricks Center at Dallas Theological Seminary. I am daily afforded the privilege of being influenced by their wisdom, insight, caution, correction, character, creativity, counsel, and candor. Most of them are younger than I am, but I regard all of them as mentors, because I learn so much by working alongside them.

I deeply appreciate Tony Burton for giving me permission to tell his story about James Settee, and Dave Ridley for letting me tell his story about Herb Kelleher. I also have Brad Smith to thank for giving me (over many years and many retellings) the core storyline for *The Story of God*, which I have now put into writing. Brad is no way to blame if I have not told the story properly.

Moody Publishers graciously published *As Iron Sharpens Iron* twenty-three years ago and has kept it in print all these years. Now they have been bold enough to trust me with updating and revising it, so as to keep pace with the times. I am thrilled by their perceptive awareness that mentoring is an "evergreen" theme that will always need to be emphasized. I get to have my name on the cover, but let there be no mistake: this book is the product of the entire Moody team. I want to express special appreciation to my editor, Kevin Emmert, for his remarkably patient—and needfully persistent—shepherding of me in completing this project. And as always, I thank Paul Santhouse and Greg Thornton for believing in me over the many years of our relationship.

My wife, Lynn, has been my invaluable and irreplaceable partner in this project. For her, that has meant too many hours with Bill holed up with his computer, or worse, with his mind fixated on mentoring when it should have been focused on husbanding. Lucky for me, she seems to instinctively know how much the practice of mentoring feeds my soul, and she graciously indulges me in satisfying that hunger. I am deeply appreciative of her support, faithful prayers, and love.

Finally, to God be the glory for any truth I have managed to express in this book. And to Him be the praise for any good that comes from the writing of it. In His infinite love He made us for Himself. And when we had fallen into sin and become subject to evil and death, He came down from heaven to share our human nature, and to live and die as one of us, offering Himself as a perfect sacrifice for the whole world. While among us, He was the perfection of iron sharpening iron. Then, just before returning to His Father, He issued a command that we must go and do likewise, according to all that He taught us. My prayer is that this book helps all of us become more faithful and effective in accomplishing that mission.

NOTES

How and Why We Came to Write This Book

1. African American communities, of course, had many outstanding churches. But in the mid-1990s, Blacks comprised only about 13–15 percent of the America population.

2. See Dan Kimball, "6 Common Perceptions of Christians," *Outreach* magazine, April 19, 2011, https://churchleaders.com/outreach-missions/outreach-missions-articles/138865-i-like-jesus-not-the-church.html.

3. Church attendance continues to drop, especially among millennials, half of whom say they have not been to church in the past six months. Even among millennials who grew up in the church, 59 percent have stopped attending church at some point. See "Americans Divided on the Importance of Church," March 24, 2014, https://www.barna.com/research/americans-divided-on-the-importance-of-church/#.VL09cYh0ycx.

   Another significant fact: more people today who identify as Christians (having made a "personal commitment to Jesus Christ that is still important to their life today") now say they "love Jesus but not the Church," with the result that they no longer attend church. Of those, 61 percent are women. See "Meet Those Who 'Love Jesus but Not the Church,'" March 30, 2017, https://www.barna.com/research/meet-love-jesus-not-church/.

4. See "The State of the Church 2016," https://www.barna.com/research/state-church-2016/.

5. See "Competing Worldviews Influence Today's Christians," May 9, 2017, https://www.barna.com/research/competing-worldviews-influence-todays-christians/.

6. One of the greatest joys of my life in the past twenty-three years has been engaging in mentoring relationships—both as a mentor and as the one being mentored—with more and more people who aren't like me. Doing so has enlarged my understanding and appreciation of different cultures, sobered me as to the realities and challenges of communicating across cultures, proven to me that the gospel really does have the power to change *anyone's* life, and taught me that heaven is going to be filled with far more people who are not like me than are like me. It's further evidence that when John 3:16 says that "God so loved the world," it means *all* the people in the world.

7. See Morley Winograd and Michael Hais, "How Millennials Could Upend Wall Street and Corporate America," Brookings, May 28, 2014, https://www.brookings.edu/research/how-millennials-could-upend-wall-street-and-corporate-america/.

8. See Mary Lyons, Katherine Lavelle, and David Smith, "Gen Z Rising," *Accenture*, https://www.accenture.com/t20170901T082427Z__w__/us-en/_acnmedia/PDF-50/Accenture-Strategy-Workforce-Gen-Z-Rising-POV.pdf#zoom=50.

9. For example, Sue Edwards and Barbara Neumann, *Organic Mentoring: A Mentor's Guide to Relationships with Next Generation Women* (Grand Rapids, MI: Kregel, 2014); Vickie Kraft and Gwynne Johnson, *Women Mentoring Women: Ways to Start, Maintain, and Expand a Biblical Women's Ministry* (Chicago: Moody Publishers, 2003); Susan Hunt, *Spiritual Mothering: The Titus 2 Model for Women Mentoring Women* (Wheaton, IL: Crossway, 2016); Natasha Sistrunk Robinson, *Mentor for Life: Finding Purpose through Intentional Discipleship* (Grand Rapids: Zondervan, 2016).

10. I must qualify this statement by saying that there are numerous titles about discipling men, which certainly overlaps with mentoring (see chapter 1). But in terms of books targeted at men, and specifically Christian men, there are not that many. One recent release that offers thirty conversation starters for men in mentoring relationships is Vince Miller's *Thirty Virtues That Build a Man: A Conversational Guide for Mentoring Any Man* (Colorado Springs, CO: Outreach, Inc. [DBA Equip Press], 2018).

Chapter 1: As Iron Sharpens Iron

1. The stone had already been worked on by two other master sculptors, both of whom abandoned it because they considered it flawed.

2. He was *not* talking about two sword blades being rubbed against each other to sharpen them (as is frequently suggested). No one of Solomon's era did that! Doing so would only dull iron blades, not sharpen them.

3. In Joel 3, the prophet warns of coming judgment, and in that context proclaims, "Beat your plowshares into swords and your pruning hooks into spears" (v. 10). In Isaiah 2, the exact opposite takes place: "And they will hammer their swords into plowshares and their spears into pruning hooks" (v. 4). In both cases, what will do the beating and hammering to bring about these transformations? In the context of those times, the iron implements would have been repurposed by using iron tools.

4. Again, as I pointed out in the Introduction, this does not suggest that a woman cannot have an influence on a man. Women can and do have great influence on men, including through mentoring relationships. Given his cultural context, it's probable that Solomon was thinking only of men, and not women, when he coined this proverb. But if we wanted to reframe it in a modern context, we might render it this way: "As iron sharpens iron, so one person sharpens another." I see nothing in that wording that substantially departs from the text or its basic meaning. That said, it seems clear that men have things to offer men that women cannot provide, and women have things to offer women that men cannot provide. If that were not the case, we would have no need for the many books on mentoring women, nor for books like this one on mentoring men.

5. Philosophers since Aristotle have debated the extent to which the human mind arrives in the world like a blank slate (Latin, *tabula rasa*), empty and waiting to be filled in, or whether it comes with pre-existing content. I believe there is abundant teaching in Scripture, corroborated by an easily observable phenomenon in the real world called *giftedness*—that God designs human beings individually and gives each one a unique identity or personhood. See my book, *The Person Called You: Why You're Here, Why You Matter & What You Should Do With Your Life* (Chicago: Moody Publishers, 2014).

6. See John Wooden and Don Yaeger, *A Game Plan for life: The Power of Mentoring* (New York: Bloomsbury Publishing, 2009)

Chapter 2: Why Men Need Mentoring

1. Humans are a body-soul unity. We are both material and immaterial.
2. Bryan Deardo, "Tony Dungy shares inspirational quotes from Chuck Noll," 247 Sports, February 28, 2019, https://247sports.com/nfl/pittsburgh-steelers/Article/Tony-Dungy-shares-inspirational-quotes-from-Chuck-Noll-129587745/.
3. It is called The System for Identifying Motivated Abilities (SIMA®), a proprietary assessment tool owned by SIMA® II, LLC, of whom I am a licensee. You can learn more about SIMA® at my website: http://www.thegiftednesscenter.com/questionswhat-assessment-does-tgc-use.
4. When I say "put people through my process," that generally represents anywhere between 6 and 12 hours of work with each person (the process is entirely personal and customized; there is no computer algorithm involved). In effect, I have engaged in a long-term research project involving 2,000 subjects that represents between 12,000 and 24,000 hours of focused inquiry.
5. See Jim Harter, "Employee Engagement on the Rise in the U.S.," Gallup News, August 26, 2018, https://news.gallup.com/poll/241649/employee-engagement-rise.aspx
6. See *State of the Global Workplace* (New York: Gallup Press, 2017), https://www.gallup.com/workplace/238079/state-global-workplace-2017.aspx?utm_source=link_wwwv9&utm_campaign=item_231668&utm_medium=copy.
7. Doug Sherman and I wrote at length about this in our book, *Your Work Matters to God* (Colorado Springs, CO: NavPress, 1987). That book is now out of print. But there are many newer books and other resources dealing with this theme of work from God's perspective. One of the best is *Every Good Endeavor: Connecting Your Work to God's Work*, by Timothy Keller and Katherine Leary Alsdorf (New York: Viking Press, 2012). Another outstanding resource is The Theology of Work Project, which looks at every book of the Bible to see what it has to say about work from God's perspective. Visit https://www.theologyofwork.org/.
8. For more, see Bill Hendricks, *The Person Called You: Why You're Here, Why You Matter & What You Should Do With Your Life* (Chicago: Moody Publishers, 2014).
9. Giftedness is not the sole possession of a fortunate few, such as superstar athletes and musicians or gifted mathematicians and brain surgeons, or "gifted and talented" students in schools. Every human being has some form of giftedness, regardless of intelligence, mental illness or psychological condition, physical disability or limitation, genetic makeup, or socio-economic status. Moreover, ever person's giftedness is unique to them. There are no two humans exactly alike. For more, see Bill Hendricks, *The Person Called You.*
10. Giftedness involves both ability and motivation. My own technical definition is this: "Giftedness is the unique way in which you function. It's a set of inborn core strengths and natural motivation you instinctively and consistently use to do things that you find satisfying and productive. Giftedness is not just what you can do but what you are born to do, enjoy doing, and do well" (*Person Called You*, 28).
11. Psychometrics attempt to quantify human behavior. I don't think that's a totally futile project, but I do think it's misguided to presume that human behavior can be completely explained through statistical analysis. As I stated earlier, humans are a soul-body unity, material and immaterial coexisting together. Science is perfectly suited as a tool to study the body. But when we get to the "soft" categories of the human soul, heart, and spirit, science quickly finds itself out of its depth. How do you "measure" sacrificial love? How do "quantify" courage. What "test" exists to perfectly predict

how someone will react when they come face-to-face with their death? These are matters that require a different calculus, and this is the territory where giftedness resides.

The reason I put the word *objective* in quotes is that virtually all psychometric tests turn out to be far less objective, and in fact highly subjective, by their own design. They present a respondent with forced-choice questions for the respondent to answer. Right there they have introduced two factors of subjectivity: (1) that the test designers are somehow smart enough to know all relevant factors, parameters, and possibilities for what the choices should be (that is, that the test designers are "neutral"), and (2) that the respondent knows himself or herself well enough to answer the questions accurately—to say nothing of whether the respondent chooses to answer the questions truthfully. If you really need a job, and the company you are applying at has a corporate culture that is highly team-oriented, how would you be inclined to answer a question like, "Do you enjoy working on a team? Yes or no?"

12. The term *knowledge worker* was first used by Peter Drucker in *The Landmarks of Tomorrow* (New York: Harper, 1959). In *Management Challenges for the 21st Century* (New York: Harper, 2001), Drucker predicated that "the most valuable asset of a 21st-century institution, whether business or nonbusiness, will be its *knowledge workers* and their *productivity.*" His prediction was spot on!

13. While the designation of "generations" is arguably a completely arbitrary exercise, there seems to be considerable consensus nowadays around what is called "pulse-rate," in which a society can be divided into generational cohorts that have a distinct personality. By that measure, William Strauss and Neil Howe divide recent American generations into: boomers (born between 1943–1960), Generation X (1961–1981), millennials (1982–2004), and Homelanders (or Generation Z, 2005–?). See "Generational Archetypes," LifeCourse Associates, https://www.lifecourse.com/about/method/generational-archetypes.html.

14. Author Gail Sheehy even dubbed the years from twenty to thirty "The Trying Twenties" in her description of young adults. See *Passages: Predictable Crises of Adult Life* (Boston, MA: E.P. Dutton, 1976).

15. Not through psychometrics (i.e., personality tests, interest inventories, etc.). Humans may be studied and analyzed through psychometrics, but persons are only understood through story. Telling me what your five highest strength-themes are, or that you are an ENTP, or a high-D, or a 5 on the Enneagram tells me *about* you but it doesn't help me *understand* you. It doesn't help me know me who you *are.* You're not a data set. You're a living actor (doer) moving through time and exercising agency that has actual effect on the world and other people. That's a narrative taking place in the real world. So the only way I can *know* you is to hear your story ("knowing" is a deeply spiritual process: it means you and I actually connect at some soul level, not just a cognitive/informational level).

16. For example, see Lillian T. Eby, Tammy D. Allen, Sarah C. Evans, Thomas Ng, and David DuBois, "Does Mentoring Matter? A Multidisciplinary Meta-Analysis Comparing Mentored and Non-Mentored Individuals," in *The Journal Vocational Behavior* 72:2 (April 2008): 254–67, https://www.ncbi.nlm.nih.gov/pmc/articles/PMC2352144/. The authors conducted a meta-analysis of 112 individual research studies on mentoring and found that "mentoring is associated with a wide range of favorable behavioral, attitudinal, health-related, relational, motivational, and career outcomes" (254).

17. In full disclosure, my sister, Bev Godby, has also had a parallel practice to mine at The Giftedness Center since about 2000. Bev specializes in college students, young adults, and women in transition. To date, she's probably worked with fifteen hundred individuals. We work with adults of all ages and stages at The Giftedness Center, but easily half our practice is with people under thirty.

18. The mandate to steward the world and its people is still in effect. Neither the Great Commandments (Matt. 22:36–40) nor the Great Commission (Matt. 28:18–20) eliminate it, but rather invest that stewardship with even greater meaning and significance.

19. Admittedly, not all men reflect so deeply on their lives. Sadly, some don't reflect on them at all. But that only strengthens the case for why men need more mentoring. Many men are actually incapable of engaging in any sort of fruitful, meaningful reflection without the assistance of another man. Do we really want any man to end up with an unexamined life?

Chapter 3: What Is Mentoring?

1. There is also a character named Mentor in *The Iliad* (the prequel to *The Odyssey*) who is mentioned one time, but he is not the same character as Mentor in *The Odyssey*.

2. Telemachus also goes on a journey in *The Odyssey*. In the first four books of the epic, he sets sail to find out what has happened to his father.

3. *Les Adventures* is a rather clever work, borrowing characters, plot lines, and other elements from an ancient and beloved epic as a framework for telling what was at the time a "modern" story that conveyed "modern" themes. In that way *Les Adventures* is similar to creative productions of our day like *West Side Story* (an adaptation of Shakespeare's *Romeo and Juliet*), *The Seven Percent Solution* (from Sherlock Holmes), *Wicked* (from *The Wizard of Oz*), or *Aladdin* (from a Middle Eastern folk tale in *The Arabaian Nights*).

4. For an account of how Mentor in *The Odyssey* is nothing like our current conception of him, and of how Fénelon's adaptation of *The Odyssey* elevated Mentor into the icon we perceive him to be today, see Andy Roberts, "Homer's Mentor: Duties Fulfilled or Misconstrued," *History of Education Journal*, November 1999, https://nickols.us/homers_mentor.pdf.

5. In this section, I am presenting the views of Gregory Nagy, Francis Jones Professor of Classical Greek Literature and Professor of Comparative Literature at Harvard University, and Director of Harvard's Center for Hellenic Studies. See, for example, his interview with B. R. J. O'Donnell, "The Odyssey's Millennia-Old Model of Mentorship," *The Atlantic*, October 13, 2017, https://www.theatlantic.com/business/archive/2017/10/the-odyssey-mentorship/542676/.

6. Shaunti Feldhahn, *For Women Only: What You Need to Know About the Inner Lives of Men* (Sisters, Oregon: Multnomah Publishers, 2004), 55–56.

7. Homer, *The Odyssey, Book III*, trans. Samuel Butler (1900), emphasis added.

8. I say "the Apostle Paul's words to Timothy," and so they are. But if one believes, as I do, in the inspiration of Scripture, they are also God's Word/words to Timothy: God Himself spoke through a mentor figure to encourage Timothy and to give him strength and godly confidence.

9. See G. Crisp and I. Cruz, "Mentoring college students: A critical review of the literature between 1990 and 2007," *Research in Higher Education* 50:6 (2009): 525–545, as cited in "Mentorship," at Wikipedia, at https://en.wikipedia.org/wiki/Mentorship#cite_ref-8.

10. *Odyssey, Book I.*

Chapter 4: Start with Your Story

1. This exercise was originally developed by Brad Smith and Pete Deison at the Center for Christian Leadership (now known as The Hendricks Center) at Dallas Theological Seminary.

Chapter 5: Whom to Look For, and What Mentors Look For in You

1. A distant mentor would be someone you follow or emulate from afar, such as a celebrity or athlete. A "virtual" mentor might be a historical figure whose wisdom and example prove

inspiring, such as Abraham Lincoln or William Wilberforce. He might also be someone whose writings or other communications heavily influence your thinking.

2. These estimates are based on my work at The Giftedness Center.

3. Paul said as much to Timothy when giving him instructions about what kind of men should lead as elders in the church. In addition to being "above reproach" and "respectable," they also needed to "have a good reputation with those outside the church" (see 1 Tim. 3:2, 7, along with 2 Tim. 2:2). Paul was not describing a popularity contest, but an assessment of character. The issue was whether the man in question actually lives out the faith he professes.

4. Proverbs 29:25 says, "The fear of man brings a snare, but he who trusts in the Lord will be exalted." Likewise, Hebrews 13:6 speaks to the confidence of the man who can say, "The Lord is my helper, I will not be afraid. What will man do to me?" No man gets very far in becoming a whole man until his fear of the Lord outweighs any fear he might have of other men—what they might think of him or what they might do to him.

5. You can read the story of Abraham's brokenness in Genesis 22:1–19 and Romans 4:13–22. David's story is found in 2 Samuel 11:1–12:23 and Psalm 51 (see also Ps. 139:19–24).

6. This popular expression comes from two lines in the poem "Invictus" by William Ernest Henley: "I am the master of my fate, / I am the captain of my soul."

7. You will notice that in this book I do not use terms like "mentee" or "protégé" to designate the person being mentored. To me, it feels too transactional to tell two people, "Okay, you're the mentor and you're the mentee." True mentoring is much more organic than that. It occurs, but quite often it is not noticed or described as "mentoring" until after it has occurred. This relates to my premise that the person who benefits from a mentoring relationship is the one who gets to decide how that relationship has helped him (see chapter 3). In most every case, he realizes that someone has served as a mentor only *after the fact*.

Chapter 6: Putting Yourself in Opportunity's Path

1. Richard J. Foster, *Prayer: Finding the Heart's True Home*, 10th Anniversary Edition (New York: HarperCollins, 2002), 328

2. The mission of the church is to *make disciples* (Matt. 28:19). A "disciple" is a learner, an apprentice—an apprentice of Jesus. The aim of discipleship is to become like Jesus and learn how to live your life as He would live it if He were you. That process is inherently developmental. Whatever else a church may be doing, if it's not intentionally and effectively making disciples, it is not fulfilling Christ's mission for it. By the way, I don't make a hard and fast distinction between "discipleship" and "mentoring," because there is too much overlap between the two. Yes, I can make technical distinctions between them. But in doing so, I think I can also show that Jesus both "discipled" and "mentored" The Twelve (among others). See the appendix on Formal Mentoring Programs.

3. In regard to "the bad and the ugly," in 1993 I wrote a book entitled, *Exit Interviews: Revealing Stories of Why People Are Leaving the Church* (Chicago: Moody Press, 1993).

4. Theologians use the term "common grace" to account for how people who have no relationship with God, and therefore remain lost and dead in their trespasses and sins (Eph. 2:1), can nevertheless live useful, productive lives and gain wisdom about living life here on earth.

5. The process I am describing here is known as Informational Interviewing. You can find out more about that through a white paper I have written on the subject, available on the Resources page of my website at http://www.thegiftednesscenter.com/new-page.

6. In the outside chance that someone says no, don't take it personally. Sure, it's disappoint-

ing, but it's not a personal rejection. The person who has turned you down has had to evaluate his availability and use of time at the moment, and apparently he's determined that getting together would not be best for him. He doesn't owe you an explanation for why he's said no. So just shake it off and move on to the next person. No harm, no foul.

7. A giftedness coach is someone who can help another person discover something about their giftedness and then apply that insight to their life—especially to their career and relationships. For more information on that, visit http://www.thegiftednesscenter.com/giftedness-coach-intro.

8. This story can be found in Linda Phillips-Jones, *The New Mentors and Protégés: How to Succeed With the New Mentoring Partnerships* (Coalition of Counseling Centers, 2001).

9. Sadly, in my part of the country (the South, and particularly Texas), people will often say that, but they don't necessarily mean it: "We should do lunch sometime." "We need to get together." "Hey, let's grab a Starbucks sometime when I'm coming your way." These gestures sound good, but then they don't ever happen. It's a cultural thing, not necessarily a personal thing. It's code for, "I've really enjoyed seeing you. It would be nice to see you more, but I know we're both very busy. But just know that I feel positive feelings for you." To those not familiar with the code, all of this can sound disingenuous and flakey.

Chapter 7: Making the Relationship Work

1. I myself have become pretty scrupulous to never call somewhere older than eighteen a "kid" or a "young person." If you're eighteen years old or older, you're legally an adult, so it's best to refer to you as such, as well as begin relating to you as an adult.

2. Starting with a trickle in the 1990s, local churches in the United States began developing "discipleship programs," a trend that accelerated in the early 2000s. More recently, some churches have started to call these programs "mentoring programs," perhaps in response to cultural perceptions. In many sectors of the church today, "discipleship" and "mentoring" are seen as amounting to the same thing. But that is not true everywhere. Some churches have formal discipleship programs for spiritual growth, and formal mentoring programs whereby volunteers mentor youth out in the community.

Chapter 8: What Should You Work On?

1. All humans are created in God's image, which means you personally and uniquely bear His image. See Gen. 1:26–27; Ps. 33:13–15; 139:13–16; Jer. 1:5; Acts 17:26–28; Eph. 2:10; and James 3:9, to name but a few relevant Scriptures.

2. Esther Trattner, "On average, Americans die with $61,000 in debt: Who pays?" MSN, MoneyWise, August 30, 2018, https://www.msn.com/en-us/money/personalfinance/on-average-americans-die-with-dollar61000-in-debt-who-pays/ar-BBMBgqM.

3. Megan Leonhardt, "Millennials ages 25-34 have $42,000 in debt, and most of it isn't from student loans," CNBC Make It, August 16, 2018, https://www.cnbc.com/2018/08/15/millennials-have-42000-in-debt.html.

4. Kathleen Elkins, "A growing percentage of millennials have absolutely nothing saved," CNBC Make It, February 12, 2018, https://www.cnbc.com/2018/02/09/a-growing-percentage-of-millennials-have-absolutely-nothing-saved.html.

5. See Timothy S. Laniak, *Shepherds After My Own Heart: Pastoral Traditions and Leadership in the Bible* (Downers Grove, IL: IVP Academic, 2006).

6. Jesus was not giving a platitude here, but stating a sobering reality that the people of His day knew well. Sheep represented the economic assets of a family (or community). In today's terms, they were like a walking bank account. Whatever else happened, a shepherd had to preserve the life of each sheep—even if it cost him his own life—lest the family lose

money out of its "bank." Jesus not only promoted that view of leadership, He modeled it by laying down His own life for His sheep.

7. Job said that trouble is as certain in life as sparks are from a fire (Job 5:7). Likewise, Jesus said plainly, "In the world you have tribulation" (John 16:33).

8. I speak with a degree of certainty about this because I've seen it happen. Very few people go through life without something major happening to them. That's actually a blessing, and Scripture exhorts us to see bad things that way (James 1:2–4). I do not consider a person who has never had anything particularly "bad" happen to them to be at all blessed. To my mind, if everything throughout their life has gone swimmingly, they are extremely vulnerable should that ever change.

Chapter 9: What Should You Watch Out For?

1. Forgiveness is an absolutely critical issue, but unfortunately too little attention is paid to it. One misunderstanding is the belief that forgiveness is required only if the person who has sinned asks for it. Another is that forgiveness is required only from the people who have been directly affected by the person's sin. The reality is, forgiveness may be more important for the person doing the forgiving than for the one being forgiven. Jesus made that plain when He said, "If you forgive others for their transgressions, your heavenly Father will also forgive you. But if you do not forgive others, then your Father will not forgive your transgressions" (Matt. 6:14–15). For more on the vital importance of forgiveness, see Bruce and Toni Hebel, *Forgiving Forward: Unleashing the Forgiveness Revolution* (Fayetteville, GA: Regenerating Life Press, 2011).

2. Jim Jones was the founder and leader of the Peoples Temple cult. In November 1978, he initiated a mass suicide and mass murder in Jonestown, Guyana, by directing his followers to drink Flavor Aid (a drink made from concentrate, similar to Kool Aid) poisoned with cyanide. 918 people died, of whom 304 were children. Jones himself is believed to have committed suicide by a self-inflicted gunshot to the head.

   David Koresh was the leader of a religious group called the Branch Davidians, who lived at a compound outside Waco, Texas. In 1993, the US Bureau of Alcohol, Tobacco, and Firearms (ATF) attempted to serve warrants to the group for illegal possession of firearms and explosives. That led to a two-month siege by the FBI, which ended when the compound was set on fire. Koresh and 79 of his followers died.

Chapter 10: Where Will This Process End Up?

1. My dad repeated this maxim so frequently that some have attributed the insight to him. Others cite John Wooden. But the true source appears to have been Dr. Henrietta Mears, for many years the Christian education director at Hollywood Presbyterian Church of Hollywood, California. See E. L. Doan, *431 Quotes From the Notes of Henrietta Mears* (Glendale, California: Regal Books, 1970), 41–42.

2. I mean no offense to Gen-Xers. The sheer size of the Baby Boom generation made it the dominant age group in American life for several decades.

3. *Forbes Magazine* defines Gen Z as people born from the mid-1990s to the early 2000s, and estimates that they make up 25 percent of the US population. See Kathryn Dill, "7 Things Employers Should Know About The Gen Z Workforce," *Forbes*, November 6, 2015, https://www.forbes.com/sites/kathryndill/2015/11/06/7-things-employers-should-know-about-the-gen-z-workforce/#7fe39708fad7.

4. You can easily find lists of the Great Books online. The Wikipedia article is a good introduction: https://en.wikipedia.org/wiki/Great_books.

5. Our accountability for what God has invested in us and with us can be seen in The Parable of the Talents, Matthew 25:14–30 (as well as other passages). Our accountability for how we influence other men can be seen in The Parable of the Two Stewards, Luke 12:42–48 (as well as other passages).

6. Grant Skeldon, *The Passion Generation: The Seemingly Reckless, Definitely Disruptive, But Far From Hopeless Millennials* (Grand Rapids, Michigan: Zondervan 2018), 34.

7. Walter Isaacson, *Steve Jobs* (New York: Simon & Schuster, 2011), 33

8. William Wilberforce (1759–1833) was a member of the British Parliament who led a movement that helped bring an end to Britain's slave trade. Charles Loring Brace (1826–1890) pioneered the foster home movement to address the problem of immigrant children living on the streets of New York. Florence Nightingale (1820–1910) is widely regarded as the founder of modern nursing. Martin Luther King Jr. (1929–1968) devoted his life to securing civil rights for African Americans.

9. At least in our culture. There are cultures in the world that are far more tribal and communal, such that whatever the patriarch or leader of the society decides is what everyone in the society then adopts.

Chapter 11: Are You Willing to Care?

1. This story is used by the permission of Anthony J. Burton. It is from a sermon he preached, wherein he astutely went on to point out that James gives us a great illustration of how it was that Jesus became a human like us in order to save us through His own death and resurrection: "Jesus couldn't save us without becoming one of us. He travelled, at enormous cost, a path God had never travelled before: he walked straight to the place of our deepest longings, our lostness and confusion, to the place of our moral struggles, our unspoken fears, our sickness and weakness and exhaustion, into that dark wood where so often there seems no clear path forward.
    - We want a map; but God gives us something better than a map: he gives us himself as a guide.
    - We want answers but God gives us something better than answers: he gives us a savior.
    - We look for a life without problems: but God offers us a new life altogether."

2. I am speaking of boomers *as a whole* and am giving my opinion as to the sins for which our generation *in general* will be remembered. Obviously there are many exceptions—as is true for any generation. You personally may have engaged in none of the sins I've listed. But it doesn't matter: we can still engage in a collective confession on behalf of our group—in this case, our generation. For examples of that in Scripture, see Neh. 1:4–11; Dan. 9:3–19; and Ezra 9:5–15. It goes without saying that God will be the ultimate Judge of both every generation and every individual.

3. See Pss. 100:5; 136:1–26.

Chapter 12: Do You Realize What You Have to Offer?

1. By the way, retirement is a cultural, not a biblical concept. You may retire from your career, but you will never retire from the Christian life. That means that until the day you die, someone somewhere ought to have the benefit of gleaning from your life.

Chapter 13: What Are the Questions Men Ask?

1. By See Guy Raz, *How I Built This With Guy Raz*, NPR, April 8, 2018, https://www.npr.org/2018/06/07/599900951/fubu-daymond-john.

Chapter 14: Some Common Themes of Mentoring

1. Which is why God reminded Samuel, "God sees not as man sees, for man looks at the outward appearance, but the Lord looks at the heart" (1 Sam. 16:7).
2. Theology of Work Project, https://www.theologyofwork.org/. In the interest of full disclosure, I am on the Steering Committee for The Theology of Work Project.
3. See Psalm 1, 23 (esp. vv. 3, 6), and 112, to name but a few passages.
4. For more, see *The Person Called You: Why You're Here, Why You Matter & What You Should Do With Your Life* (Chicago: Moody Publishers, 2014), chapter 9, "Giftedness and Your Dark Side."
5. Grant Skeldon, *The Passion Generation: The Seemingly Reckless, Definitely Disruptive, But Far From Hopeless Millennials* (Grand Rapids, MI: Zondervan 2018), 34.
6. See Olivia B. Waxman, "This Man Was Chosen to Represent the Class of 1968. Here's What He Thinks His Generation Achieved," *Time*, March 22, 2018, available at http://time.com/5209229/gun-control-1968-50th-anniversary-time-cover/.
7. Ibid.
8. W. H. Auden, "For the Time Being: A Christmas Oratorio" (1942).

Chapter 16: What Will Be Your Legacy?

1. See John Ortberg, *When the Game Is Over, It All Goes Back in the Box* (Grand Rapids, MI: Zondervan Publishers, 2007).
2. For example, see Matt. 24:42–44; Luke 12:35–40; Rom. 8:23; Gal. 5:5; 1 Thess. 5:1–11; 2 Peter 3:1–4; and Jude 1:20–21.
3. See for example, Isa. 65:17–23 and Rev. 21:24–27.
4. Getting right with God is not about "getting good enough for God." None of us can ever be or become good enough for God. Knowing that (see *The Story of God* in chapter 14), God took upon Himself the judgment that otherwise would have fallen on each of us for not being good enough for God (what the Bible calls our "sin"). That happened when Jesus was crucified and, on the cross, became our sin and thereby put our sins to death. That was an act of sheer grace on God's part. And by that grace, nothing now stands between us and a renewed relationship with God. So, "getting right with God" means trusting that what He's done in Christ covered our sin and thereby entering into a new relationship with Him whereby we walk with Him and follow His lead.
5. For example, see Dan. 7:27; Matt. 24:45–47; Luke 16:10–12; 1 Cor. 6:2–3; 2 Tim. 2:11–12.
6. Remember that the shepherd has been the dominant model of leadership (for good reason) throughout human history, until only very recently (see chapter 8).
7. From "Prayer" (2009), Music by René Clausen, Lyrics by Cardinal John Henry Newman, Adapted by Mother Teresa of Calcutta.

Appendix A: Formal Mentoring Programs

1. Enron Corporation was an energy company based in Houston, Texas. Founded in 1985, the company had outstanding performance (along with a great corporate culture that its employees loved), with $100 billion of revenues in 2000. Enron was named "America's Most Innovative Company" by *Forbes Magazine* for six years straight. Then in 2001, it was discovered that the senior executives and the company's accounting firm, Arthur Anderson, had defrauded investors out of billions of dollars, and the company imploded into scandal and bankruptcy.
2. Robert M. Kachur and David Neff, "Surviving Leadership Fast Forward," *Christianity Today*, April 18, 1986. At the time, mentoring was just becoming recognized as a key best practice

by which Fortune 500 companies were developing their future leaders. MacDonald was one of the pioneers in perceiving the critical need for leadership among pastors and churches.

3. http://daveridleyspeaks.com/. I strongly encourage business leaders particularly to invite Dave to come speak to the leaders in your organization. He was directly involved for more than twenty-five years in helping sustain the corporate culture that Herb Kelleher created at SWA.

4. Trevor Hunter, "It's Just the Culture," *Talentism*, May 24, 2018, https://www.talentism.com/research/its-just-the-culture/.

5. Visit https://www.perimeter.org/pages/reaching-the-city/reaching-the-city/church-planting-1/pages/around-metro-atlanta-1/.

6. Stephen M. Badger II, "Editorial," *Brewery Journal #3: Exploring Mutuality*, June 11, 2015.

7. The Mars Company continues to think deeply about the role of business in causing the world to flourish beyond mere profit. See Bruno Roche and Jay Jakub, *Completing Capitalism: Heal Business to Heal the World* (Oakland, California: Berrett-Koehler Publishers, 2017)

Appendix B: Formal Mentoring in Churches

1. The Great Commission is often viewed as being all about evangelism—meaning, the proclamation of the gospel. But evangelism is only the first step in becoming a disciple, or apprentice, of Jesus. The book of Acts makes that clear. For example, in Acts 2, Peter proclaims the gospel (evangelism), and three thousand people respond in faith. But then the apostles immediately begin doing exactly what Jesus told them they should do next in the Great Commission: "teaching them to observe all that I commanded you" (Matt. 28:20). So, Acts 2:42 states, "They [the new converts] were continually devoting themselves to the apostles' teaching and to fellowship, to the breaking of bread and to prayer."

The same purpose and pattern of people-development can be seen throughout the New Testament letters. For example, Eph. 4 explicitly states that the purpose of the apostles, prophets, evangelists, and pastor-teachers is "to equip [Christ's] people for works of service, so that the body of Christ may be built up until we all reach unity in the faith and in the knowledge of the Son of God and become mature, attaining to the whole measure of the fullness of Christ" (vv. 12–13 NIV).

2. "New Research on the State of Discipleship," Barna, December 1, 2015, https://www.barna.com/research/new-research-on-the-state-of-discipleship/. This was a comprehensive, multiphase research study among Christian adults, church leaders, exemplar discipleship ministries, and Christian educators. For the purpose of its research, Barna defined "practicing Christians" as self-identified Christians who say their faith is very important to their lives and who have attended a worship service, other than for a special occasion, one or more times during the past month.

3. Greg L. Hawkins and Cally Parkinson, *Reveal: Where Are You?* (Barrington, IL: WillowCreek Resources, 2007), 13, 36.

4. Ibid., 47, 52–53.

5. Barna, "New Research on the State of Discipleship."

6. Without question, education, knowledge, and information are vitally needed as one follows (or apprentices under) Jesus. So, I'm not suggesting we leave those behind, rather that we move beyond—or better yet, build upon—them to actual life-change. The current model of discipleship talks about life-change. The question is: Has it delivered that? Or can it?

7. The New Testament evidence for how the apostles themselves engaged in in-depth discipleship is sparse. But we are told that Paul spent more than a year and a half in Corinth (Acts 18:11, 18) and at least two years at Ephesus (19:8–10). The account indicates that much of his time in and around those cities was devoted to teaching. But, presumably, he engaged in

personal conversations and interactions, as well, in order to go deeper with the new believers. That surmise would be consistent with Paul's relationship with Aquila and Priscilla, tentmakers in Corinth with whom he stayed and worked alongside for what appears to have been more than a year and a half (Acts 18:1–4, 11, 18). The Acts narrative gives insight into Paul's later exhortation to the Corinthian church to "be imitators of me, just as I also am of Christ" (1 Cor. 11:1).

Several of Paul's other letters also attest to his discipleship-by-example model. He told the Philippians to follow his example and "walk [that is, live] according to the pattern you have in us" (Phil. 3:17). Likewise, he admonishes the Thessalonians to follow the example he set for them (2 Thess. 3:6–13; see also Acts 17:1–9). And he told Timothy to entrust "the things which you have heard from me" to other men, who would in turn pass them down to others (2 Tim. 2:2). In 1 Timothy, he challenged Timothy to set an example for the other believers (4:12).

Example-based discipleship is the exact model of Jesus and the twelve (see Luke 11:1; John 13:15).

8. I distinguish between "our culture" (the West) from other cultures around the world, particularly in South America, Africa, and Asia. Of course, it's becoming difficult to distinguish cultures regionally now because of the growing influence of global cities, which are remarkably similar no matter where they are located, and also are themselves marked by extreme cultural diversity. That said, much of the church in Southeast Asia and China disciples people using a model along the lines I'm suggesting: far more relational and experiential, and less driven by "content."

9. And perhaps Timothy, as well, if one assumes that he followed through on Paul's instruction to entrust what he'd learned from Paul to faithful men.

10. Much has been developed in this space in the past few years, but the first expert I would turn is Sue Mallory, *The Equipping Church: Serving Together to Transform Lives* (Grand Rapids, MI: Zondervan, 2001) and its companion, by Sue Mallory and Brad Smith, *The Equipping Church Guidebook* (Grand Rapids, MI: Zondervan, 2001).

11. For another outstanding example of discipleship/mentoring being modeled from the top, see the story of Randy Pope, pastor of Perimeter Church in Atlanta, in Appendix A: Formal Mentoring Programs.

12. Edgar A. Guest, "I'd rather see a sermon than hear one any day."

13. Remember, only one-third of Christian adults report that their church recommends meeting with a spiritual mentor. See Barna, "New Research on the State of Discipleship."

14. I am not at all saying the gospel or Scripture is outdated or outmatched. Only that our approach to communicating the gospel and relating biblical truth to human experience has not kept up with the times. We're not being heard—not because we don't have anything to say, but because we don't know how to speak in today's context.

15. Churchgoers get told all the time that sanctification is a lifelong process. Yet the discipleship programs typically offered them tend to have a three-years-and-you're-out timeframe on them. Could that be one reason why the longer one is involved in a church, the less satisfied they become? See Hawkins and Parkinson, *Reveal*.

Appendix C: Formal Mentoring Models to Consider

1. "Professional Development Programs," Caterpillar, https://www.caterpillar.com/en/careers/career-areas/college/professional-development-programs.html.
2. "Leadership Development," Deloitte, https://www2.deloitte.com/us/en/pages/about-deloitte/articles/inclusion-leadership-development.html.
3. Feruni Ceramiche, https://www.feruni.com/.
4. "2019 Academy Week," Praxis Academy, https://academy.praxislabs.org/academy.

5. "Attain Greater Margin and Balance," The Masters Program, https://www.mastersprogram.org/about.html.

6. Edgerton Gear, Inc., http://www.edgertongear.com/student-mentoring.html.

7. Bottom Line, https://www.bottomline.org/.

8. See Kate Stringer, "Mentoring Program Posts 81% College Persistence Rate With Focus on In-Person Coaching, Affordability, New Study Finds," The 74, November 15, 2017, https://www.the74million.org/article/mentoring-program-posts-81-college-persistence-rate-with-focus-on-in-person-coaching-affordability-new-study-finds/.

9. Hendricks Center Dallas Theological Seminary, https://hendrickscenter.dts.edu/.

10. "MyVECTOR," Air Force's Personnel Center, https://www.afpc.af.mil/Force-Development/MyVECTOR/.

11. "Mentoring," Mercy Street, https://www.mercystreetdallas.org/mentoring.

12. High Adventure Treks, https://www.highadventuretreks.org.

13. C.S. Lewis Institute, http://www.cslewisinstitute.org.

14. Radical Mentoring, https://radicalmentoring.com.

15. Men's Fraternity Classic, https://www.mensfraternity.com.

16. Life on Life, https://lifeonlife.org/.

17. Man in the Mirror, https://maninthemirror.org/.

18. Navigators, https://www.navigators.org/.

19. MentorLink International, http://www.mentorlink.org.

20. "Preparing Future Pastors," Made to Flourish, https://www.madetoflourish.org/events/pastoral-residency/.

21. The Fellows at The Falls Church Anglican, http://fallschurchfellows.com/.

22. "The Forge," Pine Cove, https://www.pinecove.com/forge/.

THE ART AND SCIENCE OF READING THE BIBLE

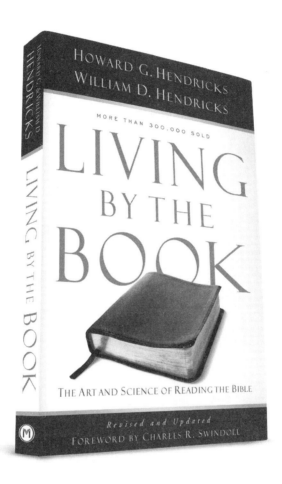

MOODY
Publishers®

From the Word to Life®

For every person who draws strength and direction from the Bible, there are many more who struggle with it. In a simple, step-by-step fashion, the authors explain how to glean truth from Scripture. This revised and expanded edition is practical, readable, and applicable.

978-0-8024-0823-5 | also available as an eBook

WHY YOU'RE HERE, WHY YOU MATTER & WHAT YOU SHOULD DO WITH YOUR LIFE

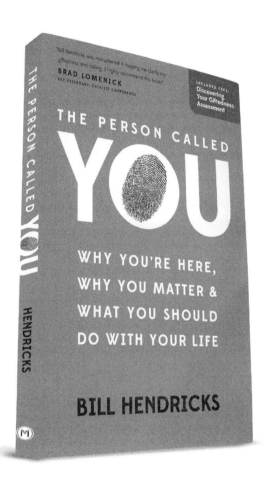

MOODY
Publishers®

From the Word to Life®

The Person Called You is a celebration, exploration, and explanation of human giftedness. Bill describes what it is (and isn't), where it comes from, how you can discover your own giftedness, and, most importantly, its potential to transform your life.

978-0-8024-1201-0 | also available as an eBook

STUDY THE BIBLE WITH PROFESSORS
FROM MOODY BIBLE INSTITUTE

MOODY
Publishers®

*From the Word **to Life**®*

Study the Bible with a team of 30 Moody Bible Institute professors. This in-depth, user-friendly, one-volume commentary will help you better understand and apply God's Word to all of life. Additional study helps include maps, charts, bibliographies for further reading, and a subject and Scripture index.

978-0-8024-2867-7 | also available as an eBook